Letter from the Publisher

Publisher and Creative Director:
B. Martin Pedersen

Design Director:
Hee Ra Kim

Designers:
B. Martin Pedersen
Hee Ra Kim
Hiewon Sohn

Associate Editor:
Sara Gonzalez

Design Intern:
Gevaughn Henry

Editorial Interns:
Amanda Farrell
Anayaé Holmes
Eavan Noonan

Japanese Advisors:
USA: Toshiaki & Kumiko Ide
Japan: Taku Satoh
Sakura Nomiyama

Chief Executive Officer:
B. Martin Pedersen

Financial Officer:
Arna T. Pedersen

Legal Counsel:
John M. Roth

Cover Art:
"King Cobra 2,"
Photo by Mark Laita

Published by:
Graphis Inc.
389 Fifth Avenue, Suite 1105
New York, NY 10016
Phone: 212-532-9387
www.graphis.com
help@graphis.com

Distributed by:
National Book Networks, Inc.
15200 NBN Way
Blue Ridge Summit, PA 17214
Phone: 800-462-6420
customercare@nbnbooks.com

ISBN 13: 978-1-931241-88-5

Some years ago, in our Branding 5 book, I presented a designer whose commissioned work that he produced for a new client, resulted in a huge surprise.

The designer had been asked to develop a new brand for this fairly common product that would distinctly separate it from the competition. After some months of explorative work, he invited the clients in to view his solutions. The two men proceeded to view the branding examples of packaging promotion and ads that were on display. As they continued to repeatedly view the work, their normal voices kept lowering until they were whispering to each other.

With this, the designer thought that he had lost the account.

The men finally approached him and related that they had been awed by what they had seen. They stated that they now had to go back and make their product better. This was, of course, the highest compliment from a client that I had ever heard of. The designer happily went into production with the work, and at the same time, the clients went to improve their product.

The designer was Steve Sandstrom from Oregon who originated the brilliant Tazo Tea brand.

When it was launched, it became an immediate success because of its unique design. Within a few years, Tazo was purchased outright by Howard Schultz of Starbucks, who saw serious competition developing.

I asked Steve later if he had thought of not charging for the production, and instead, could he receive a percentage of the company? Steve said he had never thought of it, but he would ask them since they were still good friends. He brought it up during a dinner, and they both agreed that they wouldn't have hesitated in giving him a percentage. However, time had now passed, and it was of course too late.

I then told Steve to seriously consider this with some of his future branding jobs (See page 10).

Other winning talents presented in this issue are as follows:
Design: Daeki & Jun from South Korea, with bold posters that experiment with various type styles. Ken-Tsai Lee, a pioneer of type design in Taiwan.

Advertising: Colin Corcoran (US), who produces striking advertising copy for clients.

Photography: Mark Laita (US), with extraordinary still lifes and animal photography. Canadian photographer, Steve Krug with enticing culinary work.

Art/Illustration: Braldt Bralds, a Dutch illustrator residing in America with classic paintings and illustrations.

Education: Adrian Pulfer, a legendary designer and teacher who taught at Brigham Young University in Utah. With only 10 Seniors every year in Design, he competes with SVA (School of Visual Art)'s 300 Seniors and other top design schools for Platinum and Gold Awards in our New Talent Student Annuals.

Products: New Mercedes-Benz Vision ATVR, Scate Chair from Russia, and Maison Dada's Little Eliah Pending Lamps.

Architecture: A unique Solar Egg Sauna in Sweden, and a playful family park in China.

B. Martin Pedersen
Publisher & Creative Director

We extend our heartfelt thanks to the international contributors who have made it possible to publish a wide spectrum of the best work in Design, Advertising, Photography, and Art / Illustration. Anyone is welcome to submit work at www.graphis.com.

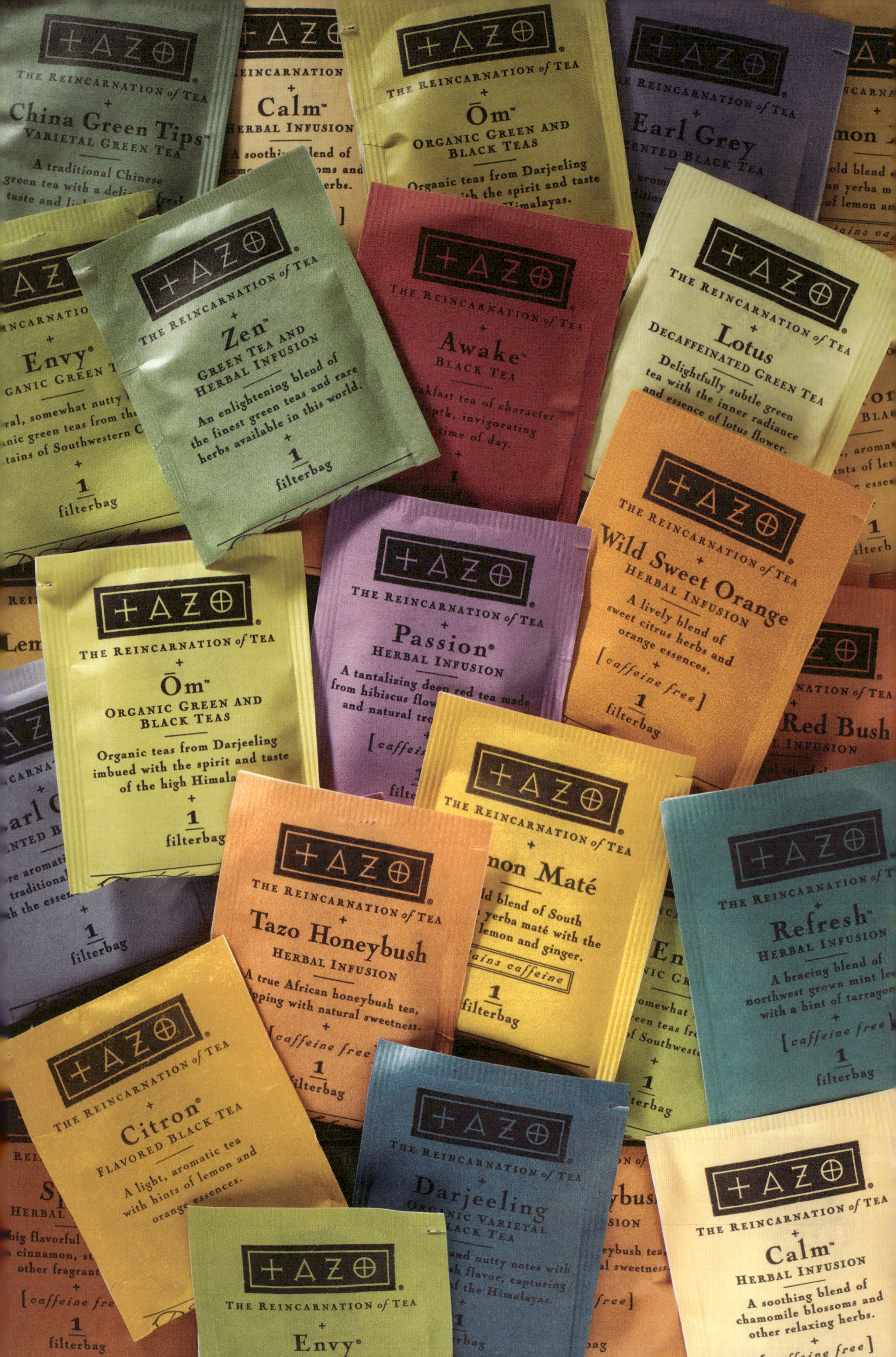

TAZO
THE REINCARNATION of TEA
China Green Tips
VARIETAL GREEN TEA
A traditional Chinese
TAZO
Calm
HERBAL INFUSION
TAZO
THE REINCARNATION of TEA
Ōm
ORGANIC GREEN AND BLACK TEAS
Organic teas from Darjeeling
TAZO
Earl Grey
TAZO
THE REINCARNATION of TEA
Zen
GREEN TEA AND HERBAL INFUSION
An enlightening blend of the finest green teas and rare herbs available in this world.
1 filterbag
Envy
1 filterbag
TAZO
THE REINCARNATION of TEA
Awake
BLACK TEA
TAZO
THE REINCARNATION of TEA
Lotus
DECAFFEINATED GREEN TEA
Delightfully subtle green tea with the inner radiance and essence of lotus flower.
TAZO
THE REINCARNATION of TEA
Wild Sweet Orange
HERBAL INFUSION
A lively blend of sweet citrus herbs and orange essences.
[caffeine free]
1 filterbag
TAZO
THE REINCARNATION of TEA
Ōm
ORGANIC GREEN AND BLACK TEAS
1 filterbag
TAZO
THE REINCARNATION of TEA
Passion
HERBAL INFUSION
Red Bush
TAZO
THE REINCARNATION of TEA
Tazo Honeybush
HERBAL INFUSION
A true African honeybush tea,
[caffeine free]
1 filterbag
TAZO
THE REINCARNATION of TEA
1 filterbag
TAZO
THE REINCARNATION of TEA
Refresh
HERBAL INFUSION
A bracing blend of
[caffeine free]
1 filterbag
TAZO
THE REINCARNATION of TEA
Citron
FLAVORED BLACK TEA
A light, aromatic tea with hints of lemon and orange essences.
[caffeine free]
1 filterbag
TAZO
THE REINCARNATION of TEA
Darjeeling
TAZO
THE REINCARNATION of TEA
Envy
TAZO
THE REINCARNATION of TEA
Calm
HERBAL INFUSION
A soothing blend of chamomile blossoms and other relaxing herbs.

Contents

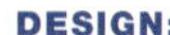

DESIGN:

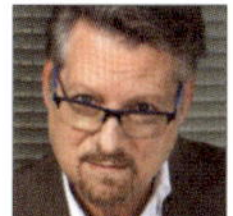

10 Steve Sandstrom (Graphis Master) / USA

Steve Sandstrom is the founding partner of Sandstrom Partners in Portland, Oregon. Sandstrom Partners has been recognized as one of the leading brand design firms in the US. Clients have included Bulleit Bourbon (Diageo), Converse, Coca-Cola, Miller Brewing, Tazo, Smith Teamaker, Sony Pictures, Cole Haan, Davos Brands, and Constellation Brands. ■ The firm has been featured in numerous books on design, branding, packaging and corporate identity, and several publications including *Graphis*, *One: a Magazine*, *Communication Arts*, *Adweek, Critique, Novum (Germany), How, Creativity, The New York Times Magazine, The Oregonian, Metropolis*, and *@Issue*. ■ Sandstrom has been involved in the creation and the revitalization of some iconic and thought-leading brands. Numerous design and advertising awards include The One Show (Advertising, Design and Interactive), *Graphis*, D&AD (London), ADC, FAB (London), *Communication Arts*, ID, Clios, ANDY Awards, Kelly Awards, Beldings, Type Directors Annual, Flash Forward, London International Advertising, and the American Advertising Federation. The combined Platinum, Gold, and Silver Awards from Graphis Annuals total over 50 from 2013 to 2019. He is a renowned workaholic and lives in Portland, Oregon with his wife Kelly, and is a proud parent of three grown children and a grandparent of two.

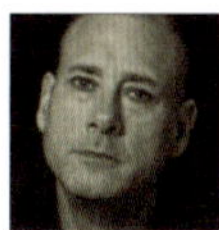

Introduction by Austin Howe

Austin Howe is founder and creative director of Austin Moffatt Barkwell Howe, Purveyors of Fine Brand Writing & Solicited Opinions Pertaining to Design, a Portland-based consultancy that works exclusively with design-driven brands and start-ups. He has collaborated with Steve Sandstrom on every kind of project imaginable over the years, dating back to the original branding for Sandstrom Partners. Austin has also worked with Bob Dinetz Design, Braley Design, Bruce Mau Design, Design Army, Fredrik Averin Design, Stitzlein Studio, Wieden+Kennedy, and Ziba. He is the author of *Designers Don't Read* and *Designers Don't Have Influences*.

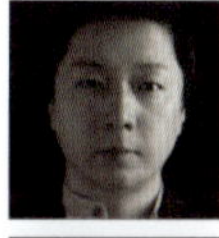

24 Daeki Shim & HyoJun Shim / South Korea

Daeki Shim & HyoJun Shim are co-founders of graphic design studio DAEKI & JUN. As the co-founders, they have been recognized for their work and have won and been nominated more than 100 times at international design awards and biennials. Most notably, they won the Grand Prix at the 2017 Red Dot Design Awards, the Judge's Choice Award at the 2017 Society of Typographic Arts (STA100) in Chicago, and the Platinum & Gold Awards in the Graphis Annual competitions in 2016 and 2017. ■ Daeki Shim received a bachelor's degree at the University of the Arts London (UAL), Central Saint Martins (CSM), and a master's degree at the University of London, University College London (UCL). He currently is an adjunct professor at the Sejong University, Seoul Tech University, and Hongik University. He also has served as a curator at the ‹Typojanchi 2015: International Typography Biennial›, a chief curator at ‹Typojanchi 2017: International Typography Biennial›, and a director of ‹Seoul Design Brand: Communication Tools› at Dongdaemun Design Plaza (ddp), and more. ■ HyoJun Shim received a bachelor's degree at the University of the Arts London (UAL), Central Saint Martins (CSM), a master's degree at the University of London, Goldsmiths and another master's degree at the University of London, University College London (UCL). He currently teaches graphic design at the Dongduk Women's University.

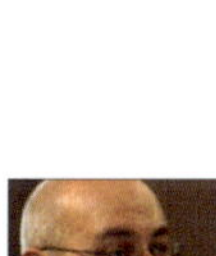

Introduction by Serge Serov *Portrait by Vladimir Makushkin*

Serge Serov is a design provider, curator, art historian, editor, educator, art director, and graphic designer. Born January 23rd,1952, he graduated from Moscow Institute of Telecommunications and St. Petersburg Academic Institute of Fine Arts, Sculpture and Architecture after Ilya Repin. He is an author of 15 books and 600 articles, an editor-in-chief for several design magazines, an organizer of 300 design events, President of Golden Bee Moscow Global Biennial of Graphic Design, Vice-President of the Academy of Graphic Design and Professor & Head of chair at RANEPA Design School. He has been a guest speaker for universities and international design events in 25 countries. His awards include Honorary Diploma of the U.N.Council for Public Awards, Rodchenko Award, and Golden Badge of Honour for Public Recognition. He is a member of Alliance Graphique Internationale (AGI), Brno Biennale Association (honorary member), Union of Designers of Ukraine (honorary member), etc.

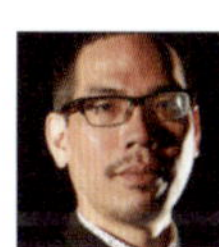

38 Ken-Tsai Lee (Graphis Master) / Taiwan

Ken-Tsai Lee is an associate professor at the National Taiwan University of Science and Technology, as well as the Visual Director for Taiwan Designers' Week, and the regional representative of the New York Art Directors Club and NY Type Directors Club. ■ He was named one of the 100 best contemporary designers in the world by Japanese design master, Shigeo Fukuda, through the design book AREA. He represented Taiwan in a traveling exhibition titled "Conforming to Vicinity – A Cross-Strait Four-Region Artistic Exchange Project 2014." ■ He leads "Ken-Tsai Lee Design Lab" in Taiwan Tech with his graduate students. He has brought the Type Directors Club's annual exhibition, "Young Guns," to Taiwan, as well as curated the Chinese Typography Design Biennial, gathering works of Chinese typography from all over the world. ■ His work has been recognized by the Taiwan National Design awards and numerous others from leading design organizations and publications worldwide, including Design for Asia Awards, D&AD, NY TDC, NY One Show, Tokyo TDC, Hong Kong Designers Assoc., Red Dot Design Award, *Communication Arts*, and *Graphis*.

(Opposite page) "Tazo Envelopes" by Steve Sandstrom

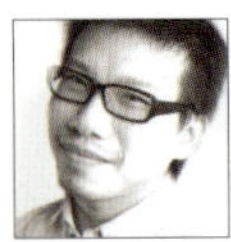

Introduction by Ben Chiu

Ben Chiu, the executive director of Taiwan Designers' Web, is closely involved with all the various design projects the company is involved in. He has been responsible for planning and delivering the annual Taiwan Designers' Week since 2009, working closely with Taiwanese designers as well as designers from across the world. He positioned himself as the provider of services to many designers and also brings various designers together to build new connections and relationships, and of course promote Taiwanese design.

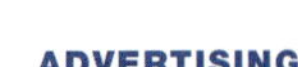

ADVERTISING:

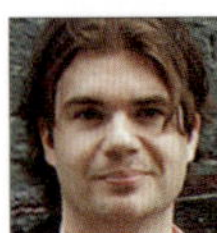

52 **Colin Corcoran (Graphis Master) / USA**

Despite being a freelancer, Corcoran is Lürzer's Archive Magazine's #1 ranked U.S.-based copywriter over the past decade. He was also the writer with the most work published worldwide in *Graphis*' 2019 & 2020 Advertising Annuals and *Communication Arts*' 2016 & 2019 Advertising Annuals. In 2017, he won the only D&AD Yellow Pencil not awarded to an agency on either coast. After 16 years in the business, he has freelanced for over 500 ad agencies, design studios, and interactive shops. After beginning his career in Minneapolis followed by stints in San Francisco, L.A. and Chicago, Colin is now based in Brooklyn.

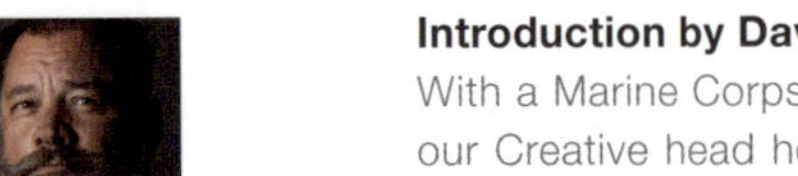

Introduction by Dave Damman

With a Marine Corps sniper for a father and a psychiatric hospital administrator for a mother, it's no wonder our Creative head honcho has no problem zeroing in on award-winning thinking. Dave has held leadership positions at top agencies across the country – including ECD at Fallon Worldwide, CCO/Managing Partner at Carmichael Lynch, and most recently, Co-President & CCO at Gallegos United. He's led the charge on breakthrough work for household names like Lee Jeans, United Airlines, Subaru and more, earning him international acclaim and the hardware to go with it. But his biggest feat yet? We'd argue it's serving John Gotti a Smith & Wollensky steak and living to tell the tale.

PHOTOGRAPHY:

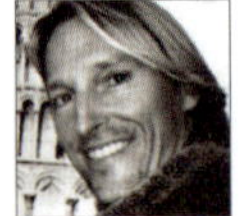

68 **Mark Laita (Graphis Master) / USA**

For over twenty years, advertising agencies worldwide have asked Mark Laita to bring his expertise, problem-solving abilities, and signature style to their most important campaigns. His clean, colorful, graphic photography has earned him a reputation for award-winning work for clients such as Adidas, BMW, Van Cleef and Arpels, and MINI. ■ Based in Los Angeles since 1986, Mark also maintains a studio in Manhattan for his New York clients. His grace, wit, and straightforward manner helps to create a relaxed and efficient work environment that can handle all aspects of print and live action imagery ranging from elaborate prop building, to complicated retouching as well as video editing. Mark's images have been featured in campaigns for clients as diverse as Estee Lauder, Budweiser, Visa, and IBM. ■ His photography was used in the introduction of Apple's iMac, iBook, G3, and subsequent campaigns for Apple products for ten years. Mark's first book, *Created Equal* was published by Steidl in 2010. His second book, *Sea* was published by Abrams in late 2011. His most recent book, *Serpentine* was released in 2013. His work has been exhibited in galleries in the U.S. and Europe.

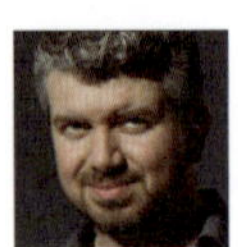

Introduction by Adam Voorhes (Graphis Master)

Adam Voorhes has a knack for blowing things up. After graduating from the Brooks Institute of Photography in 2003, he has shot anything and everything blowing up, catching fire, spitting sparks, and frozen in time and space, giving the "still" in still life a run for its money. His work ranges from colorful worlds to stark black and white spaces, from capturing carefully crafted props to macro close ups of oozing cheesy goodness. When he's not placing the fire extinguishers close to set, he can be found with a margarita in one hand and a sci-fi book in the other.

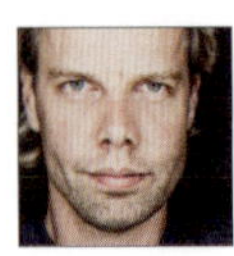

82 **Steve Krug / Canada**

Steve Krug has been an active member of the Toronto photographic industry for 20 years. Highly skilled in both commercial and editorial styles, Steve's work spans food and beverage, consumer products, locations, lifestyle and interiors. He continues to build a diverse roster of repeat clients who appreciate his creativity, attention to detail, and collaborative nature on set. An intense passion for cooking and all things gourmet help set his food and beverage photography apart. He is represented by Fuze Reps of Toronto.

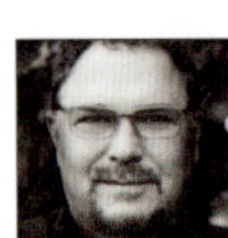

Introduction by Rob Fiocca

Toronto-based director/photographer Rob Fiocca has an exceptional eye for beauty. He has established himself as one of the most sought out and well-respected artists on the leading edge of the commercial industry. For over 25 years, his creative and commercial work has garnered international awards. His client list is stocked with advertising agencies such as Leo Burnett, JWT, and Cossette. ■ As a director, Rob applies his mastery of light and texture to memorable spots for clients such as McDonald's, Kraft, Schneiders, and Kellogg's. His appreciation for the story of food and the poetry within the details has made this medium a natural translation of his unique vision. ■ When not shooting for clients, Rob's love of travel to far flung places like South Africa and Iceland have allowed him to capture beautiful images that have been featured in galleries and private collections.

(Opposite page) "Blue Blubber Jellyfish" by Mark Laita

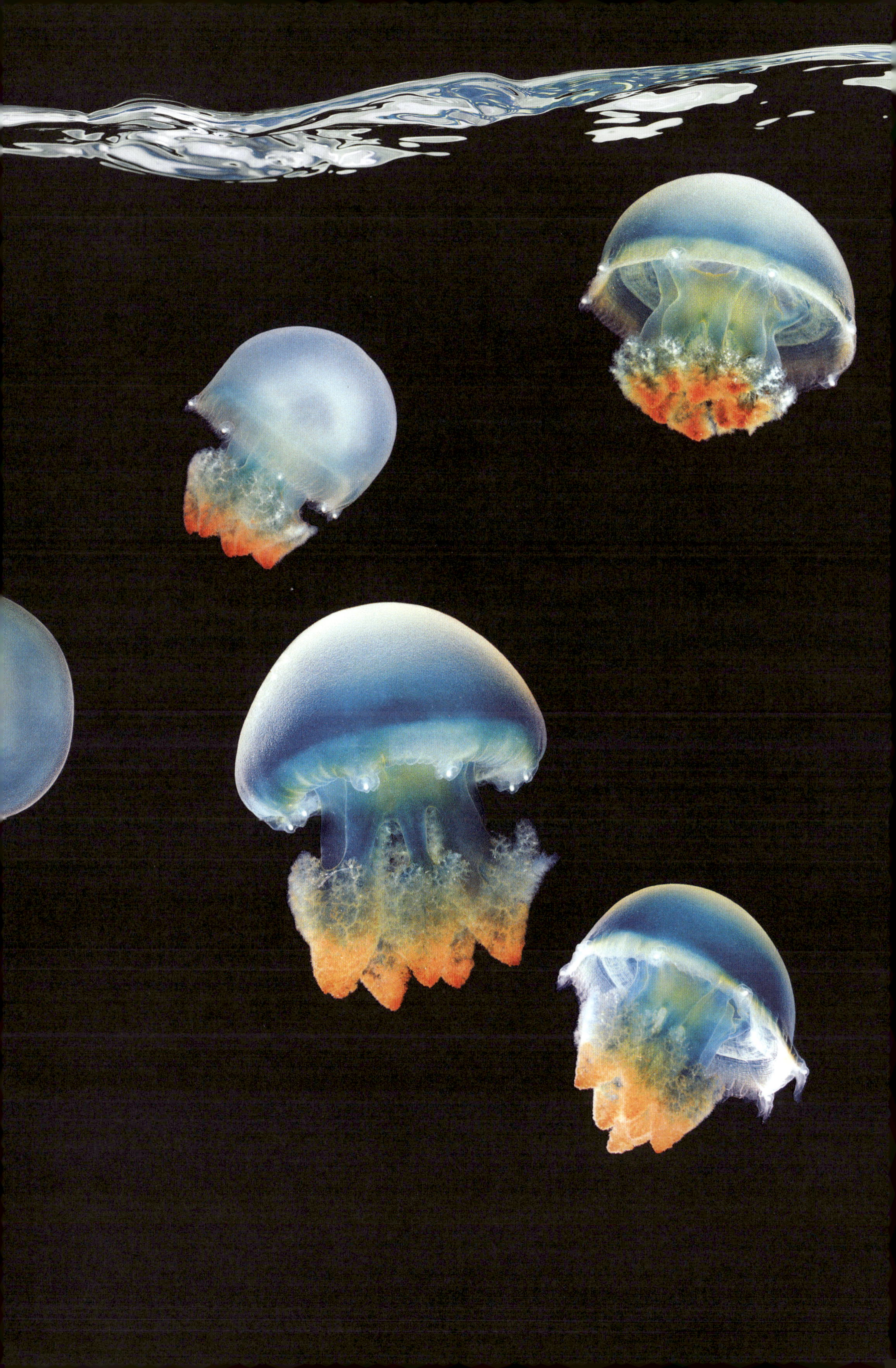

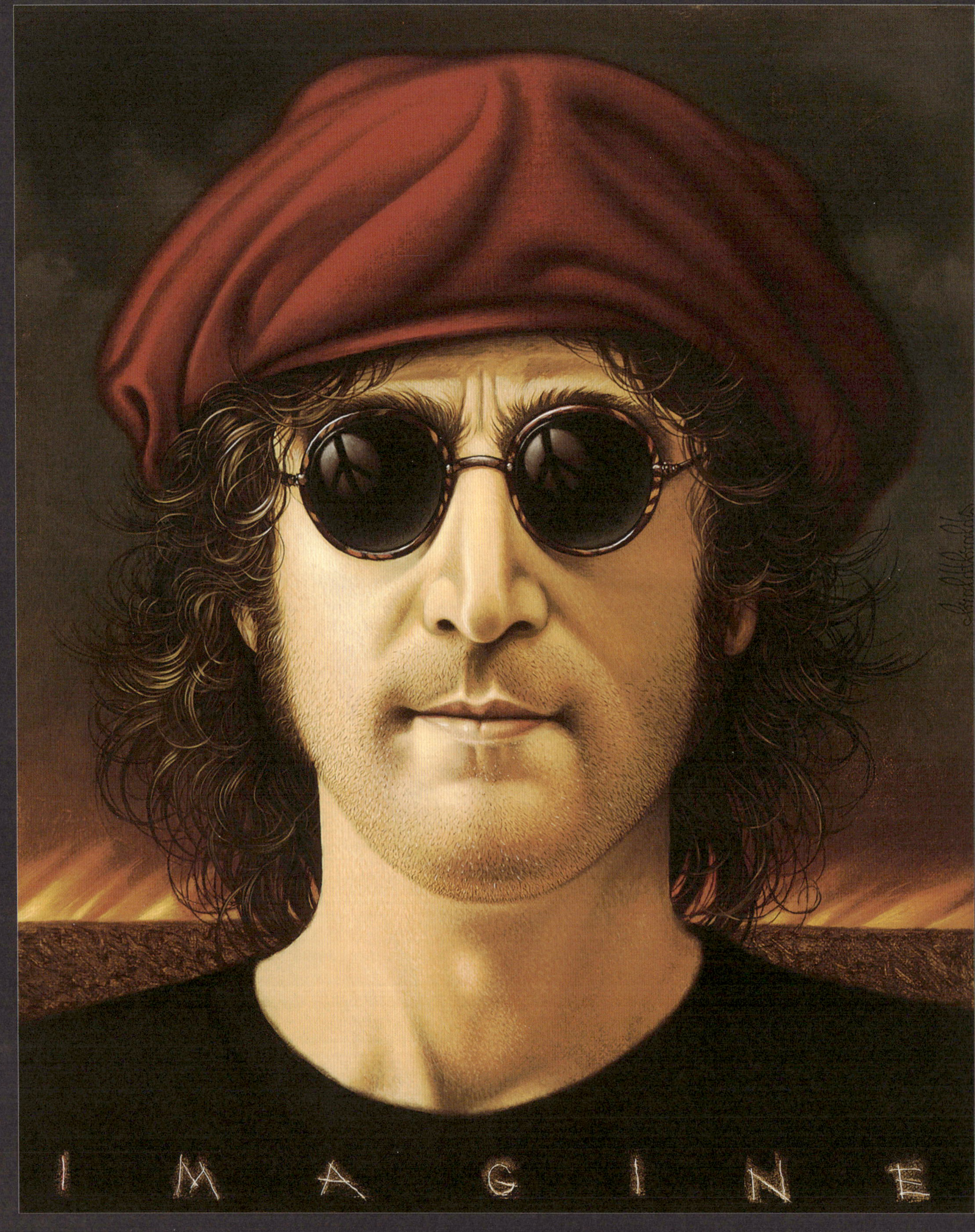
I M A G I N E

(Opposite page) "Imagine" (Lennon) by Braldt Bralds

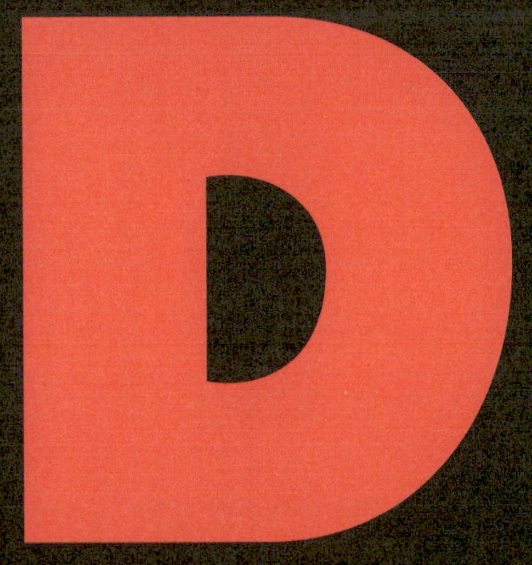

DESIGN

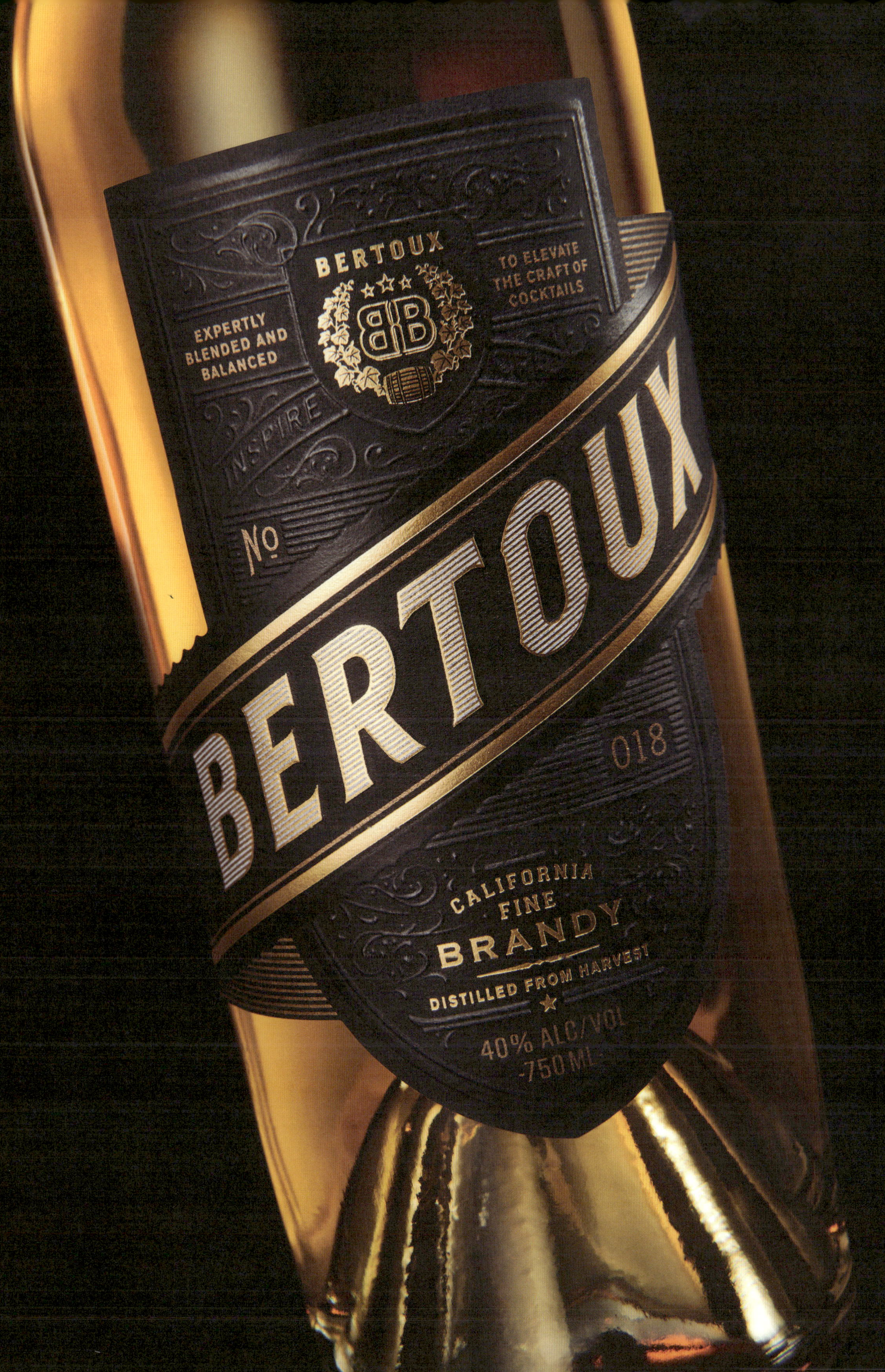
BERTOUX
EXPERTLY BLENDED AND BALANCED
TO ELEVATE THE CRAFT OF COCKTAILS
INSPIRE
№
BERTOUX
018
CALIFORNIA FINE
BRANDY
DISTILLED FROM HARVEST
40% ALC/VOL
750 ML

STEVE AND THE TEAM CREATE A BRAND THAT NOT ONLY EXISTS, BUT CARRIES A VISCERAL SENSE OF BEING; THE BRAND NOT ONLY LIVES, BUT ANNOUNCES ITS PRESENCE AS IF IT HAD ALWAYS BEEN A PART OF THE FABRIC OF OUR CULTURE.

Diana Pawlik, *Head of Marketing for BERTOUX*

STEVE'S DESIGN GOES WELL BEYOND MOST PEOPLE'S DEFINITION. HE SEEMS TO CREATE FULLY REALIZED, ENDURING WORLDS WHERE THE BRAND JUST FITS IN AS IF IT ALWAYS EXISTED.

YOU DON'T SIMPLY END UP WITH STRATEGIC WORK THAT LOOKS BEAUTIFUL, INSTEAD HE GIVES YOU SOMETHING YOU CAN FEEL, SENSE, TASTE, AND TOUCH. THE MAN IS A MAGICIAN.

David Baldwin, *Founder/CEO of Baldwin&, Raleigh*

ONLY ONE WORD IS NEEDED TO DESCRIBE STEVE: GENIUS. HE'S ONE OF A KIND. HIGHLY RECOMMEND WORKING WITH HIM AND THE SANDSTROM TEAM, WHO ARE, QUITE LITERALLY, THE WHOLE PACKAGE.

Andrew Chrisomalis, *CEO of Davos Brands*

HE IS A LEGEND IN THE DESIGN WORLD. HE IS WILLING TO SAY AND DO UNPOPULAR THINGS IN THE SPIRIT OF WHAT IS RIGHT FOR A BRAND. HE CREATED TIMELESS PACKAGING FOR BULLEIT BOURBON OVER 20 YEARS AGO, AND TODAY, IT IS STILL INTACT.

Ed Bello, *Global and US Brand Director, Bulleit Frontier Whiskey*

(Page 9) Client: Bertoux Distillers–Bertoux is a brandy developed specifically for making fine cocktails. It's named for the inventor of the bicycle/motorcycle sidecar, and a Sidecar is also the most famous brandy cocktail. / (Opposite page) Bulleit Bourbon Aged 10 Years. Client: Diageo. Design: Steve Sandstrom. Photo: Polara Studio. Primary and secondary packaging for an extra aged version of Bulleit Bourbon (also designed by Sandstrom).

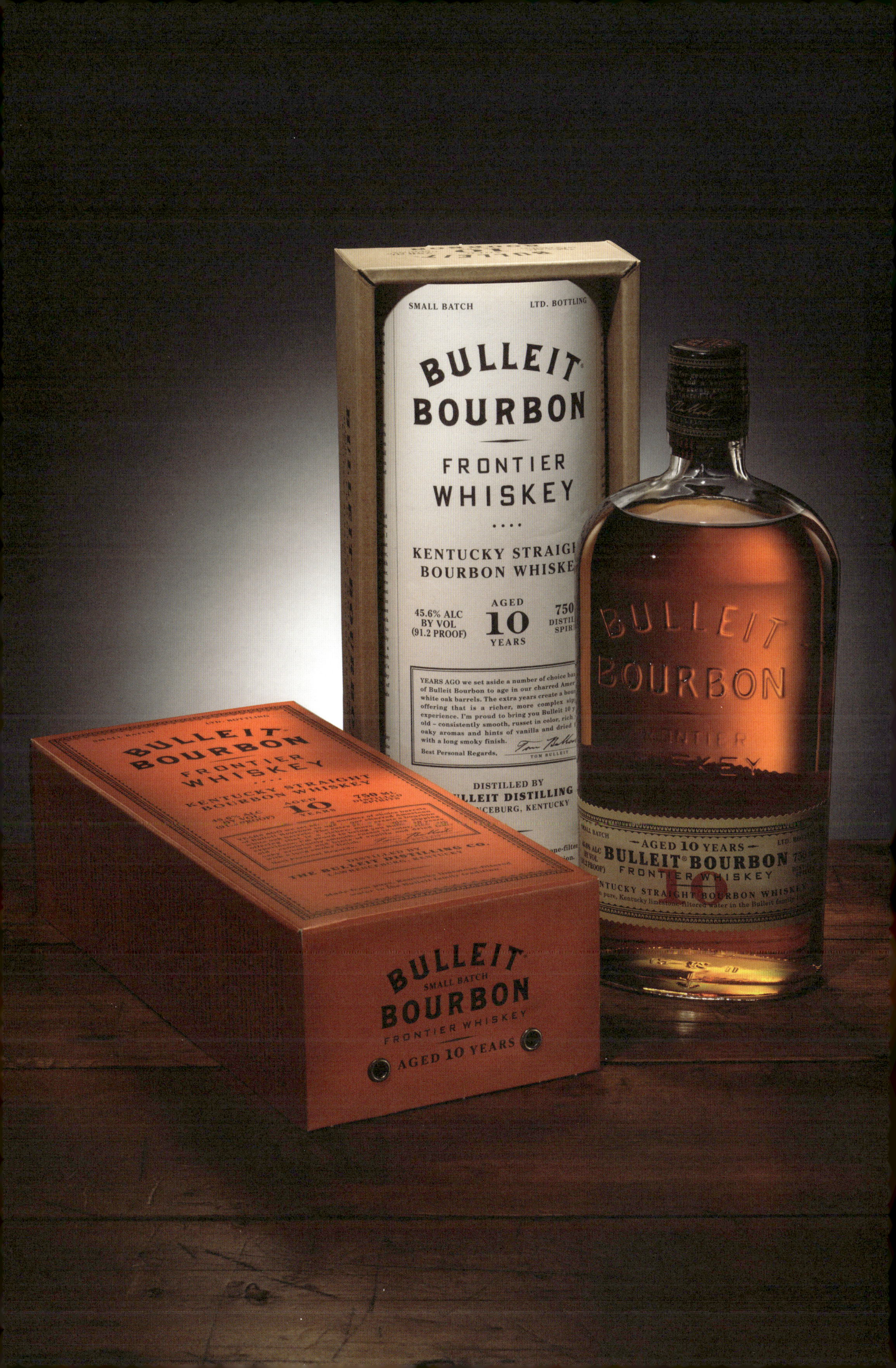

SMALL BATCH
LTD. BOTTLING
BULLEIT
BOURBON
FRONTIER
WHISKEY
45.6% ALC
BY VOL
(91.2 PROOF)
AGED
10
YEARS
Best Personal Regards,
DISTILLED BY

BULLEIT
SMALL BATCH
BOURBON
FRONTIER WHISKEY
AGED 10 YEARS

AGED 10 YEARS
BULLEIT BOURBON
FRONTIER WHISKEY

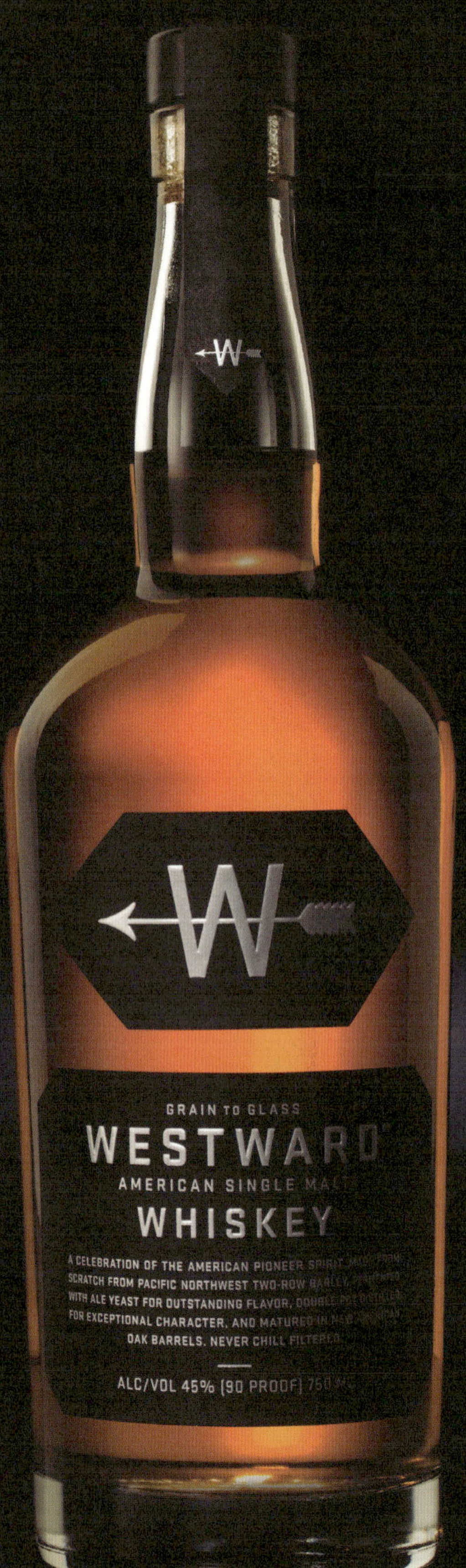
GRAIN TO GLASS
WESTWARD
AMERICAN SINGLE MALT
WHISKEY
ALC/VOL 45% [90 PROOF]

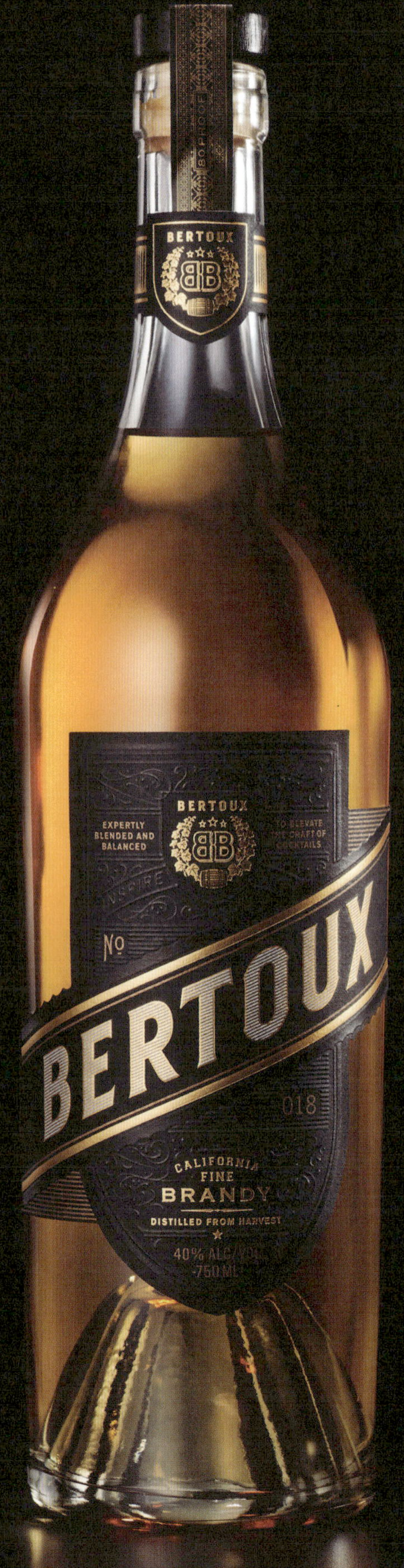
BERTOUX
EXPERTLY BLENDED AND BALANCED
№
BERTOUX
018
CALIFORNIA FINE BRANDY
DISTILLED FROM HARVEST
750 ML

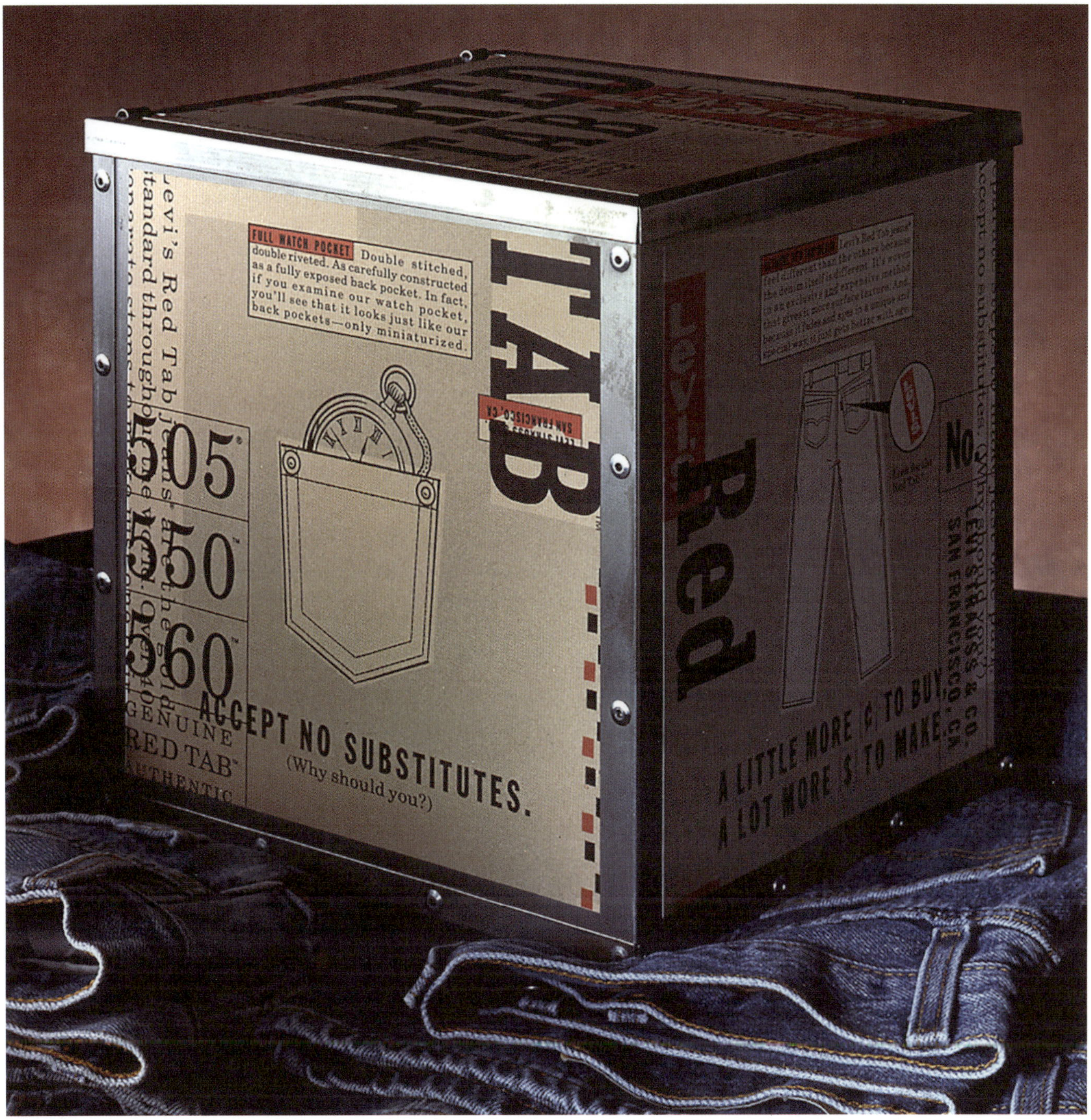

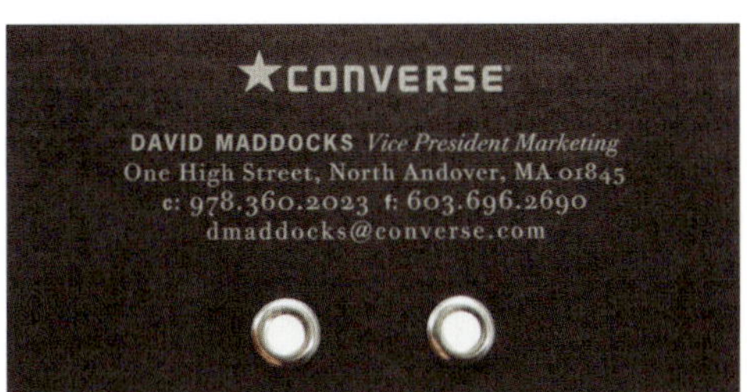

(Page 12, Left) Westward Whiskey. Client: House Spirits. Design: Steve Sandstrom. Photo: Polara Studio. An American single malt whiskey. The brand identity and labeling feature a single typeface. / (Page 12, Right) Client: Bertoux Distillers–Bertoux is a brandy developed specifically for making fine cocktails. It's named for the inventor of the bicycle/motorcycle sidecar, and a Sidecar is also the most famous brandy cocktail. Photo: Polara Studio / (Page 13, Top) Metal and paper display cube for Levi's Red Tab jeans, part of a broad campaign in collaboration with FCB/San Francisco in the early 90s. Photo: Mark Hooper. / (Page 13, Bottom) Executive business cards for Converse (2005) featuring the highly recognizable small grommets that serve to vent each pair of Chuck Taylor All Star shoes. Photo: Mark Hooper.

Introduction by Austin Howe *Creative Director and Author*

Assume for a moment that I do not like Steve Sandstrom. What would I have to begrudgingly acknowledge about him and his work? I'd probably be forced to admit that he has quietly become one of the world's most important and iconic designers. I say "quietly," because despite the fact that Sandstrom Partners has won more creative awards than most small countries, he's not much of a self-promoter. Otherwise, he might take credit for single handedly blowing up and reinventing traditional packaging in the mid-nineties, with the original Tazo Tea branding. He literally invented "packaging as branded content." His proprietary superpower is melding authentic (and painstakingly researched) historical references with modern quality cues to create these fully- and wondrously-realized brand worlds that have never existed before (see St-Germain, Bulleit, etc.). He'd never admit to being the greatest craftsman working in design today, even though clients similarly obsessed queue up to work with him. Now, assume for a second that I love and admire the man. Then I'd have to add that Steve Sandstrom is one of the smartest, wittiest, most talented, loyal, gracious, and interesting people I've ever had the pleasure of working with.

IT IS VERY GRATIFYING TO BREATHE NEW LIFE AND RELEVANCE INTO A BRAND THAT HAD LOST ITS WAY.

Steve Sandstrom, *Executive Creative Director, Sandstrom Partners*

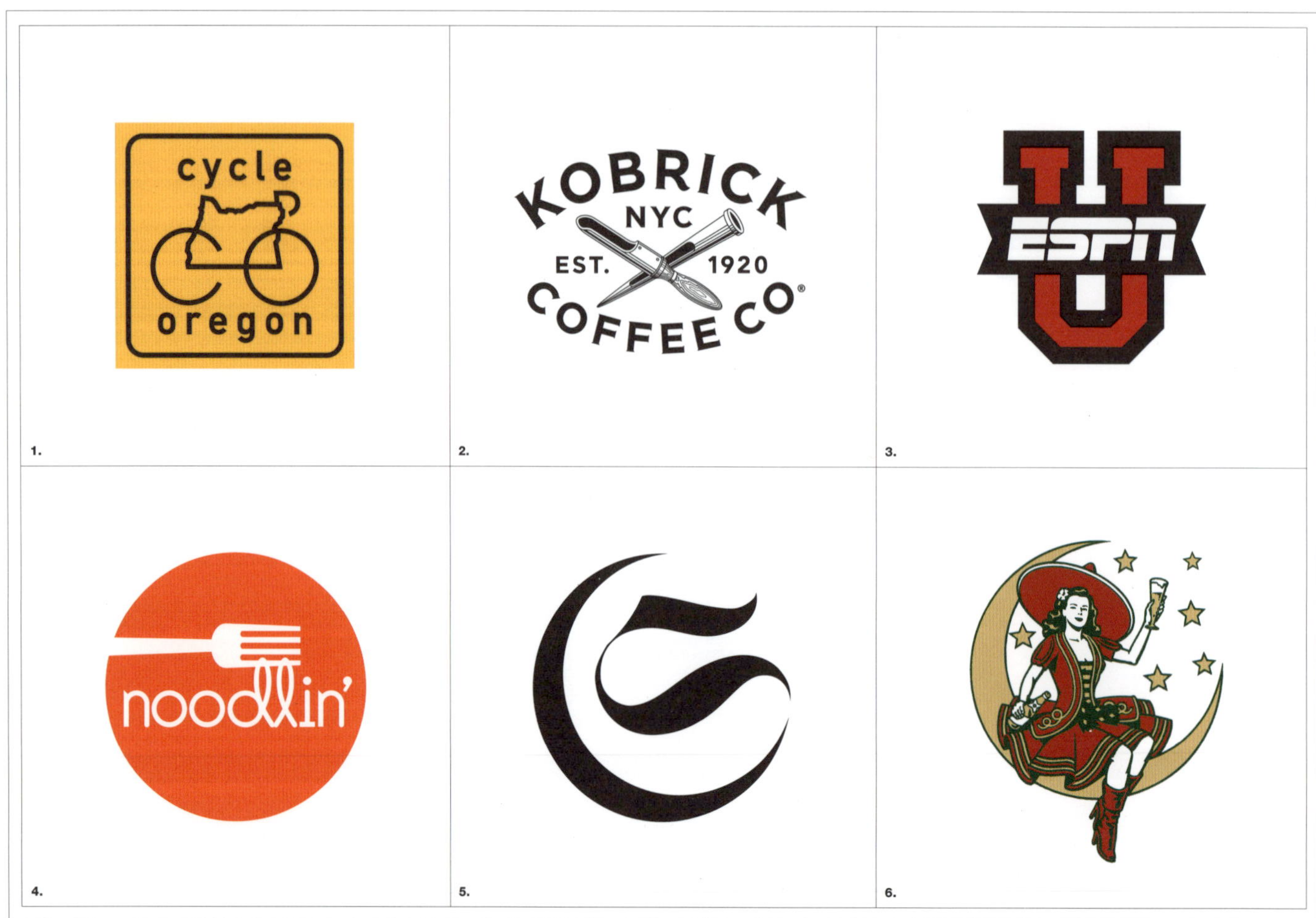

1. *Client: Cycle Oregon–Organized bike rides to promote the beauty of the state, and raise funds to help support rural communities.* **2.** *Kobrick Coffee is a fourth generation, family-owned specialty coffee roaster for the finest chefs and restaurants in New York and beyond.* **3.** *Client: ESPN–ESPNU is a cable television network featuring collegiate sports.* **4.** *Client: The Holland, Inc.–A fast-casual restaurant with a variety of noodle/pasta dishes.* **5.** *Client: Storycode. Creators of a digital publishing platform. The mark is inspired by William Shakespeare's signature.* **6.** *Client: Miller Brewing–Miller High Life iconography. Illustration by Larry Jost.*

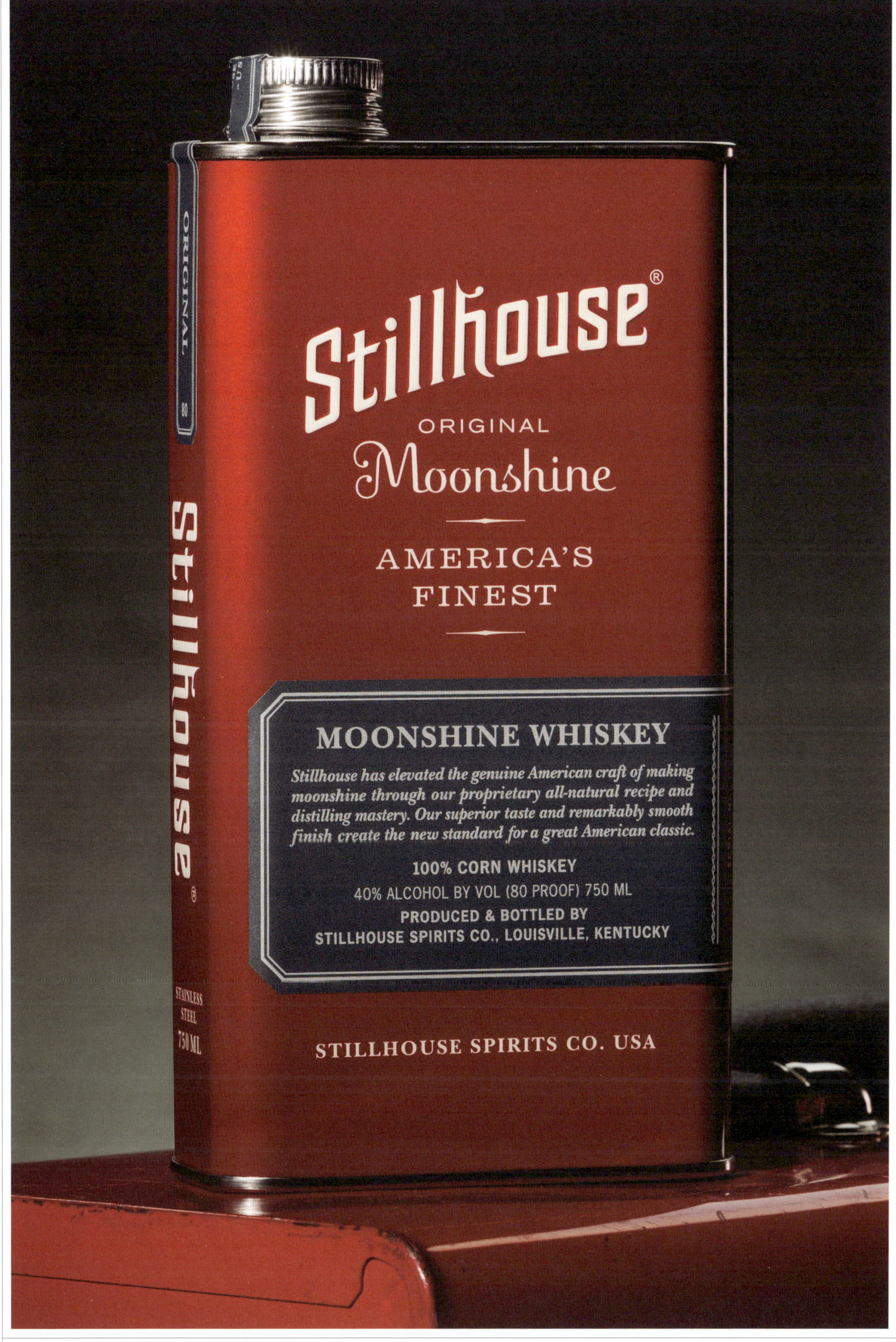

Original Moonshine Whiskey. Client: Stillhouse Spirits Co. Concept and design: Steve Sandstrom. Photo: Polara Studio. Completely custom, stainless steel "turpentine" can plays off the inexperienced misperceptions of harsh taste and threatening quality of moonshine, while supporting the outlawed and risk-taking lore of moonshine culture.

What inspired or motivated you into your career?
I was a Fine Arts major at the University of Oregon (BFA Drawing and Painting). But I had taken some graphic arts and offset printing classes in high school and community college, so I knew how to create and prepare artwork for commercial reproduction. I thought I would need to move to New York to make a proper commitment of becoming a fine artist, but that was not affordable to me. And I couldn't tolerate the idea of more debt. I ended up moving back into my parent's home and renting a small studio space in downtown Portland with the hopes of becoming an illustrator.

Eventually, I interviewed with small advertising agencies and got a job as an art director/production artist. It was a five person agency with larger offices in two other cities. I didn't really know that much about advertising, but this was not an impressive place with any notable creative credentials or accolades to tout. We had mostly industrial or wood products accounts and a couple of smaller independent banks. However, I learned about the Portland ad scene, made some good connections, did some work that started to get noticed, did some freelance work on the side to make ends meet, and learned about business and how to estimate a job from concept through final execution. This led to a job with another small agency focused more on design and packaging projects than advertising.

I had a progressive rock radio station client that had been my freelance account for several years. The radio station became increasingly popular and the work I was able to create for them made a bigger and bigger impression on the city through a wide range of promotions. This led to work for another station in Worcester, Massachusetts with a similar rock format. (The identity I created for that station in 1981 is still being used). The aggressive attitude and high production value of my work for radio impressed Peter Moore, who was the creative director at Nike Design. He hired me as a senior art director/designer. My main focus was supporting the apparel side of the company's business and also overall brand work as needed.

What is your work philosophy?
I have a ridiculous work ethic. I'm tougher on my own work than that of others. Otherwise, I strive to subvert expectations.

Who is or was your greatest mentor?
My art instructor in high school was Robert Boardwell. When Bob was a college student, he studied photography with Minor White, one of the most significant photographers of the 20th century. In high school photo class, Bob taught us to mix our own chemicals from scratch for black and white film and print developers using Minor White's custom formulas. He taught us as if we were advanced college students.

Bob also studied calligraphy with Lloyd Reynolds at Reed College while pursuing his Masters degree. (Look up Steve Jobs commencement address to Stanford University about calligraphy at Reed.) Lloyd Reynolds was named Calligrapher Laureate of Oregon by the governor for introducing, educating, and promoting the art form with significant influence throughout the country. Bob taught us the same assignments and lessons being taught at Reed while we were sophomores in high school art class. He also taught us aerodynamics; each student was tasked to design and carve their own airplane out of blocks of balsa wood. We shaped the air foils on the wings and positioned them and stabilizers on the fuselage for long gliding, or more aggressive trick flights. Our grades were A if it flew, and F if it didn't.

During lunch, Bob would let us listen to recordings of Alan Watts' lectures on Zen teachings and Eastern Philosophy. It was daily mind-blowing inspiration without drugs.

He won a science award for tracking the Russian "Sputnik" satellite with photography, and he helped develop photo-screen printing. He was a kind of Renaissance man with a mind and talent for any art form or medium and how science could be engaged in each. He gave me tremendous support and encouragement, guidance, and belief.

What is it about Design that you are most passionate about?
Solving a problem well enough that the problem shouldn't seem to have existed.

What is the most difficult challenge you've had to overcome?
I was a child of blue collar means. I had to pay my way. I was also born a white hetero male. I think that privilege was enough to believe that I've had no challenges of any significance.

Who were some of your greatest past influences?
I'm a West Coast guy, so all the Michaels in the Bay Area come to mind. One of my early favorite designers was your publisher, B. Martin Pedersen. When I first saw his Nautical Quarterly publication it floored me, beautifully done. And Peter Moore at Nike, of course. I've been greatly influenced, as a fan of advertising, by writers such as Bill Borders, Dave Newman, Steve Sandoz, Peter Wegner (now a significant and brilliant fine artist), Jim Riswold, Austin Howe, Jim Haven, Palmer Petterson, the list is long. And also architects, industrial designers, athletes, musicians, songwriters, dancers, filmmakers, photographers, illustrators. So many.

What are the most important ingredients you require from a client to do successful work?
A trusting relationship is critical. Being open to things that may not be expected or pre-conceived. A commitment to quality execution.

What would be your dream assignment?
The key, I think, is to seek the dream from whatever the assignment that you're given.

You've helped brands re-establish themselves, what is most important when doing so?
Whenever I've had the chance to work on a once famous or iconic brand, I deeply feel the importance of the work as it relates to history and a potential future. To bridge the time when the brand was last great to the current and next generation, is to be done with respect and the enthusiastic energy of discovery. It's like brand archeology. It is very gratifying to breathe new life and relevance into a brand that lost its way.

What is your proudest professional achievement?
Coming to the office with work to do each day.

How do you define success?
I've received a lot of important creative industry awards over my career. It's an incredible thing to be honored and respected by your peers. But it's something more when that body of work helps clients achieve success and to see the impact it makes on their business and their lives.

What part of your work do you find most demanding?
Dealing with the culture of fear that is pervasive in almost all of corporate America. Few companies incorporate the importance of failure into their culture. It takes many attempts to actually innovate, but not many people have an allowance to fail within a corporate structure in order to create something

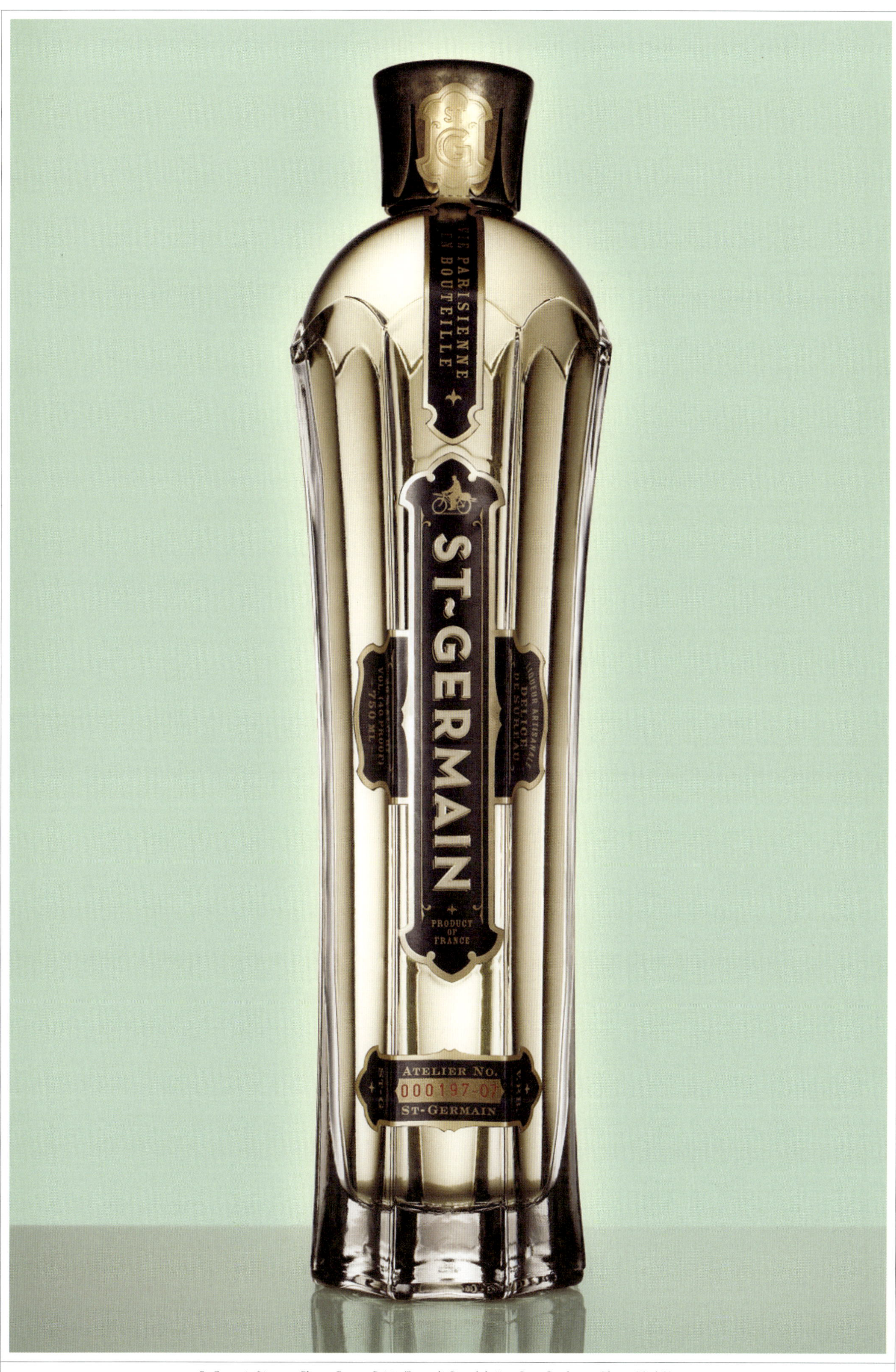

St-Germain Liqueur. Client: Cooper Spirits/Bacardi. Brand design: Steve Sandstrom. Photo: Mark Hooper.
The first liqueur made from fresh, hand-picked, wild elderflowers from the foothills of the Alps.

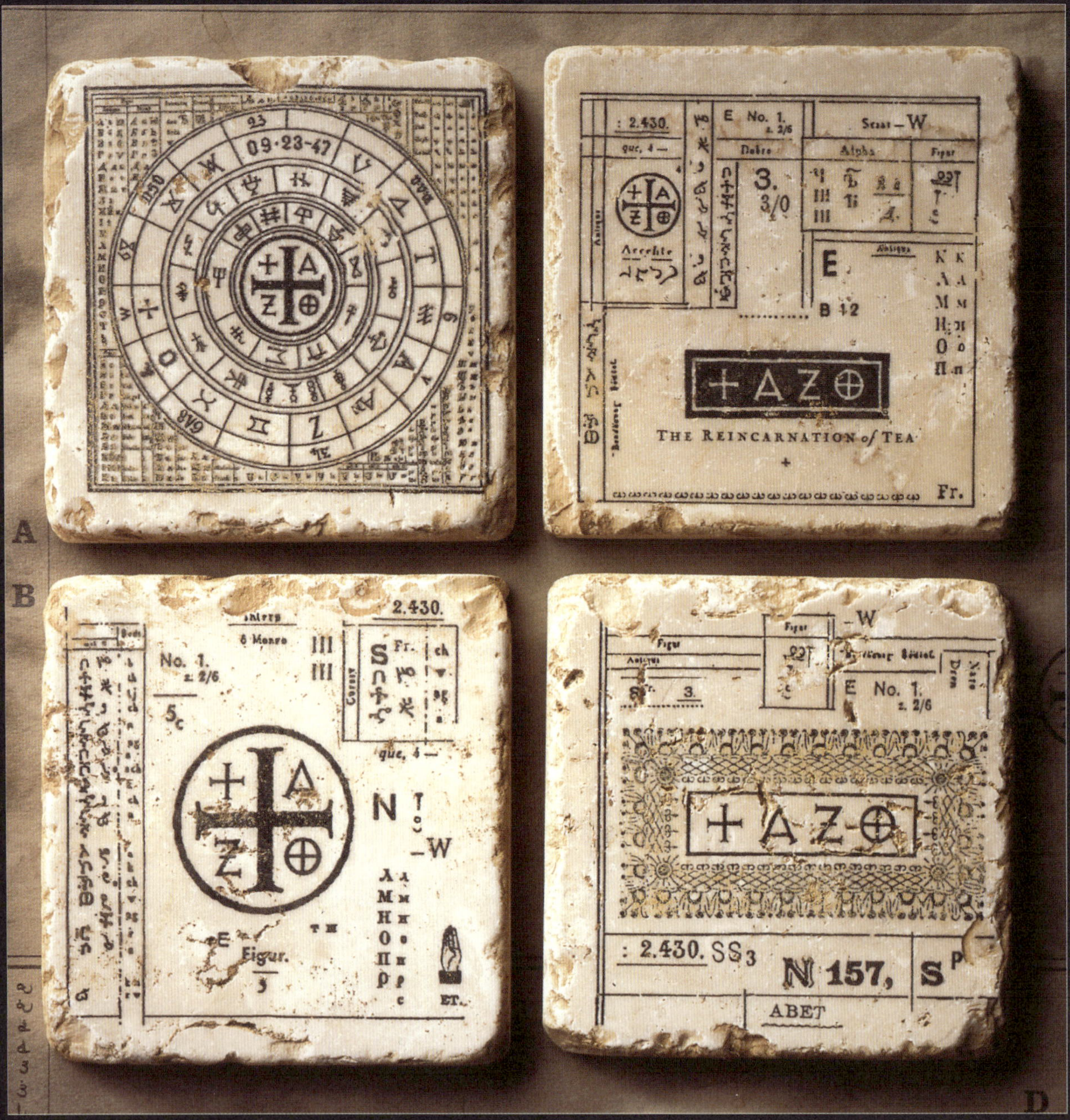

"The original brand story conceived for Tazo was full of historic and cultural references which we integrated with our own versions. One example is a Tazo testimonial from Socrates, 339 B.C., 'Better than hemlock without the bitter afterlife.' To expand this brand mythology, we created our own artifacts such as the Tazo Stone, our fictional twist on the discovery of the Rosetta Stone that scholars used to translate Egyptian hieroglyphs. The Tazo Stone was the ancient repository of many Tazo blends, and was uncovered after centuries in a cave on the shores of the Red Sea during an unusually low tide. Furthering the Tazo Stone story led us to create ceramic coasters (above) as replicas of stone fragments also found in the cave." Photo: Mark Hooper.

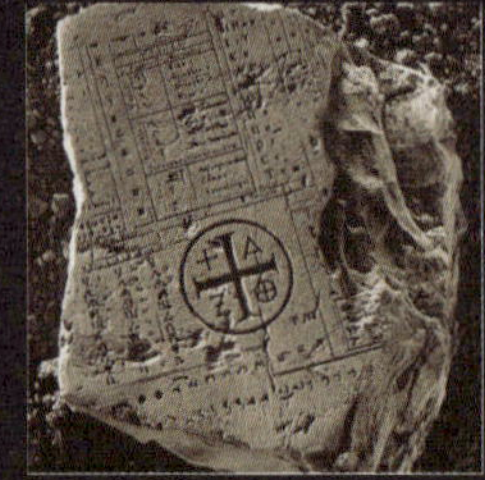

STEVE SANDSTROM'S INITIAL PACKAGING CONCEPT WAS SO STRONG, IT INSPIRED TAZO'S FOUNDERS TO GO BACK AND IMPROVE THEIR (TEA) PRODUCT.

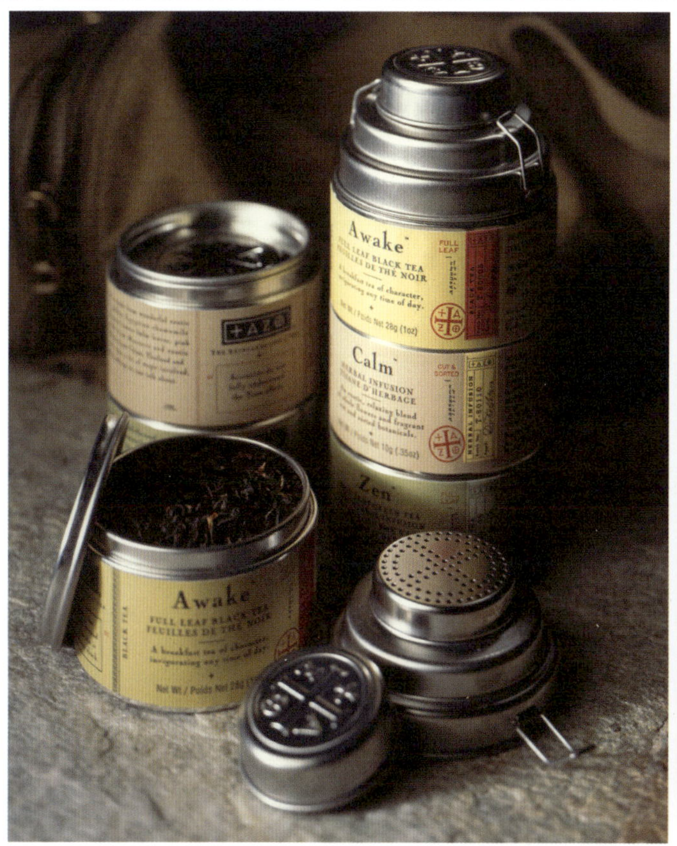

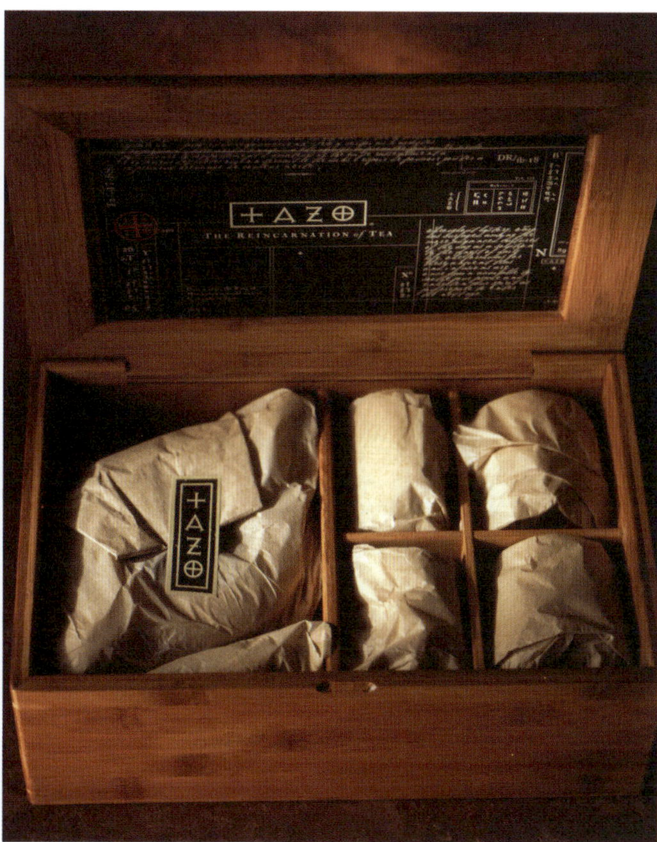

(Left) Stacking tins of three loose leaf teas from Tazo. The cap system includes a stainless steel infuser that can rest across a tea cup for brewing. (Right) Bamboo gift box containing a custom Tazo tea pot and four cups. Photo: Polara Studio.

new or significant. A lot of mostly flawed research is utilized. Mostly flawed because it is not actual science and people don't always know what they want until they see and experience it.

What professional goals do you still have for yourself?
To see how long I can remain relevant and passionate, and create meaningful, exceptional work.

What has been your most memorable project?
There are many. To list only one would be the creation of the tea brand Tazo. It was our first chance to create a brand from scratch–even before there was a name and before any products had been developed. Our client had sold their previous tea company and so they knew plenty about the tea industry and business, but they wanted to do something quite differently the next time around. The client was introduced to me by my friend, creative collaborator, and brilliant writer, Steve Sandoz. On the client side were Steve Lee and Steve Smith. If you're not counting, that's four Steves in one meeting. Our brief was derived from an idea that Smith had in mind, "Marco Polo meets Merlin."

Origin stories about tea are all myths. No one truly knows. That gave us a chance to create our own history for Tazo (named by Sandoz) and we ran with that in humorous and often inspirational ways. We wanted the brand to be multicultural and not "American," so we kept ourselves in check from being perfect at marketing. Sandoz and I were able to enlist our main client, Steve Smith, deep into the concept. He became a great believer in the power of creating something beyond expectations. He was also a remarkably creative and driven individual. Together, we helped awaken a sleepy category, and created a brand that influenced not only the tea category, but well beyond.

Starbucks purchased Tazo and eventually misguided it from a brand with tremendous energy and potential to an average line of products no one needs to care about. We resigned from the account once we were clear that they had no vision. Steve Smith left soon after. But our Tazo experience taught us how to bring more depth and value to a brand, and it informed the way we approach much of the work we've done for others since. Including another tea company–Steven Smith Teamaker.

What do you wish you had known when you first started out?
What I know now. Except then I wouldn't have enjoyed the time it took to learn it.

What interests do you have outside of your work?
Family. Travel. However, as a designer, my work integrates into much of my being so there isn't much outside of it.

What do you value most?
Relationships. I could never spend enough time with them, but I deeply value them.

Where do you seek inspiration?
Everywhere. Rudolph Arnheim wrote about how our eyes are our primary source for learning. The audio world is rich and provides us with so much, yet when we consider what audio alone can teach us about a bird, it's minimal–perhaps its chirp and the flutter of its wings. Yet the visual learning of a bird is robust. So my eyes (and other senses) are always teaching me. I once created an identity system based on the inspiration of a parking garage ticket. The small grommets on the side of Converse Chuck Taylor All Stars inspired me to put them on the shoe box and business cards of company executives. Everyone recognizes them. I just saw them as a brand story.

Where do you see yourself in the future?
Here, hopefully.

Sandstrom Partners www.sandstrompartners.com
See his Graphis Master Portfolio on graphis.com.

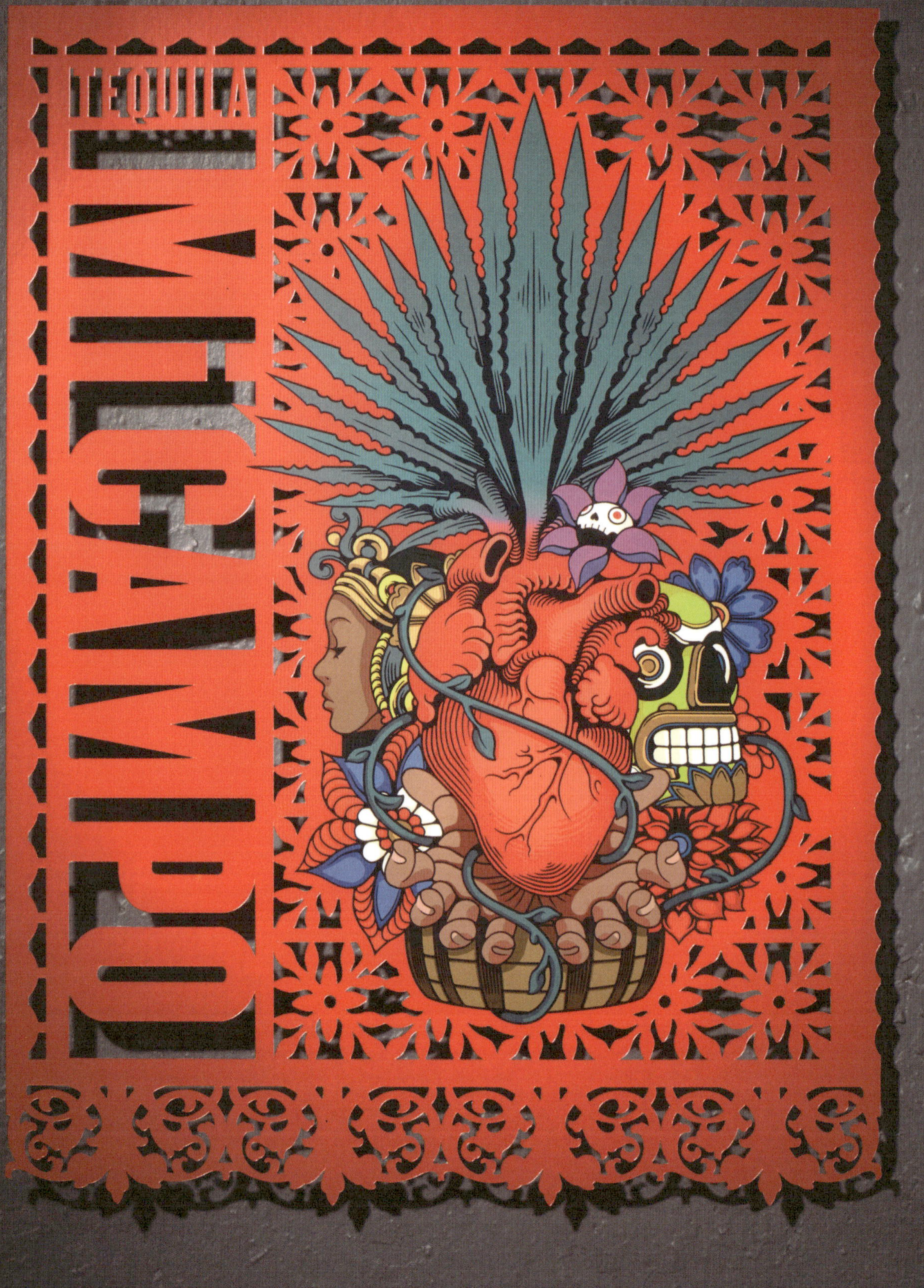

Mi Campo Tequila. Client: Constellation Brands. Design: Steve Sandstrom. Illustration: Raul Urias. Photo: Polara Studio.
Mexican "papel picado" inspired display and promotional poster (18x24 inches).

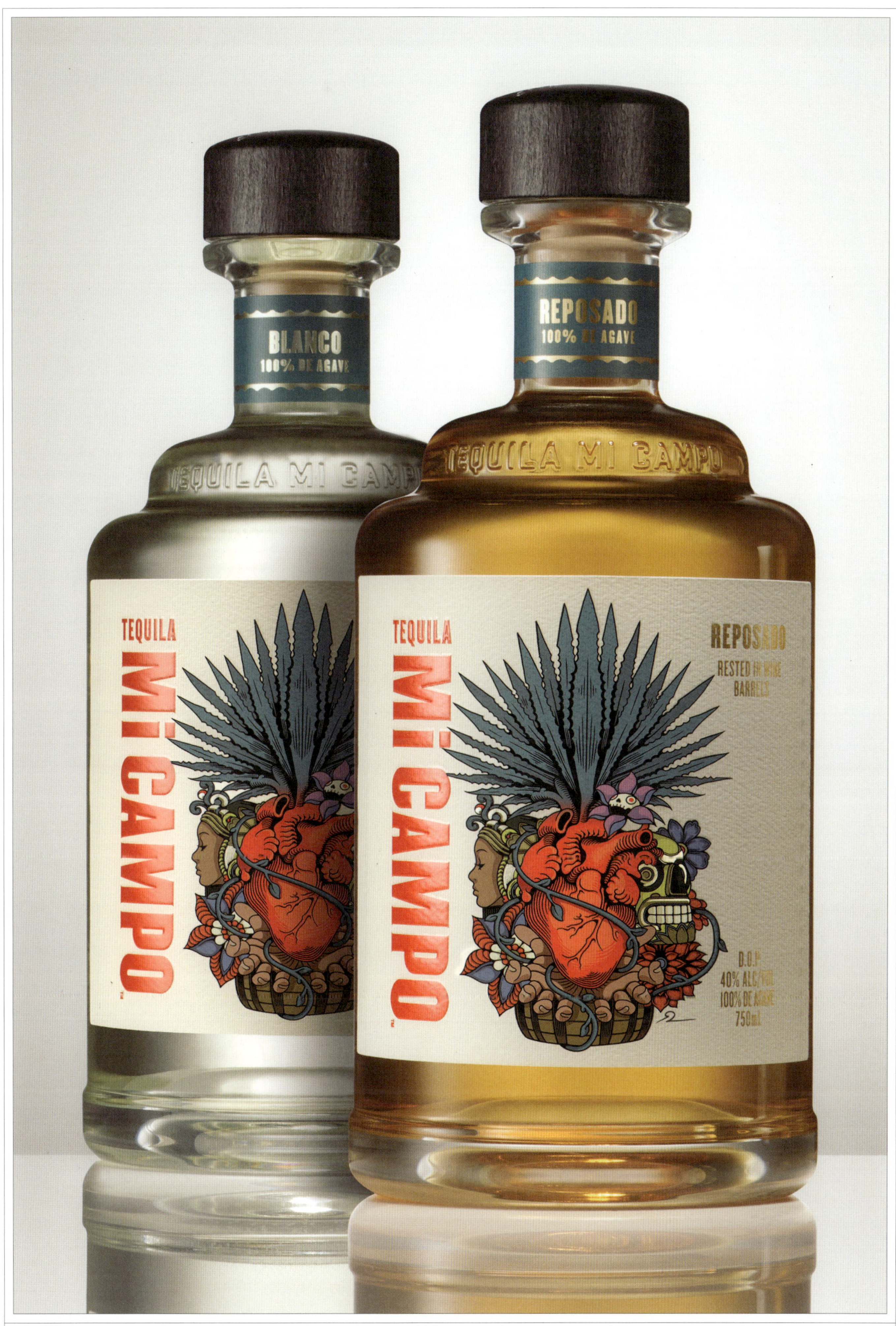

Mi Campo Tequila. Client: Constellation Brands. Design: Steve Sandstrom. Illustration: Raul Urias. Photo: Polara Studio.
The shoulders of the custom bottle are inspired by the shape of a traditional margarita cocktail glass (inverted).

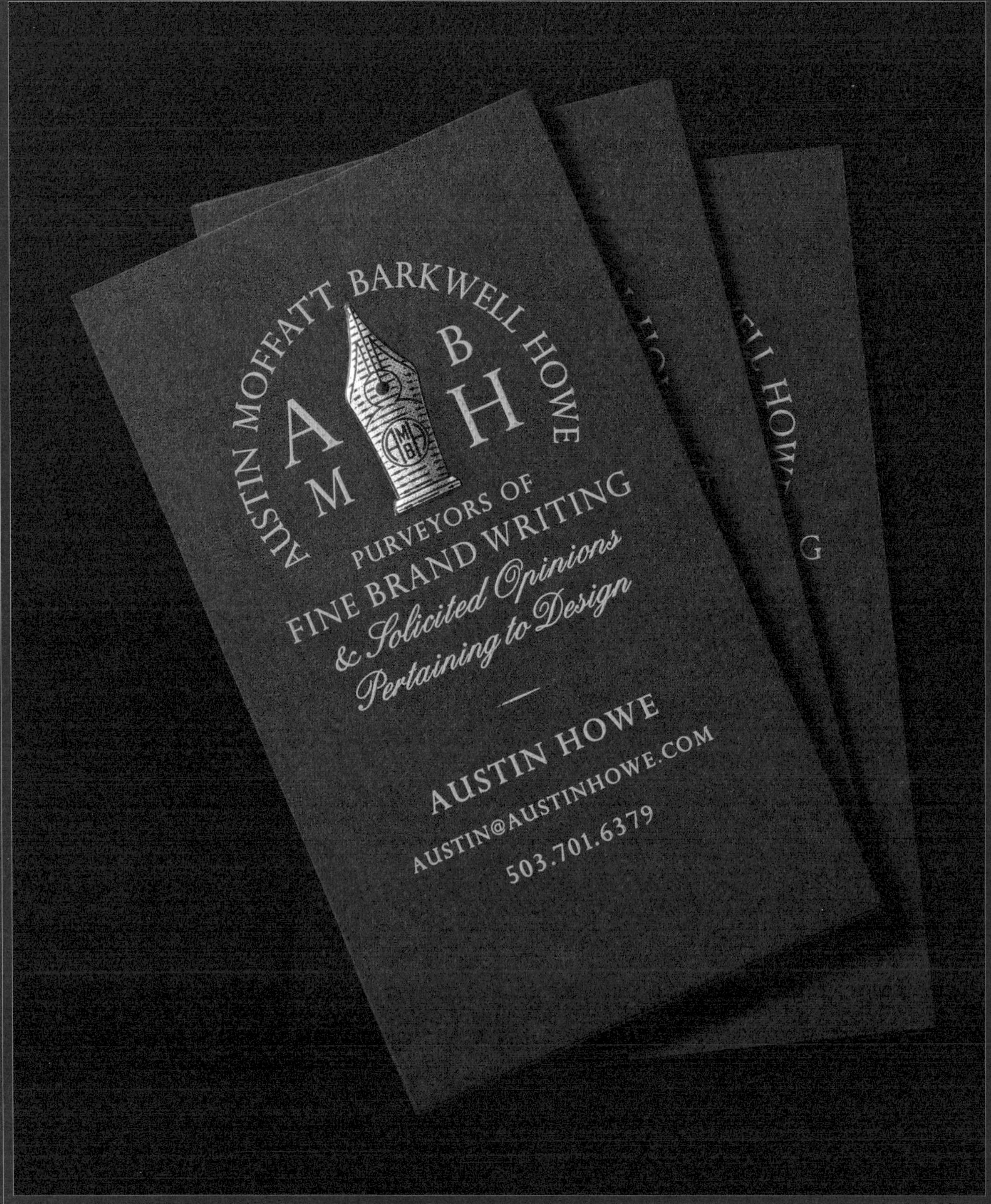

Engraved business cards for Austin Howe, accomplished writer, creative director and brilliant collaborator. Howe is the author of two books on design. Illustration: Larry Jost. Photo: Polara Studio.

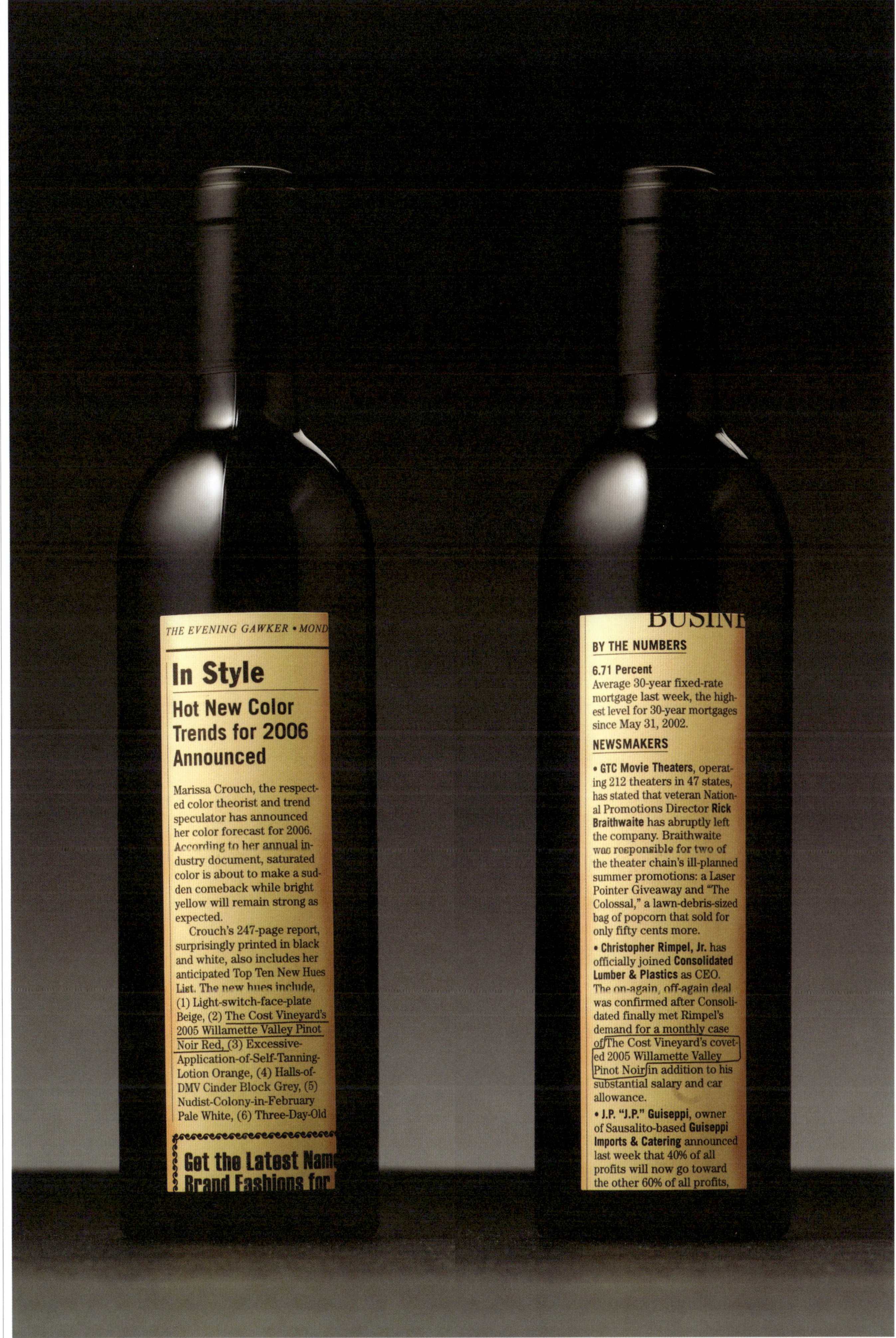

Packaging for The Cost Vineyard 2005 Pinot Noir. Each case carton contained 12 different labels designed as (fictional) newspaper clippings including classified ads, advice columns, and other sections of the paper. The wine is mentioned (and crudely highlighted) within the articles. Concept/writing by Lane Foard. Photo: Polara Studio.

WHAT MAKES DAEKI & JUN REMARKABLE IS THE COMBINATION OF CREATIVE TALENT AND EXPERIENCE THEY GAINED FROM NOT ONLY COMMERCIAL PROJECTS, BUT ALSO DIVERSE, SELF-INITIATED PROJECTS.

Byung-Hak Ahn, *Designer, Professor & Chair of Visual Communication Design Dept. at Hongik University*

DAEKI & JUN HAVE ALWAYS SUGGESTED NEW AND EXPERIMENTAL DESIGN CONCEPTS & DIRECTIONS. THEY HAVE PROVIDED THE BEST RESULTS, BEYOND EXPECTATIONS, WITHOUT A SINGLE MODIFICATION.

THEIR CREATIVE SPIRIT OF EXPERIMENTATION AND PROFESSIONALISM IS RECOGNIZED GLOBALLY. I WILL CONTINUE TO WORK WITH THEM ON DESIGN PROJECTS IN THE FUTURE.

Insu Lee, *Illustrator*

THEIR WORK HAS BEEN FULL OF 'EXPERIMENT' WHICH IS COMPATIBLE WITH 'DIVERSITY.' THAT'S THE REASON FOR ME TO LOOK FORWARD TO THEIR FUTURE WORK.

Hoon-Dong Chung, *Designer, Associate Professor & Dean of the Communication Design Dept. at Dankook University, Graphis Master*

THEY ALWAYS SHOW NEW POSSIBILITIES OF GRAPHIC DESIGN. THEIR WORK IS QUITE ABSTRACT AND SYMBOLIC. THEY LEAD IMAGINATION TO THE AUDIENCE, WHICH CROSSES THE BOUNDARIES OF RIGID THINKING.

Kyungsun Kymn, *Dir. at Typojanchi 2015: The 4th International Typography Biennale, Chairperson at Korean Society of Typography(KST), Professor at Seoul National Univ.*

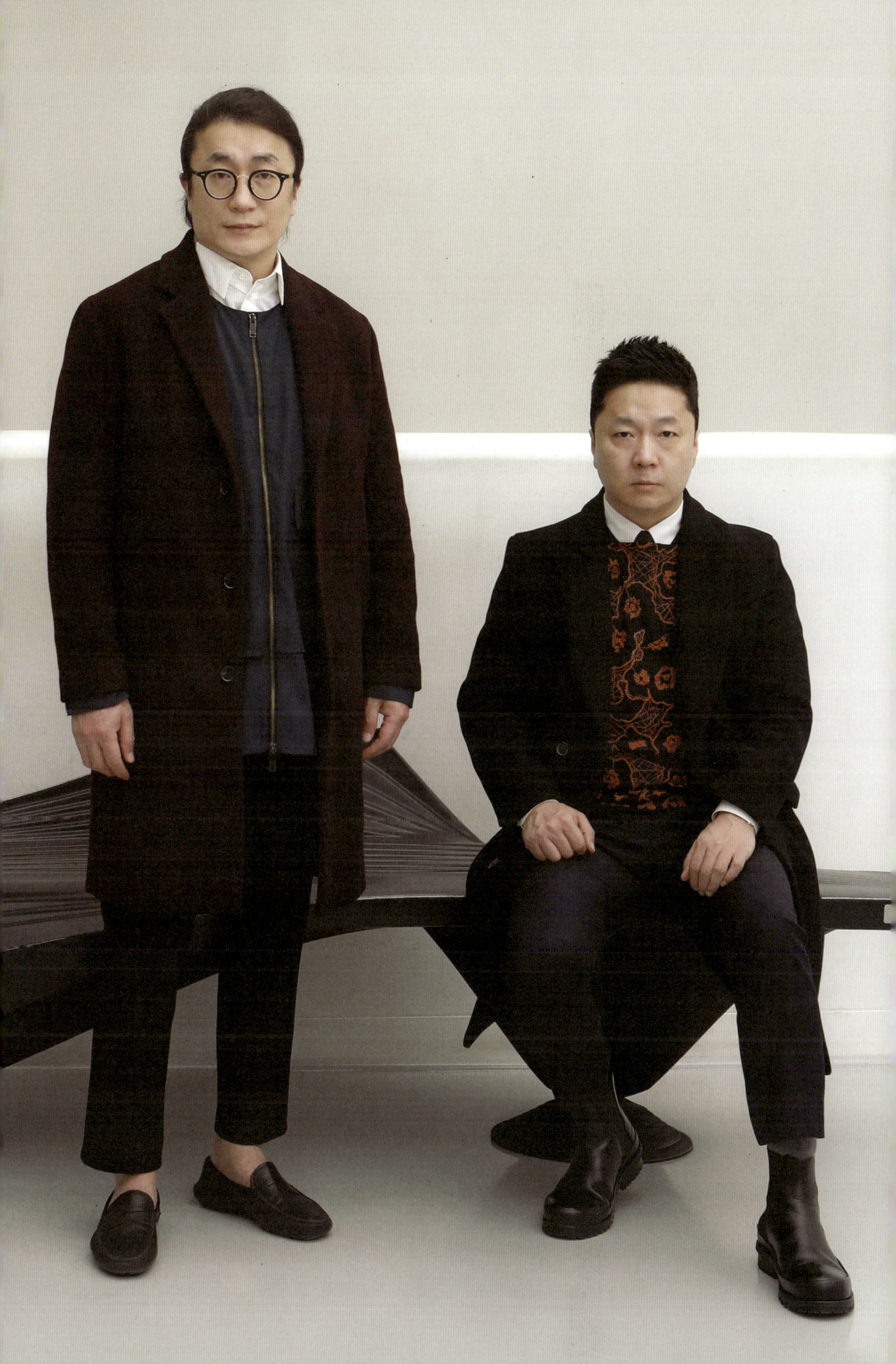

Landscapes,
unlike their
representations,
are constituted
in space-time.
They are
always changing,
in the process
of being
and becoming,
never exactly
the same twice over.

Interpreting Landscapes

Christopher Tilley

Title: Now & Here; Design Studio: DAEKI & JUN / Korea National University of Arts; Art Director & Designer: Daeki Shim, Hyun Cho
Client: 2015 Asia/Next-Poster Experimental Design Exhibition

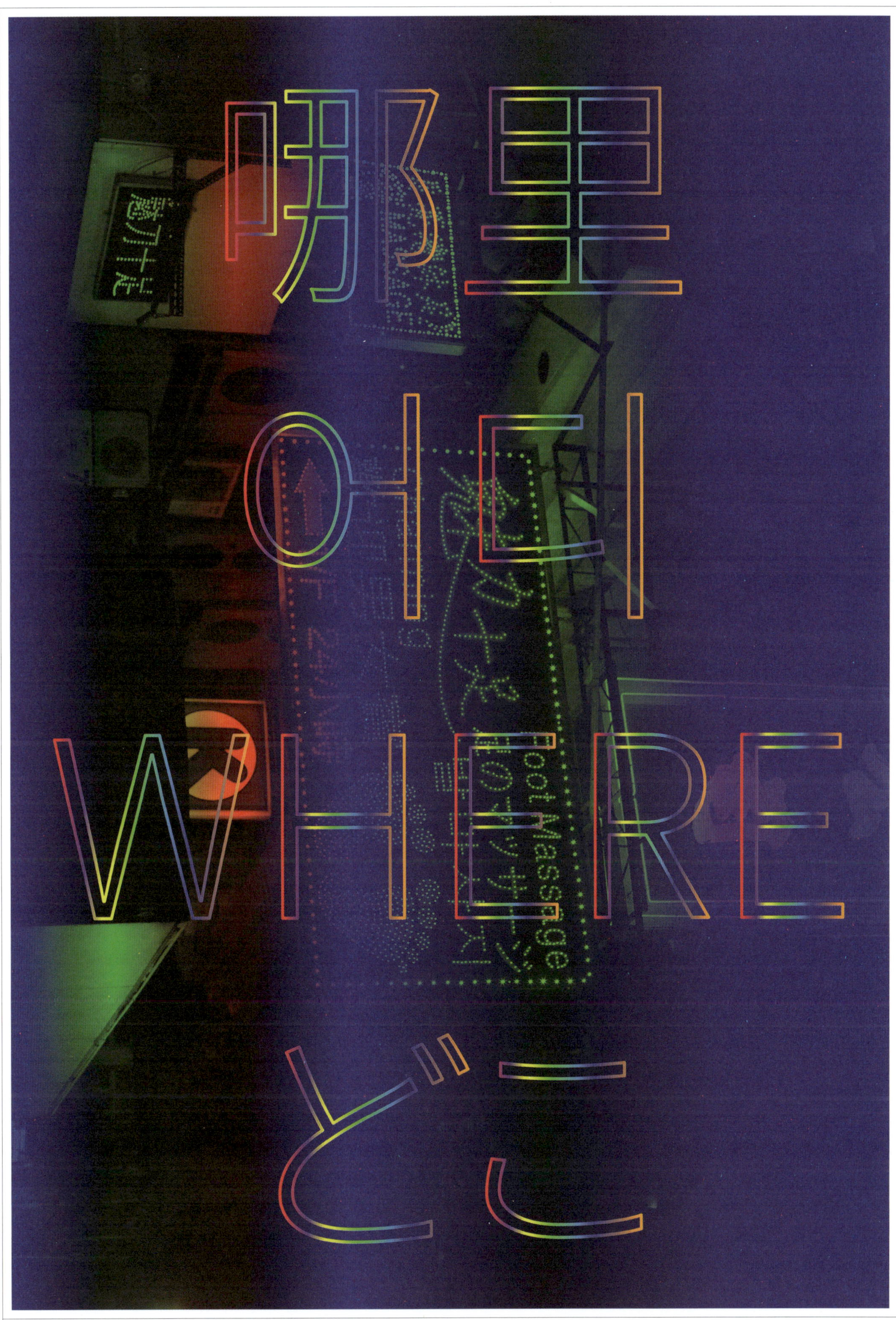

Title: Where 01: Multilingual; Design Studio: DAEKI & JUN; Art Director & Designer: Daeki Shim, HyoJun Shim
Client: International Poster Invitation Exhibition / Beijing Design Week 2015

Introduction by **Serge Serov** *Golden Bee Global Biennial President, HOD cathedra of RANEPA Design School*

South Korean design has gained enormous respect in the international professional society. Young South Korean designers, Daeki Shim and HyoJun Shim, are confidently following this path. ▪ They have set in motion the energy of colored light, creating an atmosphere of a miracle, a mysterious profoundness and a total incomprehensibility of a visual image; things that are really in demand in contemporary aesthetics. Personally, I am attracted to the presentation of their posters. They apply the image and text to the mirror with special paints, and the poster enters into a dialogue with the viewer, taking them into its own looking-glass space. They turn a poster into a natural phenomenon. ▪ The brothers Shim were invited to Vladivostok. There they showed their work and held a workshop with students of the far Eastern Federal Uni. They were greeted enthusiastically and impressed the students. Their magnificent works connecting East and West, history and modernity, were so close to the minds of Russian students. The world is one.

WE FIND INSPIRATION FROM OTHER FIELDS SUCH AS TECHNOLOGY, ARCHITECTURE, ART, AS WELL AS PHILOSOPHY. WE ARE INSPIRED BY THE VARIOUS CULTURES WE'VE EXPERIENCED IN OUR LIVES.

Daeki Shim & HyoJun Shim, *DAEKI & JUN design studio*

I WORKED WITH THEM CLOSELY AND ALWAYS ENJOYED THEIR CHALLENGING AND EXPERIMENTAL ATTITUDE. THIS MAKES THEM HIGHLY QUALIFIED TO BE INTRODUCED TO ALL OF YOU.

Byung-Hak Ahn, *Designer, Professor & Chair of Visual Comm. Design Dept. at Hongik University, Director of the 5th Typojanchi, Intl. Typography Biennale 2017*

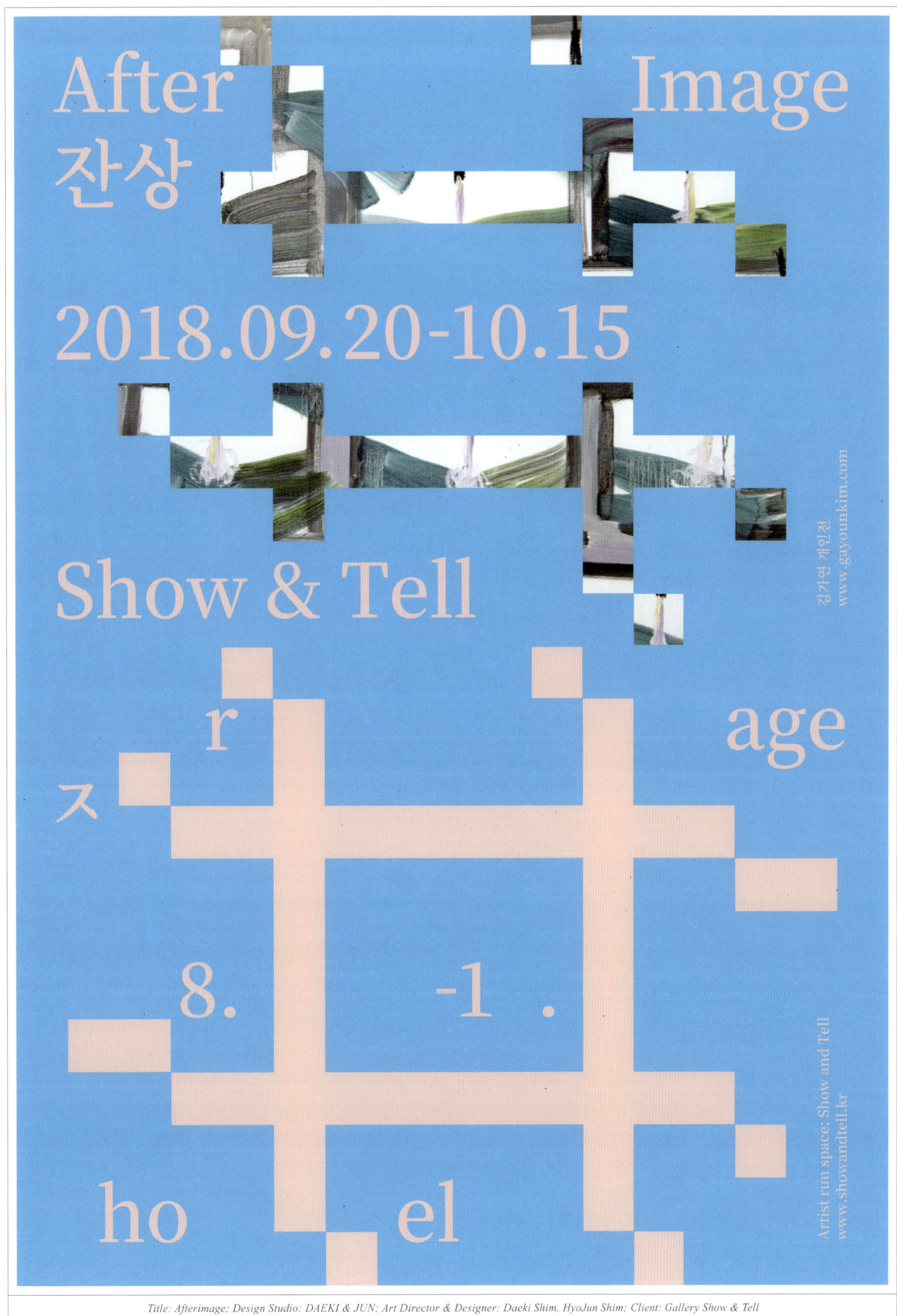

Title: Afterimage; Design Studio: DAEKI & JUN; Art Director & Designer: Daeki Shim, HyoJun Shim; Client: Gallery Show & Tell

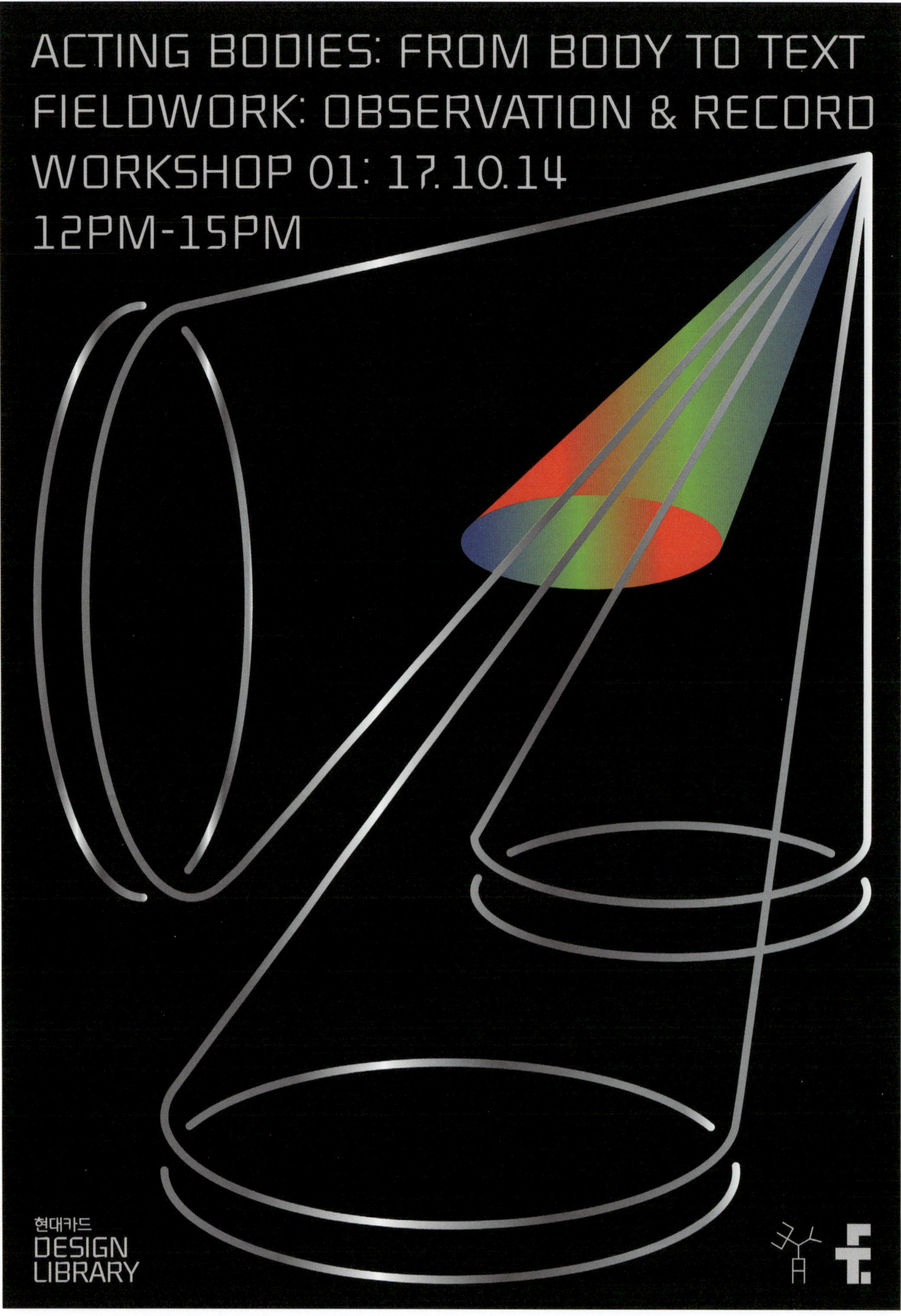

Title: Fieldwork: Observation & Record; Design Studio: DAEKI & JUN; Art Director & Designer: Daeki Shim; Assistant Designer: Yonghoon Park (intern)
Clients: Hyundai Card Design Library, Korea Craft & Design Foundation (KCDF), Typojanchi

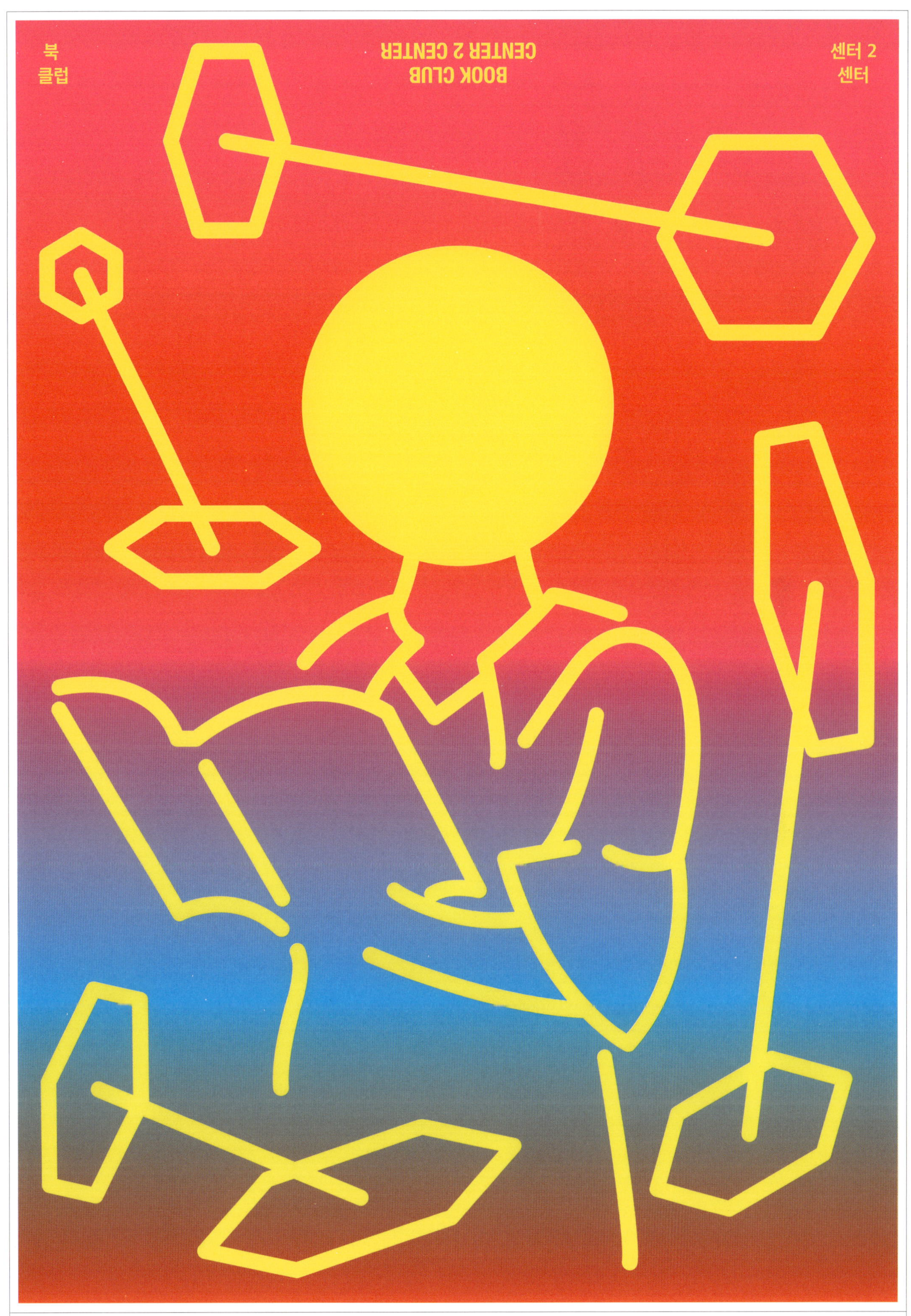

Title: Book Club 01, 02: CENTER 2 CENTER; Design Studio: DAEKI & JUN; Art Director & Designer: Daeki Shim, HyoJun Shim
Assistant Designer: Somin Lee (intern); Client: CENTER 2 CENTER

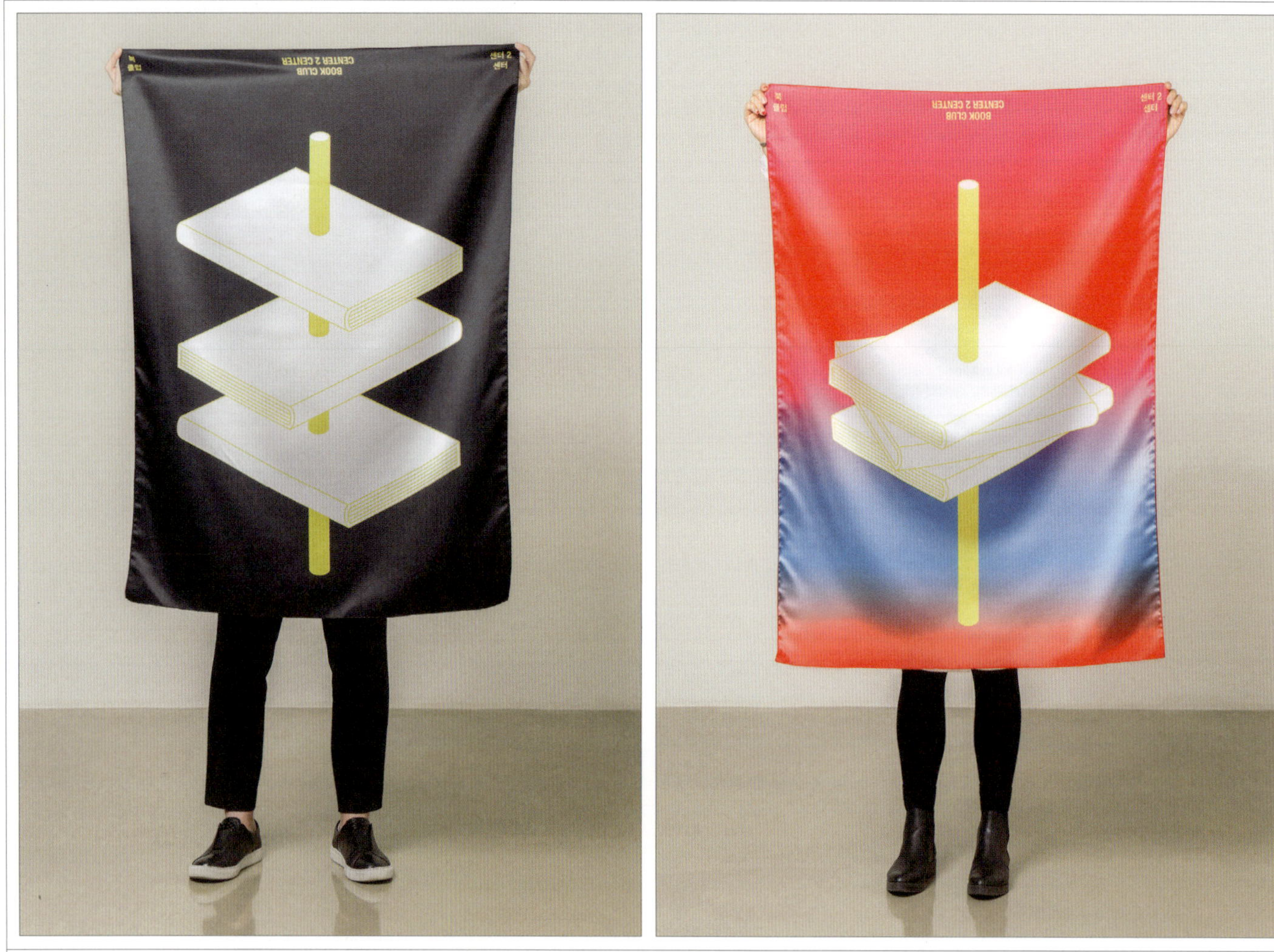

Title: Book Club 01, 02: CENTER 2 CENTER; Design Studio: DAEKI & JUN; Art Director & Designer: Daeki Shim, HyoJun Shim Assistant Designer: Somin Lee (intern); Client: CENTER 2 CENTER

Who among your contemporaries today do you most admire?
New is not always the right answer. However, if the same graphic design style has been repeated for a long time, we think that designers who fall out of mannerisms and develop new design styles will attract attention. In this regard, we note the design work of young designers, The Rodina and Jonathan Castro, who are pioneering their own style. Also, we highly value Metahaven's informal visual style and research methodology.

Who is or was your greatest mentor?
We can't talk about a specific mentor. Many mentors have advantages and disadvantages and we have always tried to see many advantages from them. Our mentors are not limited to the field of graphic design. We are inspired by artists from various cultures and arts. We also majored in graphic design as undergraduates, but majored in anthropology in the master's program. Perhaps the disadvantage was that we majored in anthropology, instead of graphic design. But it is also an advantage to be able to look at design from a different perspective than other designers.

Where do you seek inspiration?
We often find inspiration from other fields such as technology, architecture, art, as well as philosophy. We are inspired by the various cultures we've experienced in our lives. For us, it means that we can be inspired from anywhere and everything. For example, we have been inspired by Nick Sousanis's book "Unflattening" in recent years. Also, in the early 2000s, there was an exhibition for the architectural group Archigram at the Seoul Arts Center in Seoul, and we got a lot of inspiration from their work. We are also inspired by writings and exhibitions by designers such as Andrew Blauvelt and Ellen Lupton.

Who have been some of your favorite people or clients you have worked with?
We have worked with various clients. Some of the most memorable clients we have worked with are: illustrator Insu Lee, and the managers of Dongdaemun Design Plaza (ddp), where we continue to work together. They always accept our challenging proposals with open eyes. We trust each other in the relationship between client and designer. That's why we think the design results are good.

What would be your dream assignment?
Lotte Sky Tower and Fashion Group Shinwon once wanted to do some of the space design with us. But we were too busy to work on the project together at the time. If possible, we would like to design everything from branding to space design in cooperation with fashion brands or fashion designers. We think there will be a good opportunity one day.

DAEKI & JUN design studio www.daekiandjun.com

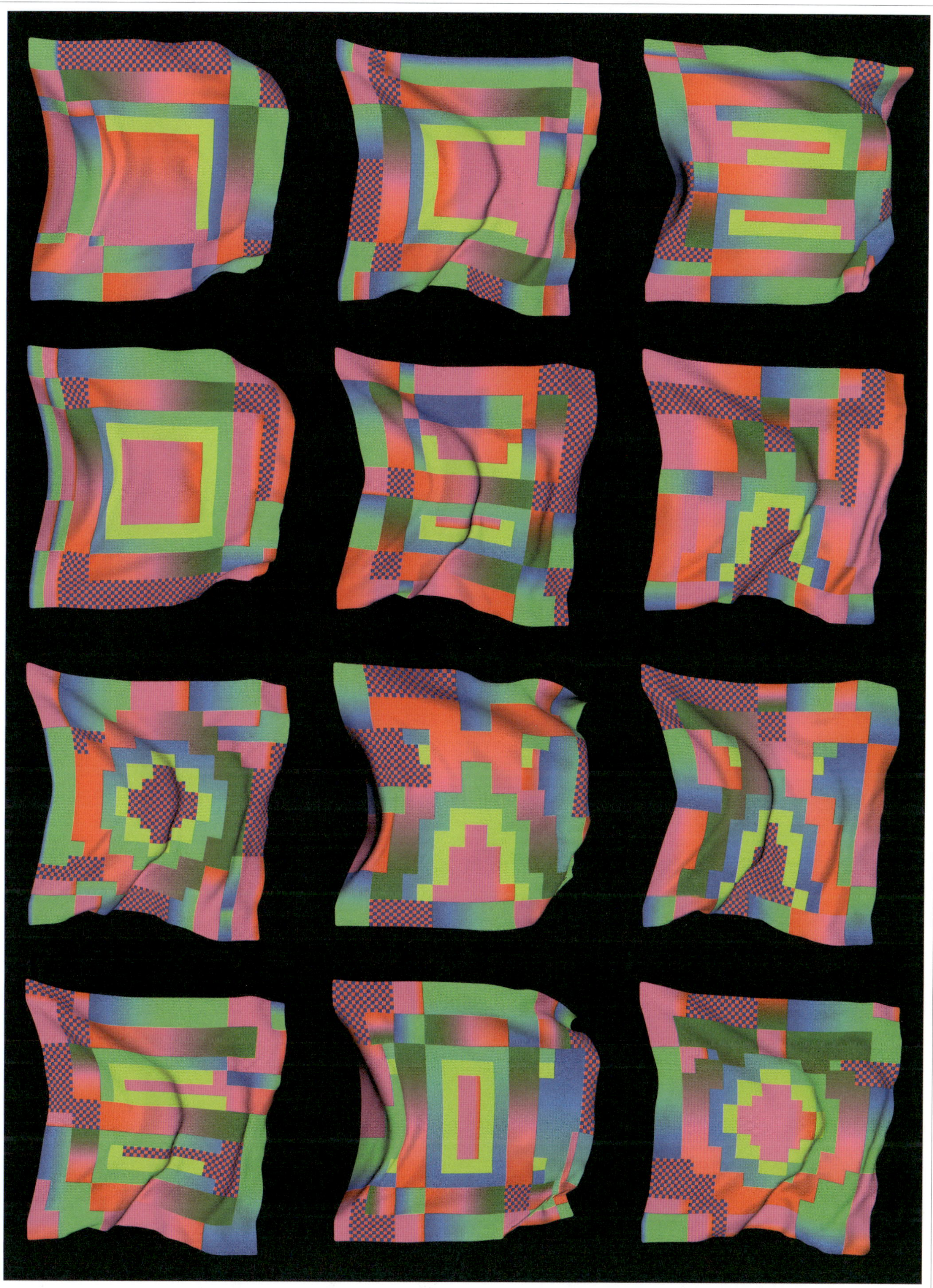

Title: Defamiliarizing Hangeul; Design Studio: DAEKI & JUN; Art Director & Designer: Daeki Shim, HyoJun Shim
Assistant Designers: Ahreum Lee (intern), Jaeun Lee (intern); Client: National Hangeul Museum

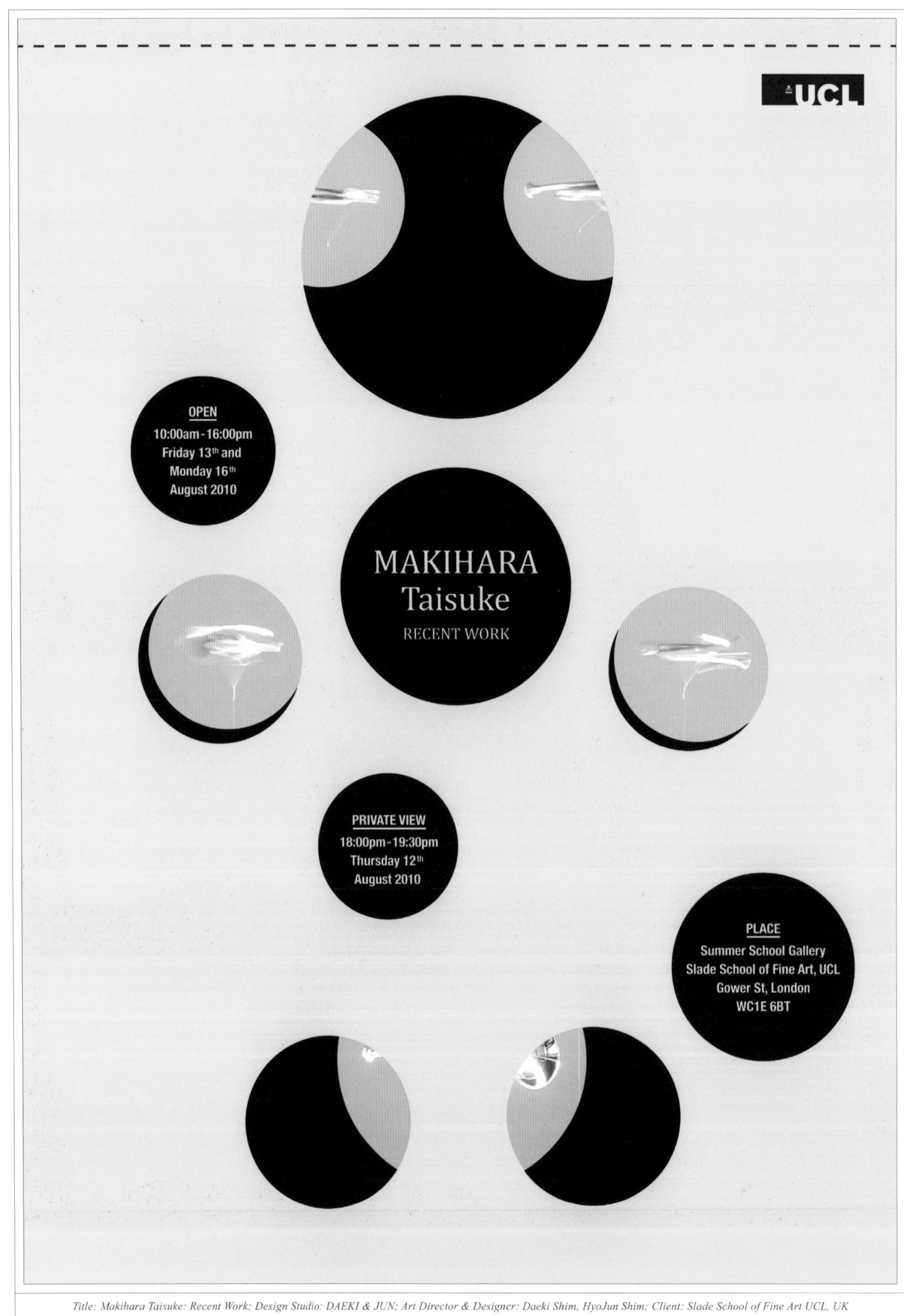

Title: Makihara Taisuke: Recent Work; Design Studio: DAEKI & JUN; Art Director & Designer: Daeki Shim, HyoJun Shim; Client: Slade School of Fine Art UCL, UK

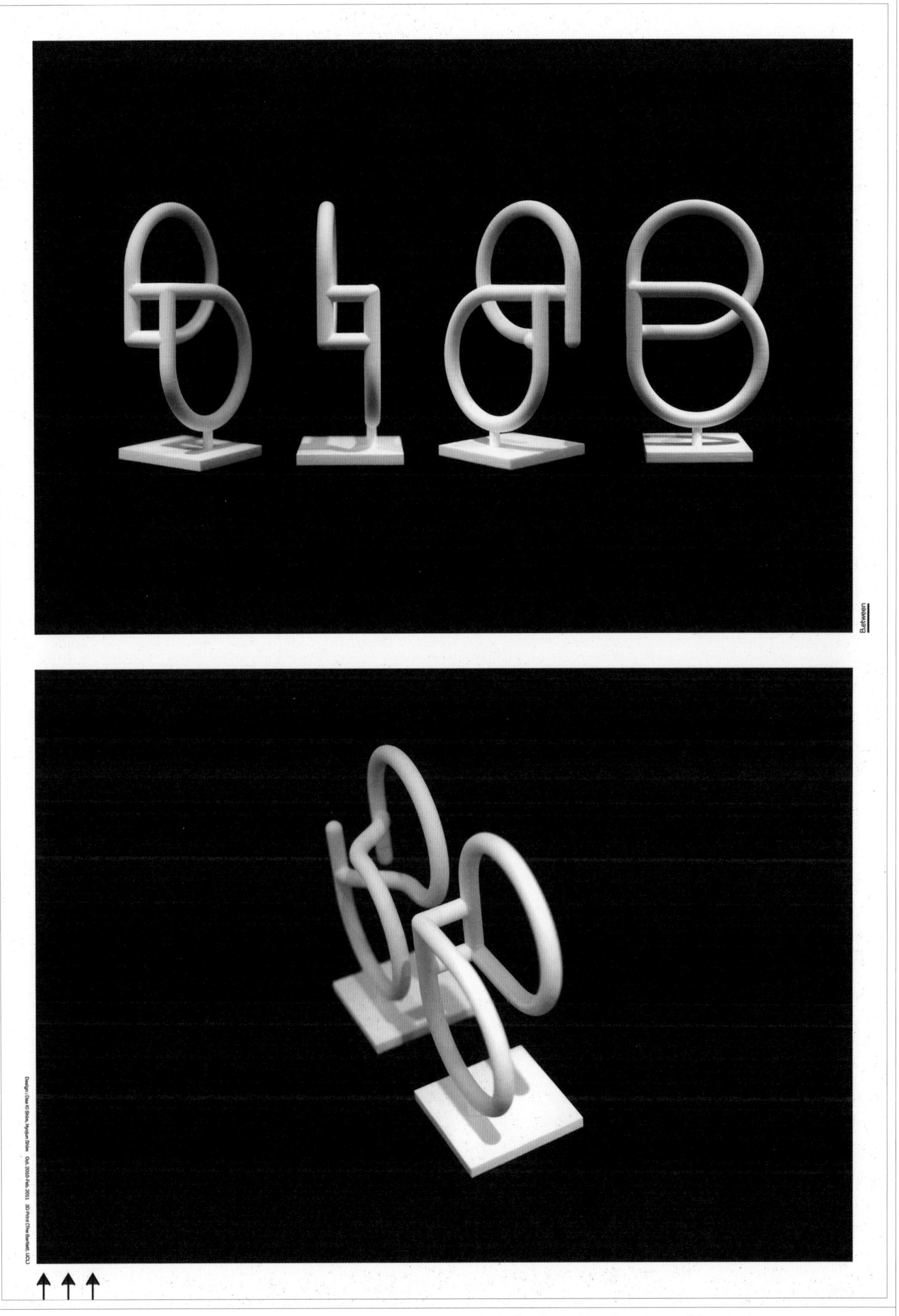

Title: Between; Design Studio: DAEKI & JUN; Art Director & Designer: Daeki Shim, HyoJun Shim; Client: Between Gallery, London

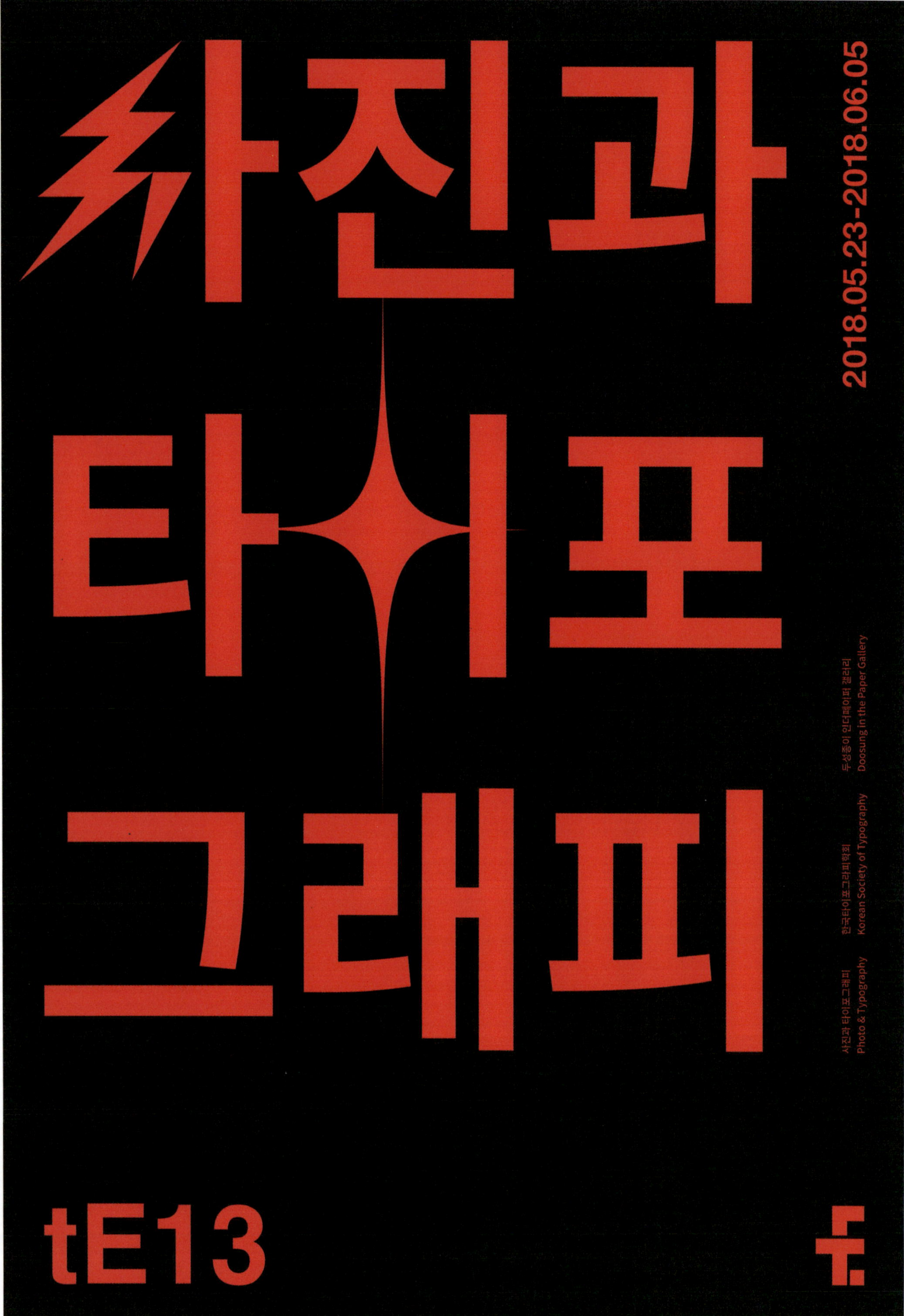

Title: TE13: Photo & Typography; Design Studio: DAEKI & JUN; Art Director & Designer: Daeki Shim; Designer: Su Yeon Lim
Clients: Korean Society of Typography, Doosung in the paper gallery

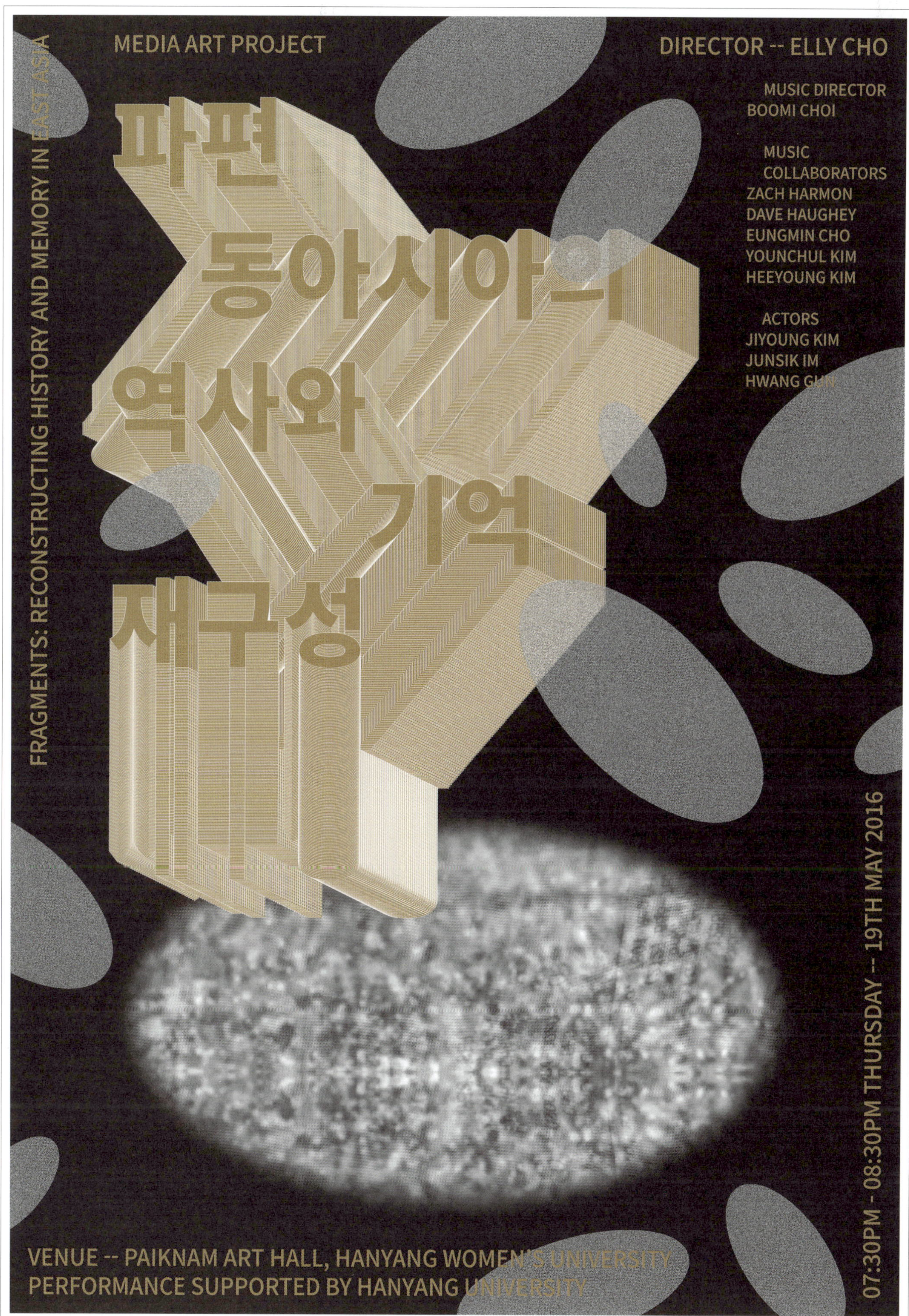

Title: Fragments 01: Reconstructing History and Memory in East Asia; Design Studio: DAEKI & JUN
Art Director & Designer: Daeki Shim, HyoJun Shim; Client: Paiknam Art Hall

KEN'S FORESIGHT OF THE IMPORTANCE OF THE TDC IN ASIA ALLOWED US TO OPEN THE TDC EXHIBIT IN TAICHUNG, TAIWAN. HIS WARMTH AND FRIENDLY NATURE ENABLED TDC TO HAVE A SUCCESSFUL PROGRAM FOR THE PAST 12 YEARS.

Carol Wahler, *Executive Director of the Type Directors Club*

WITH HIS UNIQUE STYLE, LEE RECONCILES IN A DISCONCERTING WAY, CHINESE CALLIGRAPHY, ABSTRACTION, AND MATHEMATICAL RIGOR.

Stereolux / Scopitone

HE HAS BEEN A VERY INFLUENTIAL SENIOR DESIGNER IN THE EAST SINCE I WAS A STUDENT, ESPECIALLY HIS EXPERIMENTAL ATTEMPT TOWARDS CHINESE CHARACTER DESIGN.

HIS PERSISTENCE IN DESIGN THROUGH ALL THESE YEARS IS VERY APPRECIATED.

Mann Lao, *Founder/Creative Director at Chiii Design*

HE IS ONE OF THE MOST REPRESENTATIVE DESIGNERS IN TAIWAN. HE SUCCESSFULLY TRANSFORMS DESIGN INTO CONTEMPORARY ART.

Chi-Yi Chang, *President of Taiwan Design Research Institute*

KEN-TSAI'S DESIGN WORKS AND CURATING ACTIVITIES, PROMOTING THE DIALOGUE BETWEEN THE EAST AND THE WEST, HAS OPENED UP NEW HORIZONS FOR DESIGN PRACTICE.

Wei-Hwa Chiang, *CEO, Taiwan Building Technology Center & Vice-President, National Taiwan University of Science and Technology*

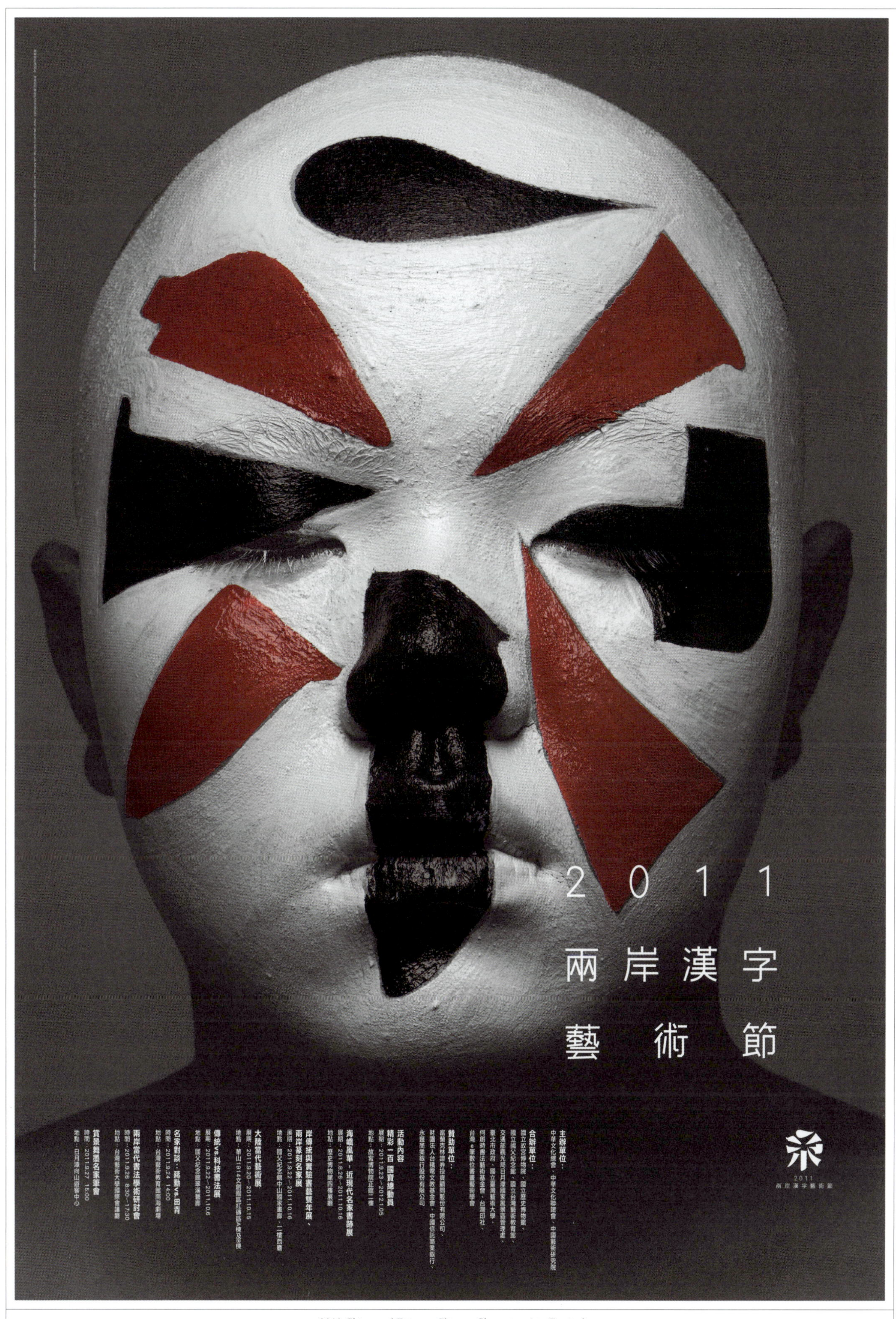

2011 China and Taiwan, Chinese Character Arts Festivel

Introduction by Ben Chiu *Taiwan Designer's Web Executive Director*

Designer's Web has been working with Ken-Tsai Lee since 2008. Every time Lee presents his work, he delivers incredible quality designs and items. He never ceases to amaze the design community in Taiwan and always raises the bar with the best designs. It has been a very enriching, enlightening as well as joyful process working with him over the past 9 years. We are proud to say that we are the only design company that hosts design events in Taiwan and we also have the most international publishings in terms of graphic work, we are therefore grateful to have Lee on board.

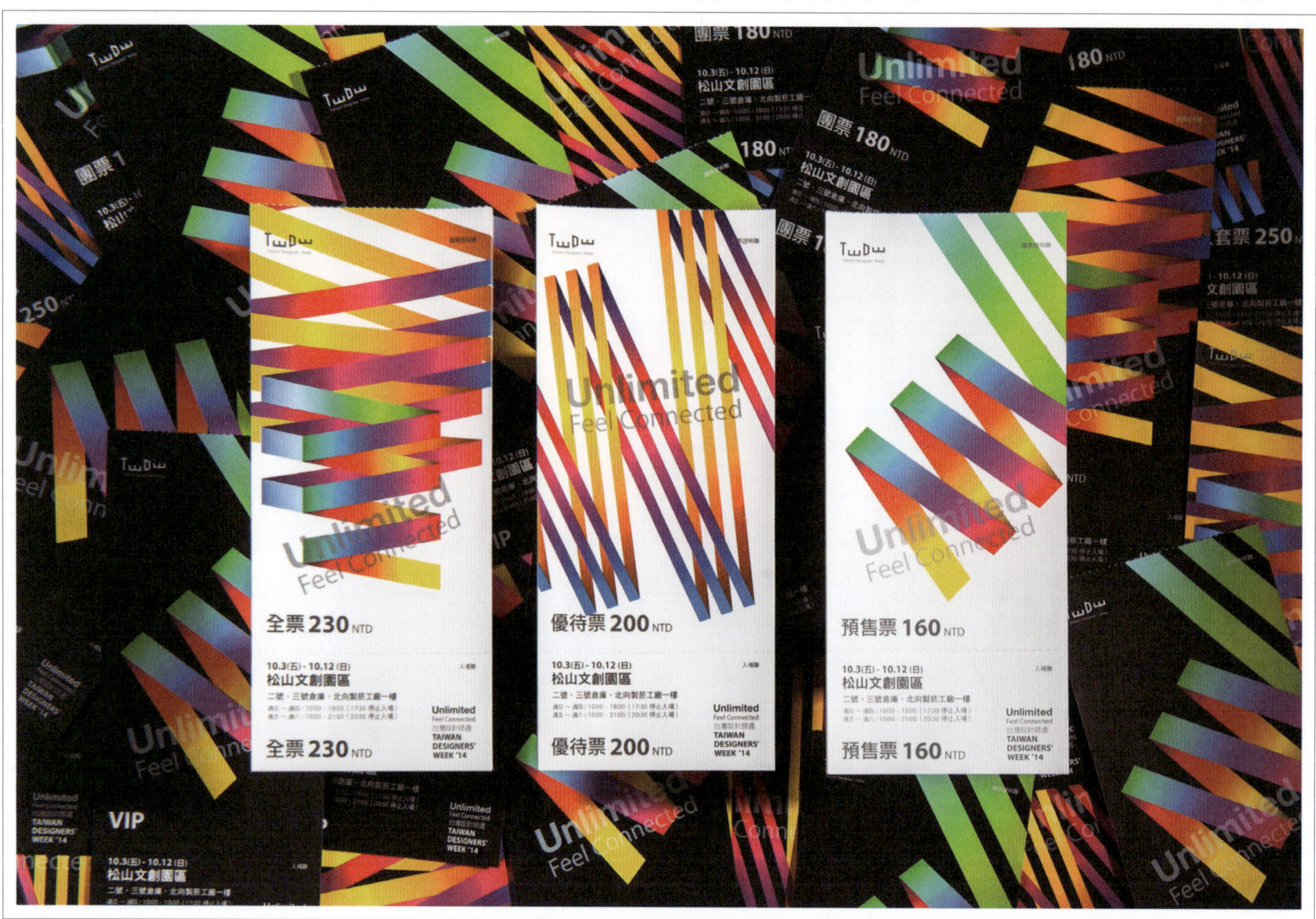

(Above) Taiwan Designers' Week 2014 / (Opposite page) Type for Wearing; Photo by Rendell

DON'T NARROW THE DEFINITION OF DESIGN AS SURFACE VISUALS. WHAT REALLY MOVES PEOPLE IS THE STORY BEHIND IT.

Ken-Tsai Lee, *Designer*

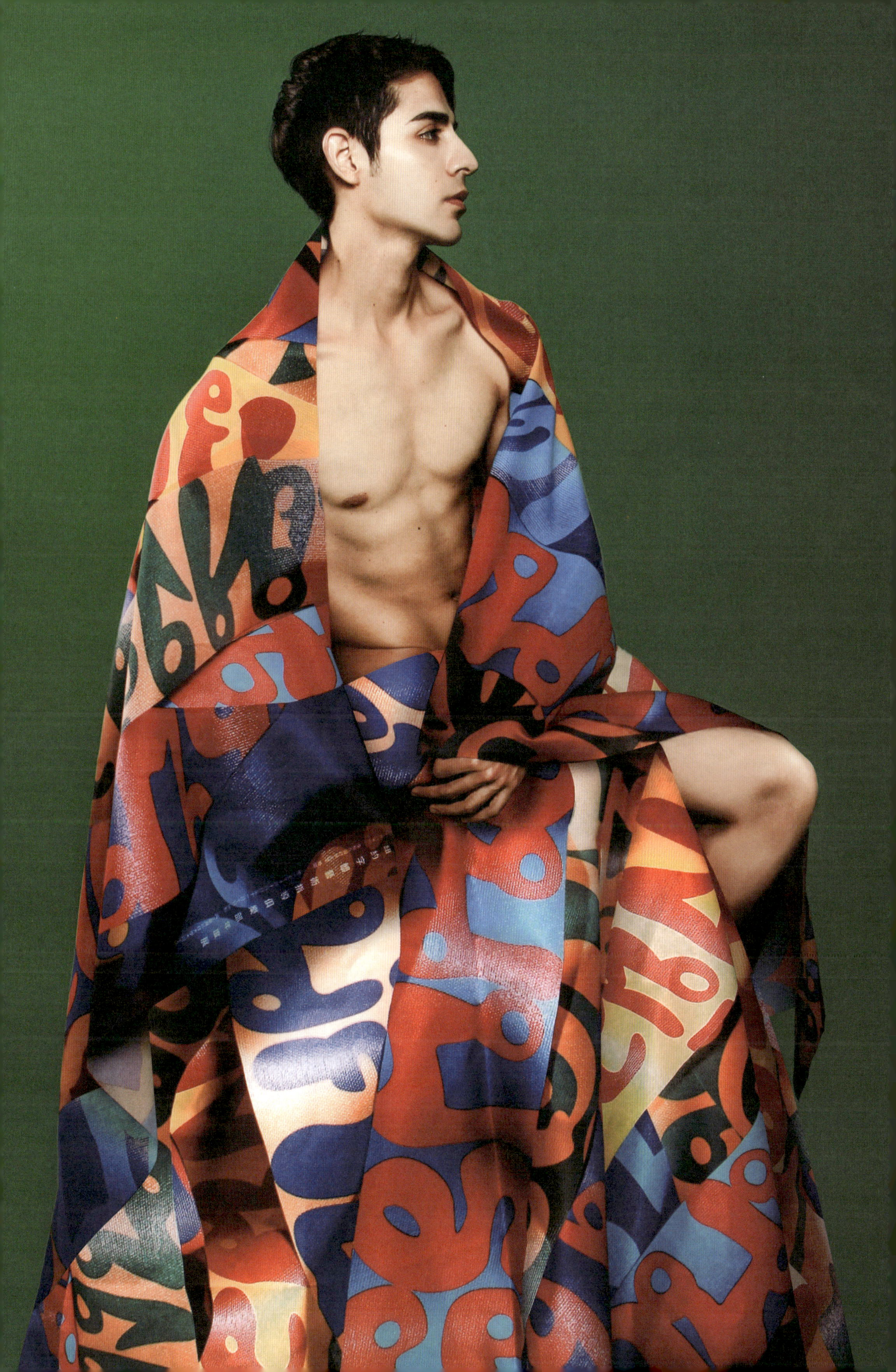

What advice would you have for students starting out today?
Open your eyes to see the world, don't define the design as just a graphic type on paper. Don't narrow the definition of design as only visuals on the surface. What really moves people is life and a story. Going through life and understanding the story behind the design will be more attractive than the visual surface.

How do you define success?
When design becomes a movement that also can influence society. To change people's behavior and change the concept of generations. If I can do that, I think I would say it's a success.

Who among your contemporaries today do you most admire?
Design is not just a design on paper, but more importantly, design is life planning and design path planning. A designer who can break everyone's perception of the design path and open up new ideas; this is what I admire most.

If I need to name a name I most admire, I would name Shepard Fairey, from the wrestler poster he posted on streets when he studied at RSID. He then became a trendy brand, through the "Hope" poster designed for the Obama election.

What has been your most memorable project?
"I am Lee Ken-Tsai," the first project I did during my first month in New York. In 2002, I quit a teaching job and went to NY at age 34. I started to learn English from the lowest level in language school. Before I went to NY, I was not only teaching in a university, I also got over 100 design awards locally and internationally. I was invited to publish a book which collected my design works by publishing houses.

I quit my job because I found that English was very important for me. In the end, I decided to quit the job because I believed that you live life only once. I wanted to know what I could do in NY, as people said: "If you can succeed here, you will succeed anywhere." The second week in NY, someone introduced a Taiwanese born American designer to me. I didn't speak english, he didn't speak chinese; we communicated with a digital dictionary. I almost cried when I got back home; the worlds we lived in were too different. "Fifteen minutes of fame," said Andy Warhol. If I write my name in different languages, print them in posters, and post them in the streets of NY, people will be curious about who Lee Ken-Tsai is. I asked my assistant to print posters in NY, he sent 100 kl posters by ferry to me and I went to Manhattan almost every night, from 12 am to 6 am. I once got arrested by the cops and was held in the police station for a few hours. After the judge said nothing, I got released in court. It changed the way I show my posters; I took posters and photos with landmarks of NY together. The project changed how I look at design. An artist friend said I'm doing art. I've never thought about what art is. Design solves problems, art is self-expression. I believe that was the definition between art and design in the textbook I studied when I was studying design. I started to become interested in the area between art and design, and "learning rules are for breaking rules," became my philosophy in design. I don't call it design, I called it "creation."

How does the design world differ in Taipei vs New York?
Compared to New York, clients in New York better understand the value of design, they also respect the design profession. Taiwan's clients always directed the designers on how to do design, they just needed designers to be their hands.

Since 1990, some Taiwanese designers have said, designers need to do self-made posters to show a designer's thoughts, not just follow the clients' direction. People don't respect designers. Clients think if they pay money, designers should follow their ideas. Even with Type, clients direct how big or small designers do it. Can't believe it, right?

At the time I agreed with this idea. But designers need to develop their thoughts and ideas, not just be the hand of clients, Especially with design in less developed countries. It was the 90's, I had just graduated from school- the first time I went to China to attend a design competition in 1996, I saw the winners' works all were self-made posters, I was angry.

If design is something that doesn't need to consider what clients need, just like school projects, then designers just want to get awards. That is so easy, so I started to do self-made posters, and just a few years later, the posters got awards. So what?

The ultimate fact is that a designer in an area where the design is underdeveloped, may have to face customers who do not respect the designer. But they have a more important task; the public will realize the importance of design.

Ken-Tsai Lee
See his Graphis Master Portfolio on graphis.com.

A DESIGNER WHO CAN BREAK EVERYONE'S PERCEPTION OF THE DESIGN PATH AND DEVELOP NEW IDEAS; THIS IS WHAT I ADMIRE MOST.

Ken-Tsai Lee, *Designer*

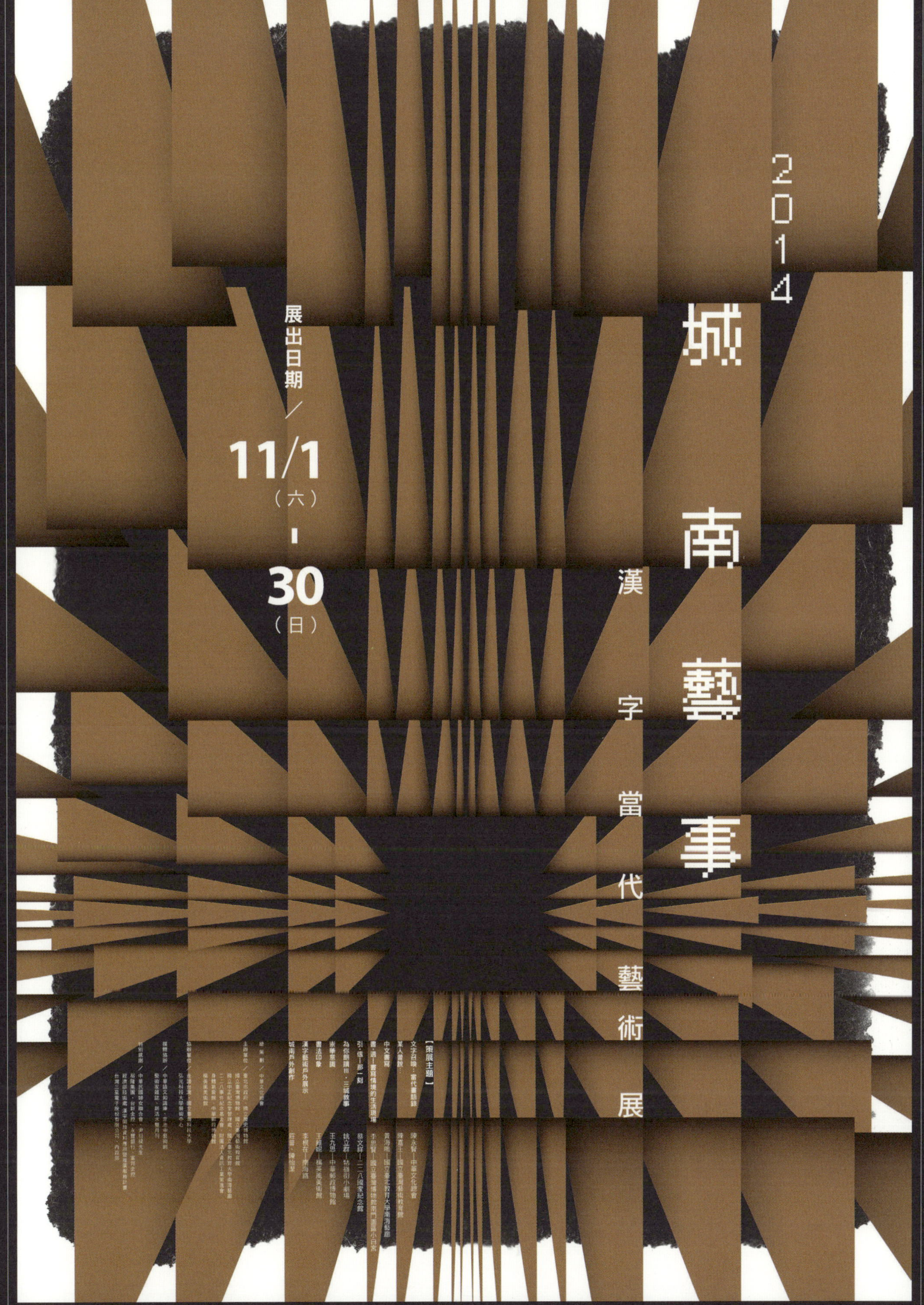
2014
城南藝事
漢字當代藝術展
展出日期／
11/1（六）－30（日）
【策展主題】
文字召喚：當代書語錄
陳永賢｜中華文化總會
某人曾說⋯
中文書寫
黃海鳴｜國立臺北教育大學南海藝廊
書・語｜書寫情境的生活現場
李思賢｜國立臺灣博物館南門園區小白宮
引・信｜那一刻
蔡文祥｜二二八國家紀念館
為你朗讀III・三城故事
姚立群｜牯嶺街小劇場
米筆意識
王九思｜中華郵政博物館
書法印象
楊英風美術館
漢字藝術戶外展示
李根在｜南海路
城南戶外創作
莊普、陳怡潔
總策劃／中華文化總會
Taipei South Town Art Festival 2014

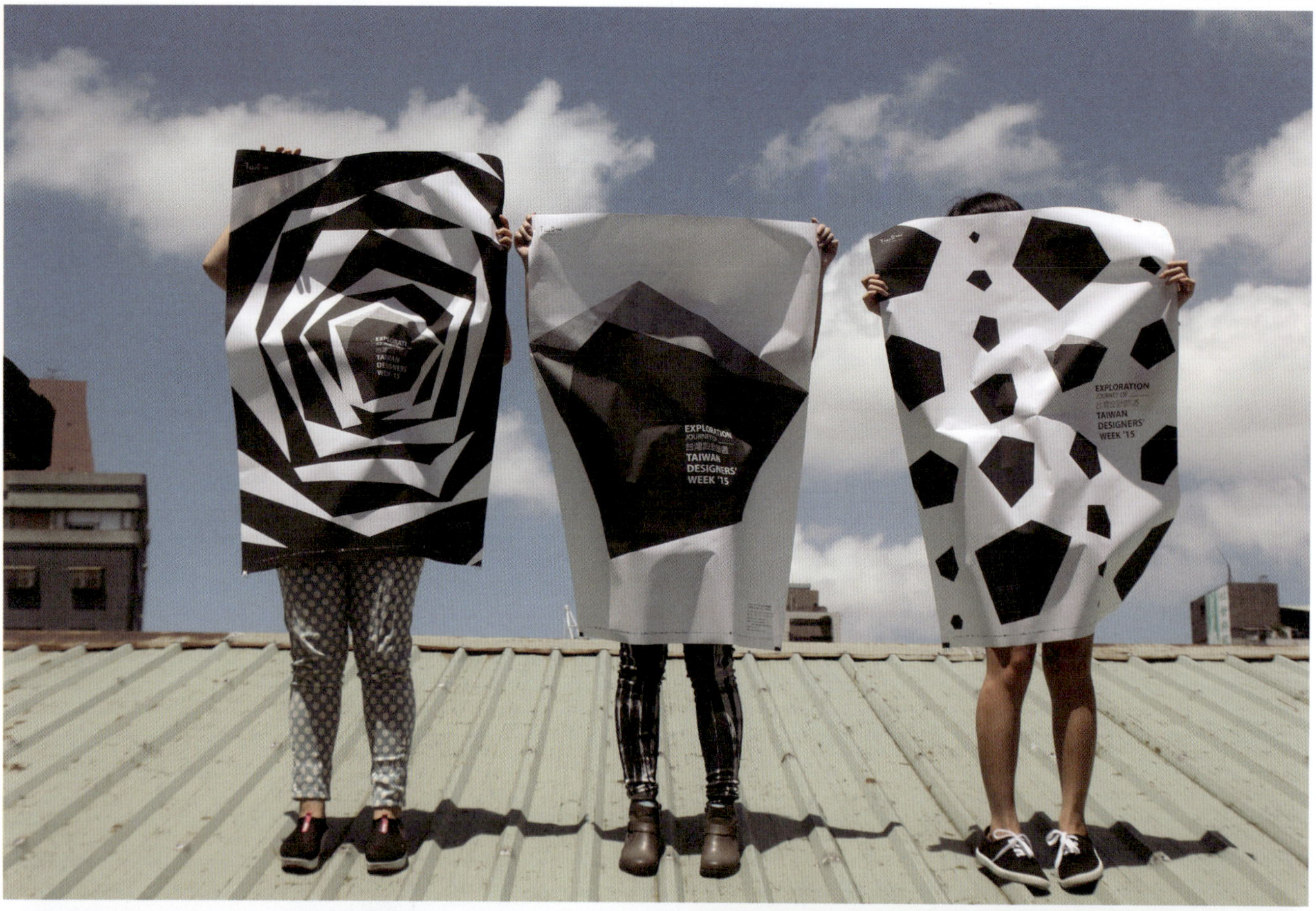

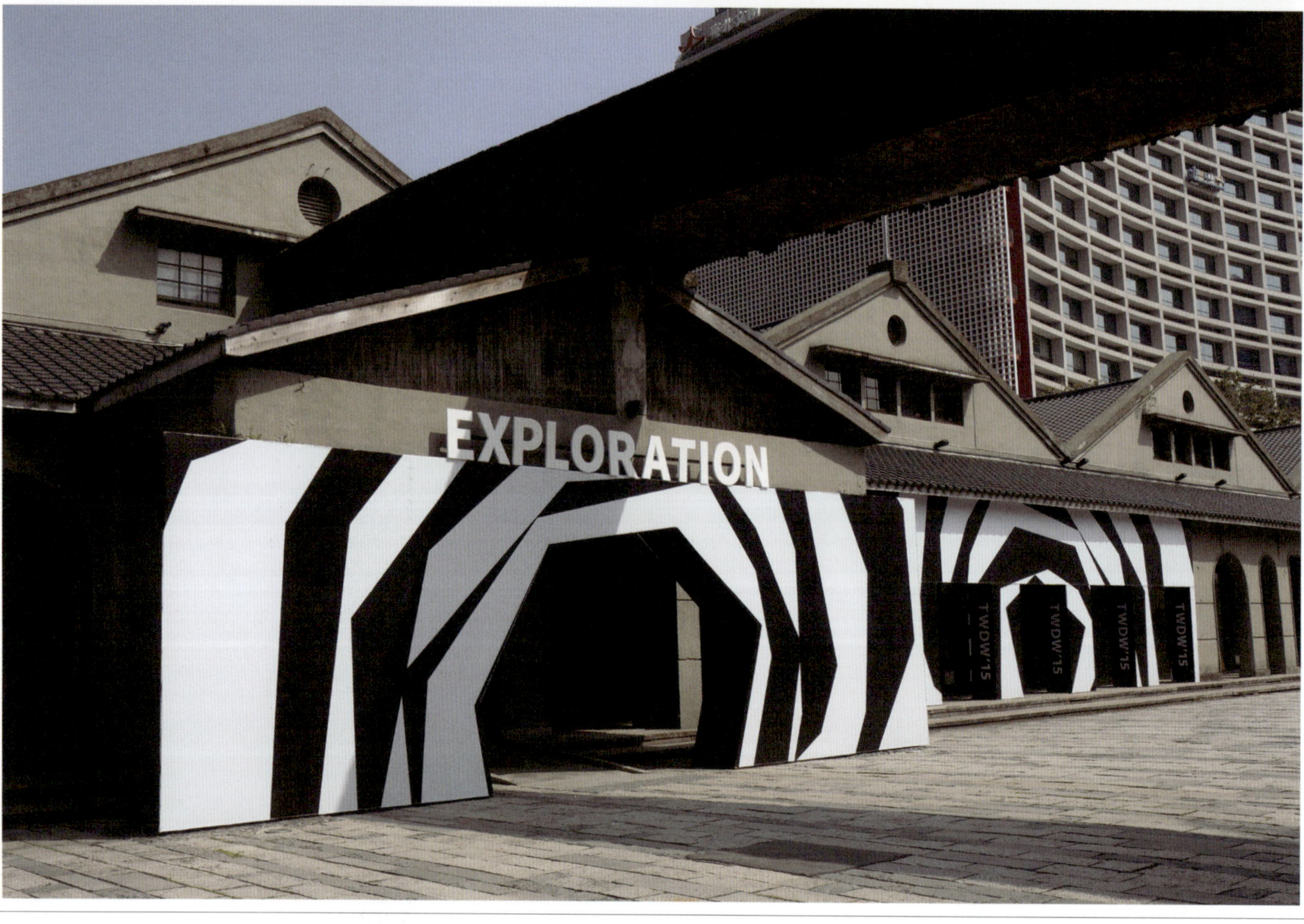

Taiwan Designers' Week 2015

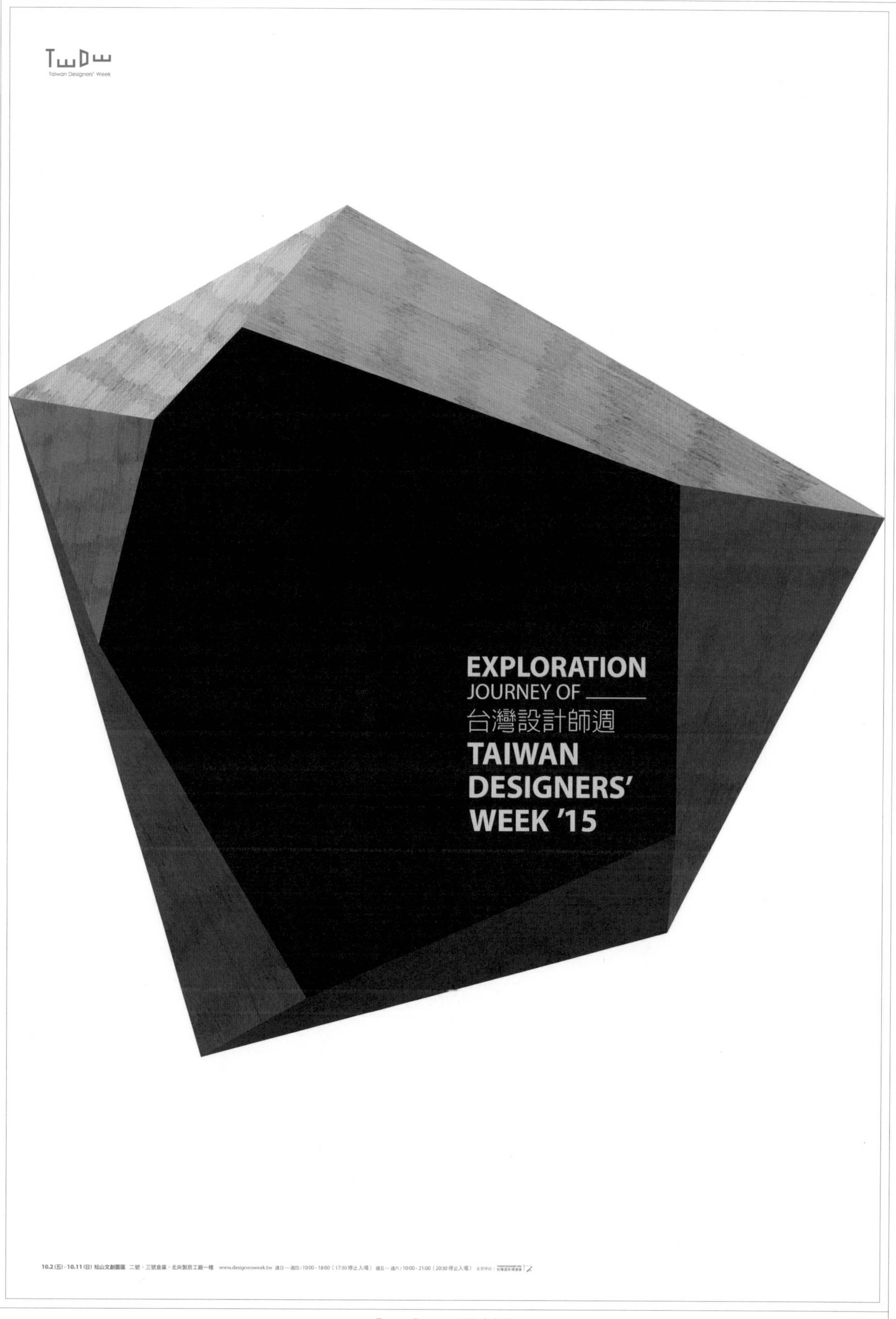

Taiwan Designers' Week 2015

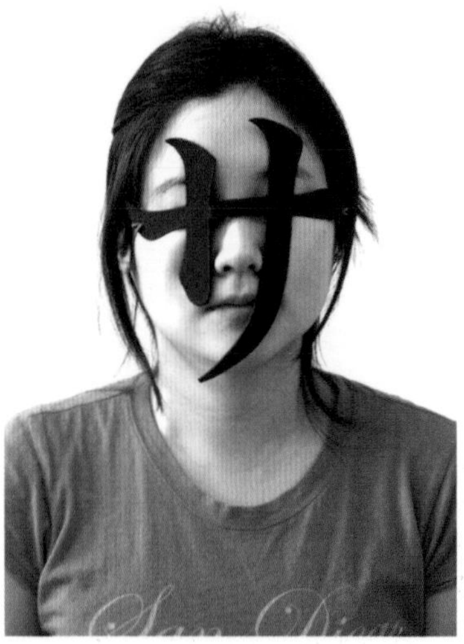

Japanese Face

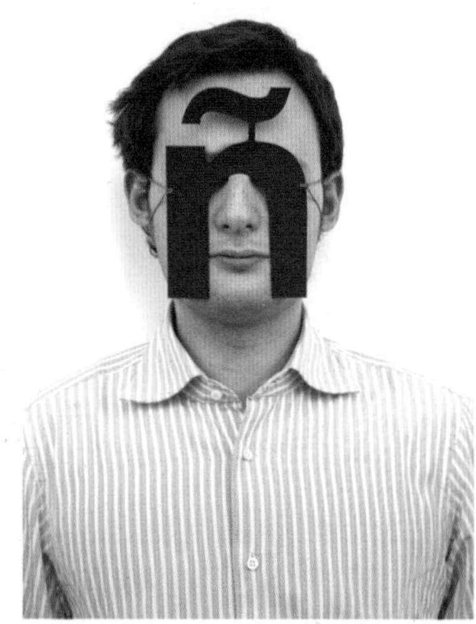

Spanish Face

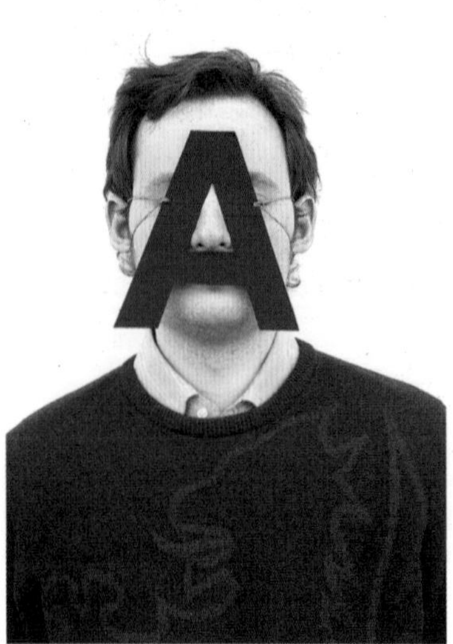

American Face

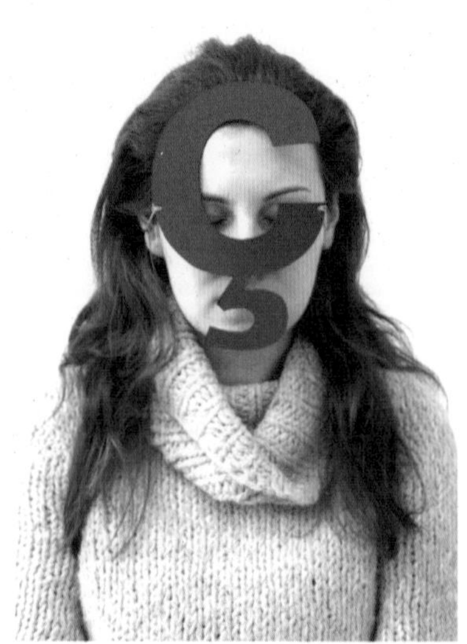

Turkish Face

Type Faces

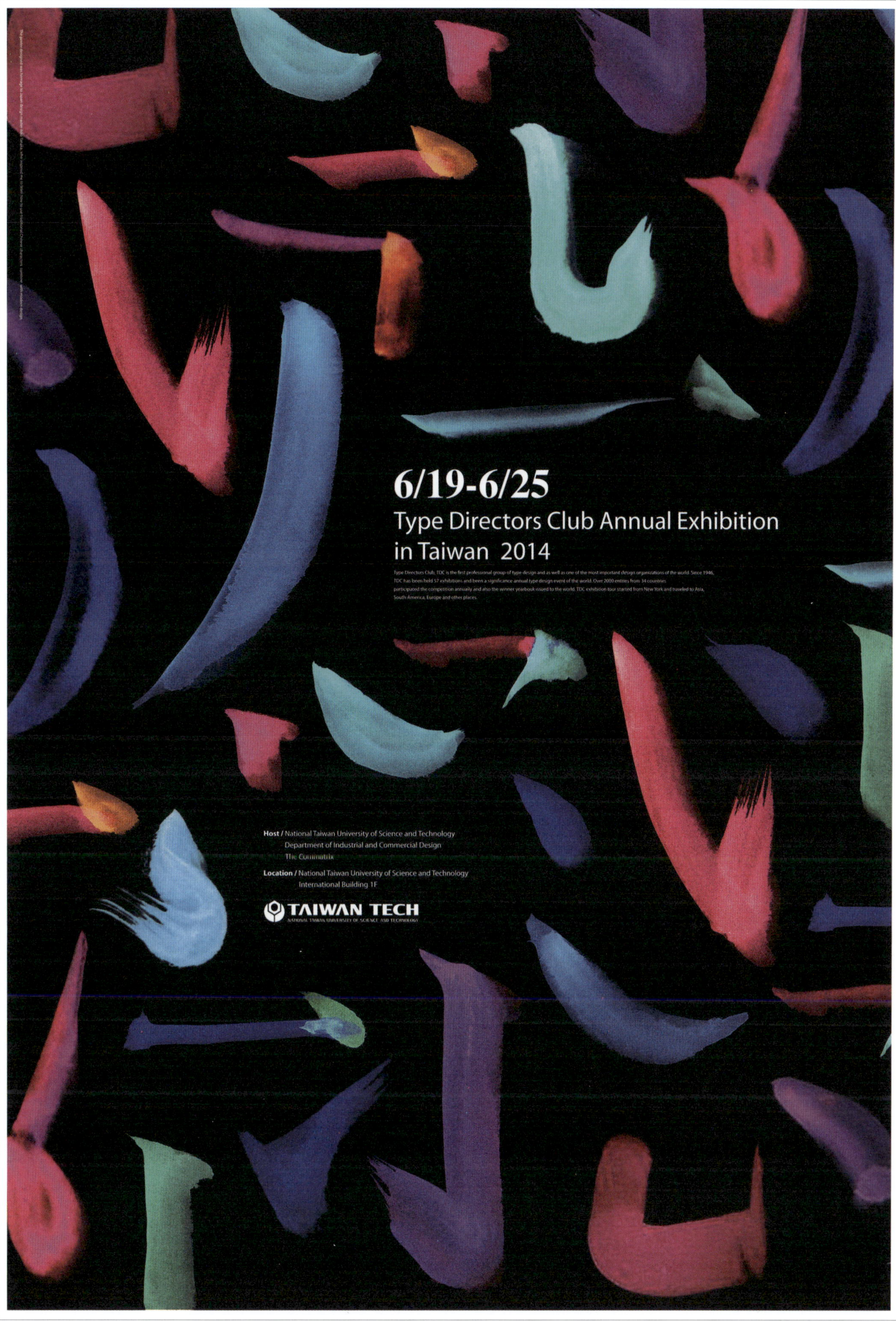

Type Directors Club Annual Exhibition in Taiwan 2014

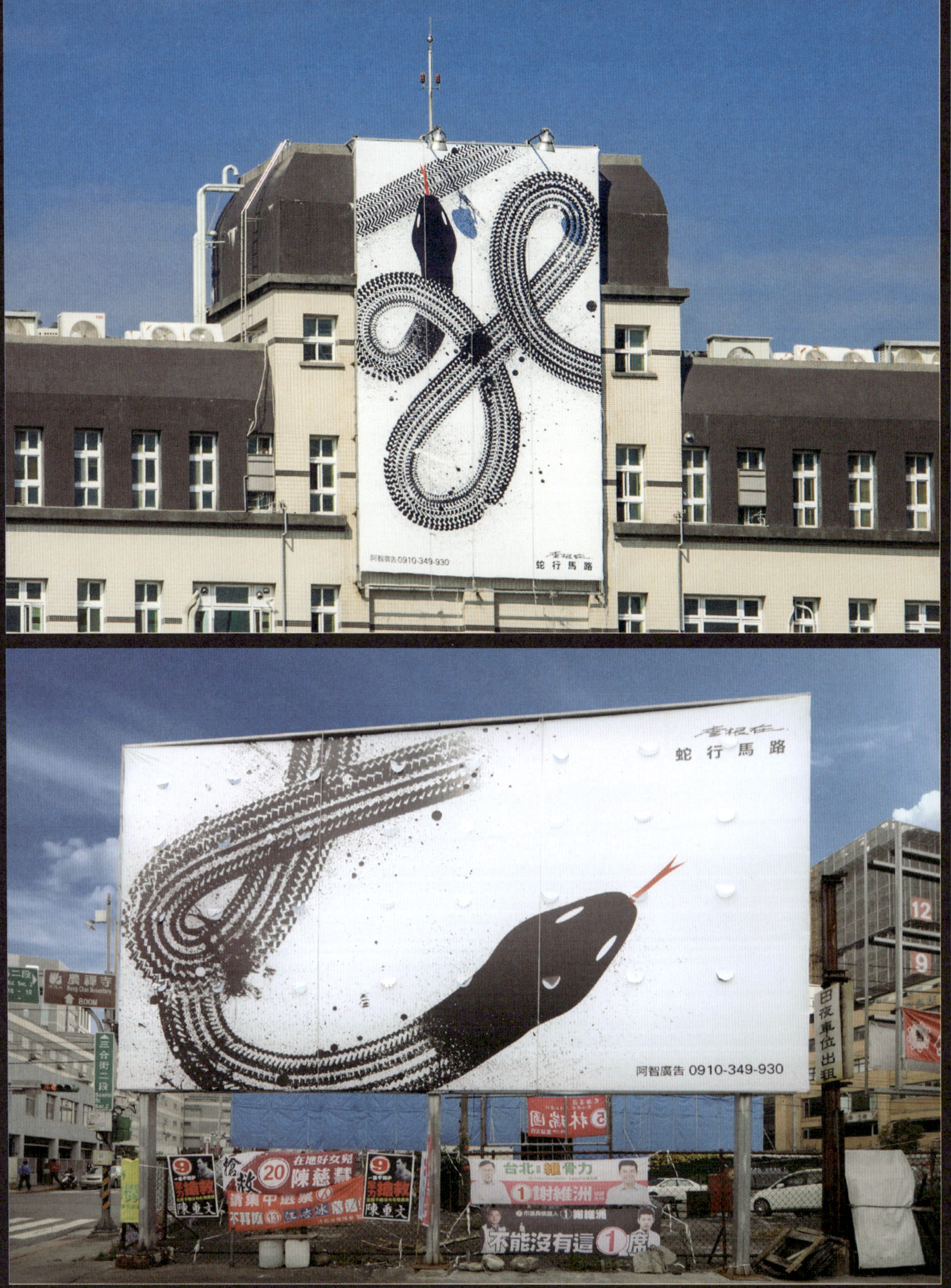

Motorcycle Snaking Would Cause Death

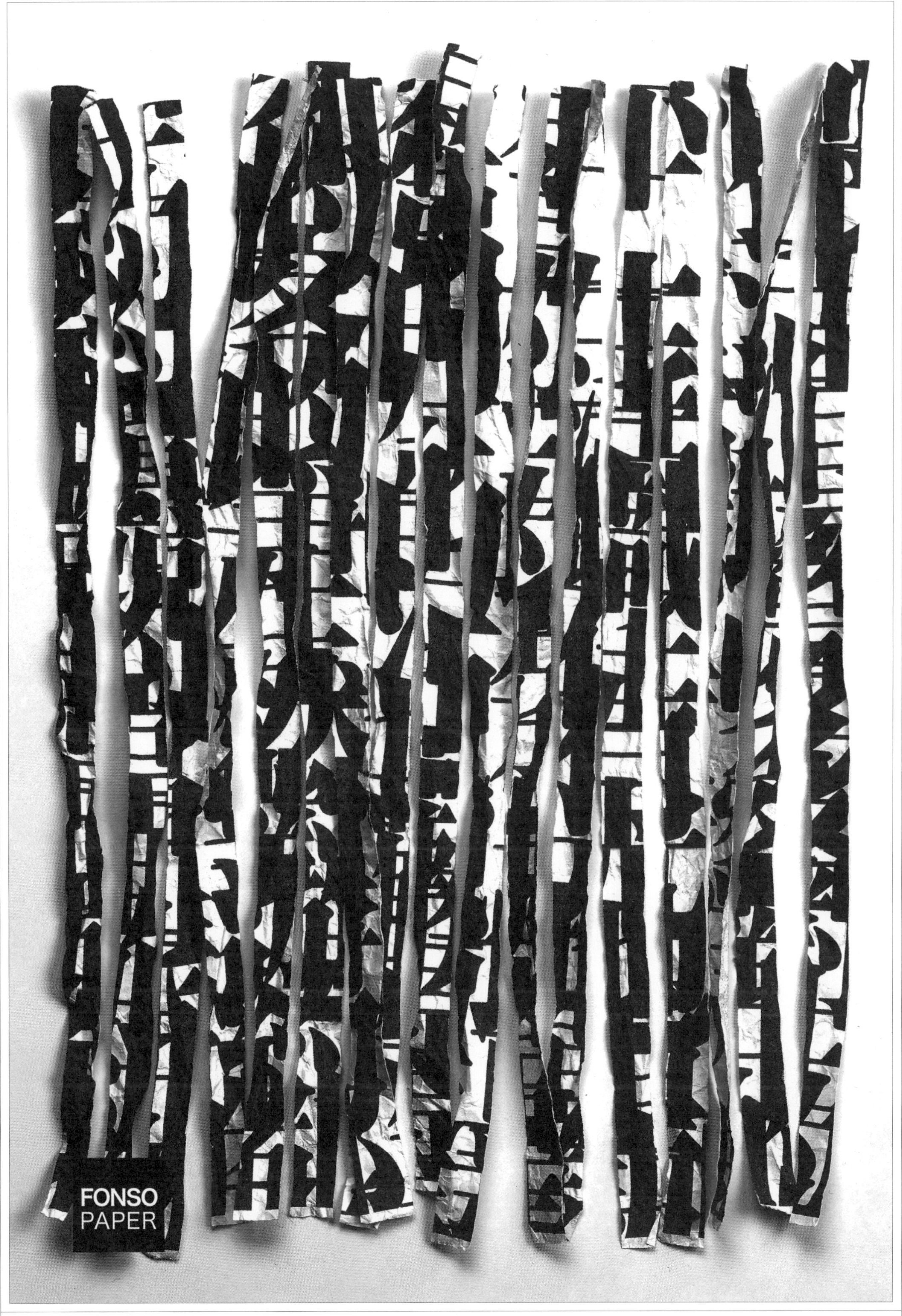

Fonso Recycling Paper Promotion Series

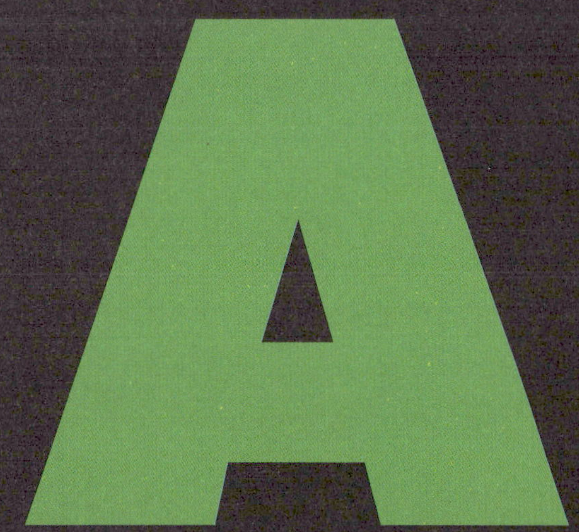

ADVERTISING

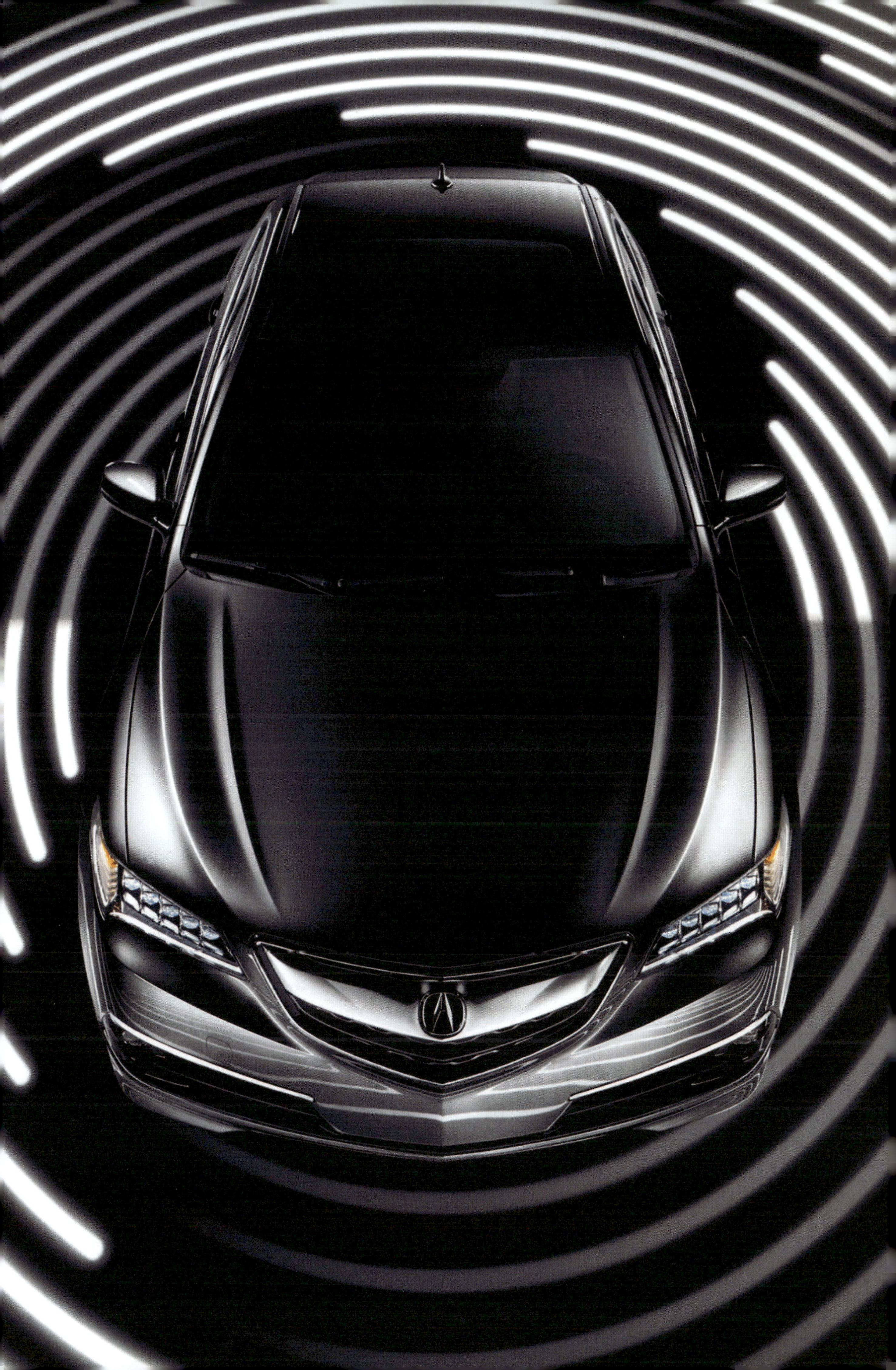

GETTING FIRED FOR BEING THE WORST ASSISTANT ACCOUNT EXECUTIVE IN THE WORLD WAS HIGHLY MOTIVATING.

Colin Corcoran, *Copywriter & Creative Director, The Independent Copywriter*

COLIN IS A PAIN IN THE ASS. HE SWEATS THE DETAILS AND MAKES YOU SWEAT THEM EVEN MORE. HE PUTS IN THE WORK, MOVING FAST AND THROWING A LOT OF PUNCHES.

THAT'S WHY HE'S THE SELF-PROCLAIMED FREELANCE HEAVYWEIGHT CHAMPION OF THE WORLD. LUCKILY, HIS ACCOLADES KIND OF BACK THAT UP.

Steve Mapp, *Director*

NOT ONLY IS GOOD WRITING HARD TO FIND, SOMEONE WHO CAN DELIVER WRITING WITH WIT AND HUMOR IS BECOMING A LOST ART. HE CAN DO SO WITHOUT LOSING SIGHT OF THE PRODUCT OR SERVICE BEING ADVERTISED.

Mike McKay, *CCO of Eleven Inc.*

COLIN HAS A TALENT FOR WEAVING WORDS TOGETHER IN AN ELOQUENT, MEMORABLE MANNER. WHAT SEPARATES HIM FROM BEING MERELY A WORDSMITH, IS HIS ABILITY TO BEND WORDS AROUND VISUALS TO FORGE A SEAMLESS STORY.

Eric Strohl, *Founder/Principal of Strohl, Inc.*

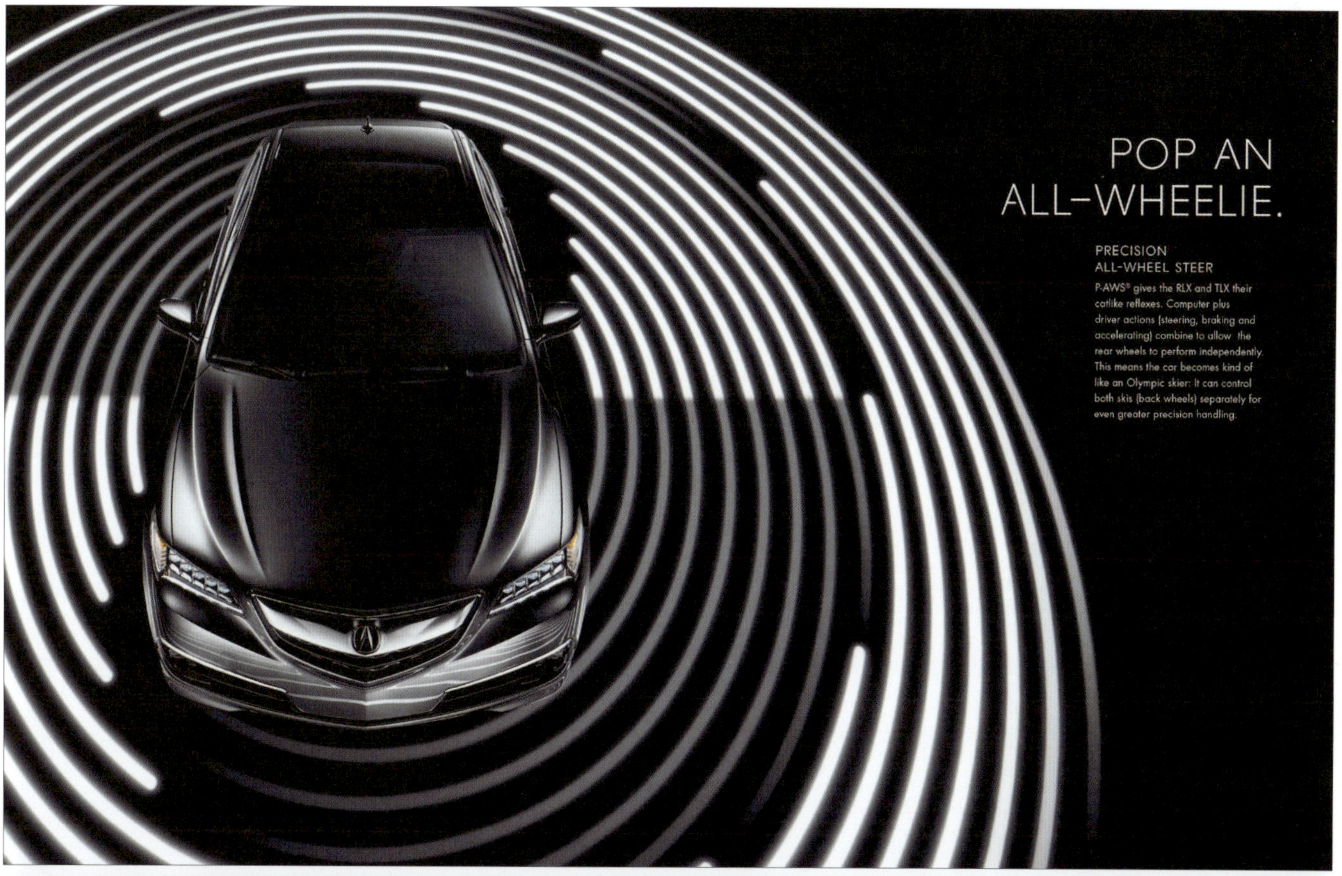

POP AN
ALL-WHEELIE.

PRECISION
ALL-WHEEL STEER

P-AWS® gives the RLX and TLX their catlike reflexes. Computer plus driver actions (steering, braking and accelerating) combine to allow the rear wheels to perform independently. This means the car becomes kind of like an Olympic skier: It can control both skis (back wheels) separately for even greater precision handling.

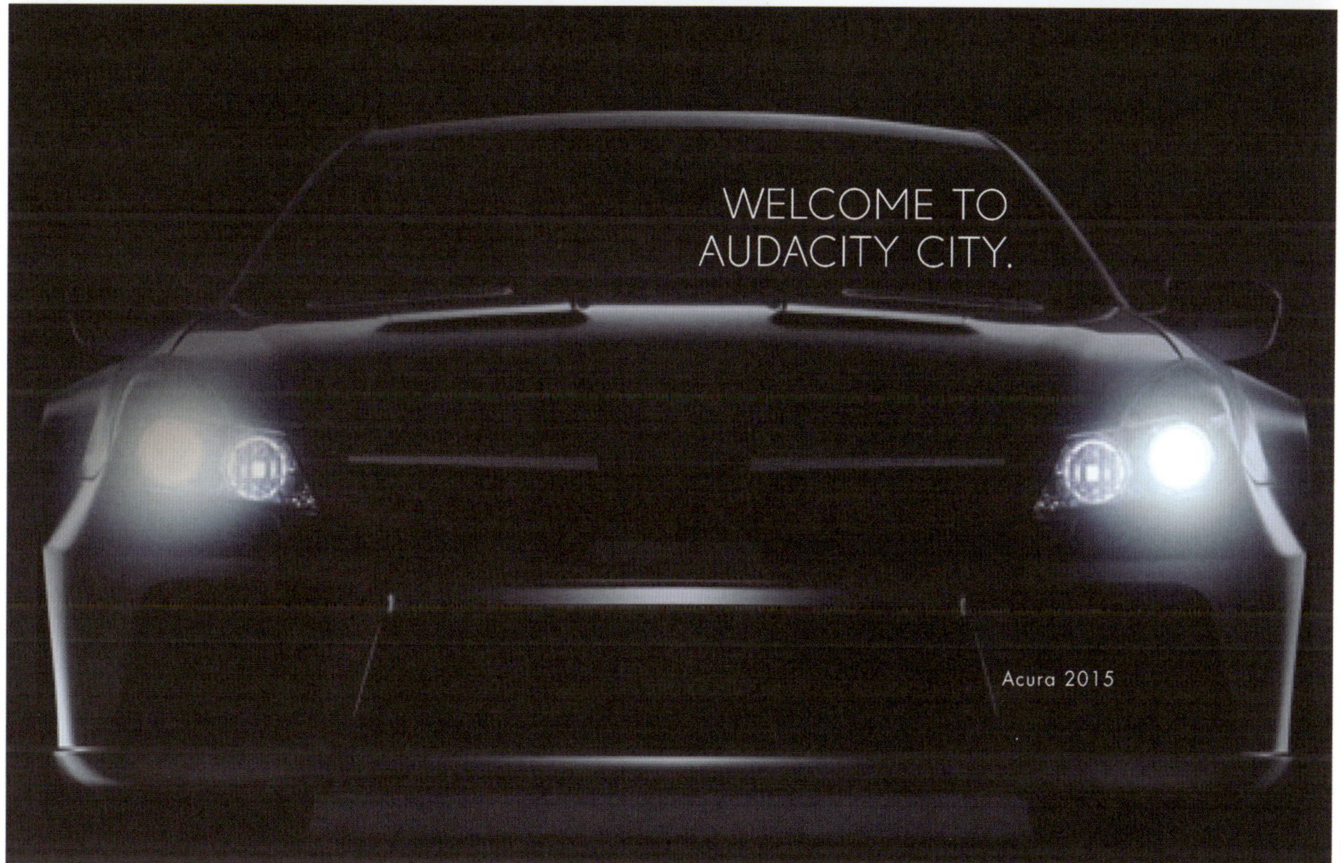

(Page 51, 53-57) Client: Acura (2015 Full-Line Brochure Pages); Agency: mullen / la; Creative Director: Margaret Keene; Copywriters: Colin Corcoran, Theo Wallace

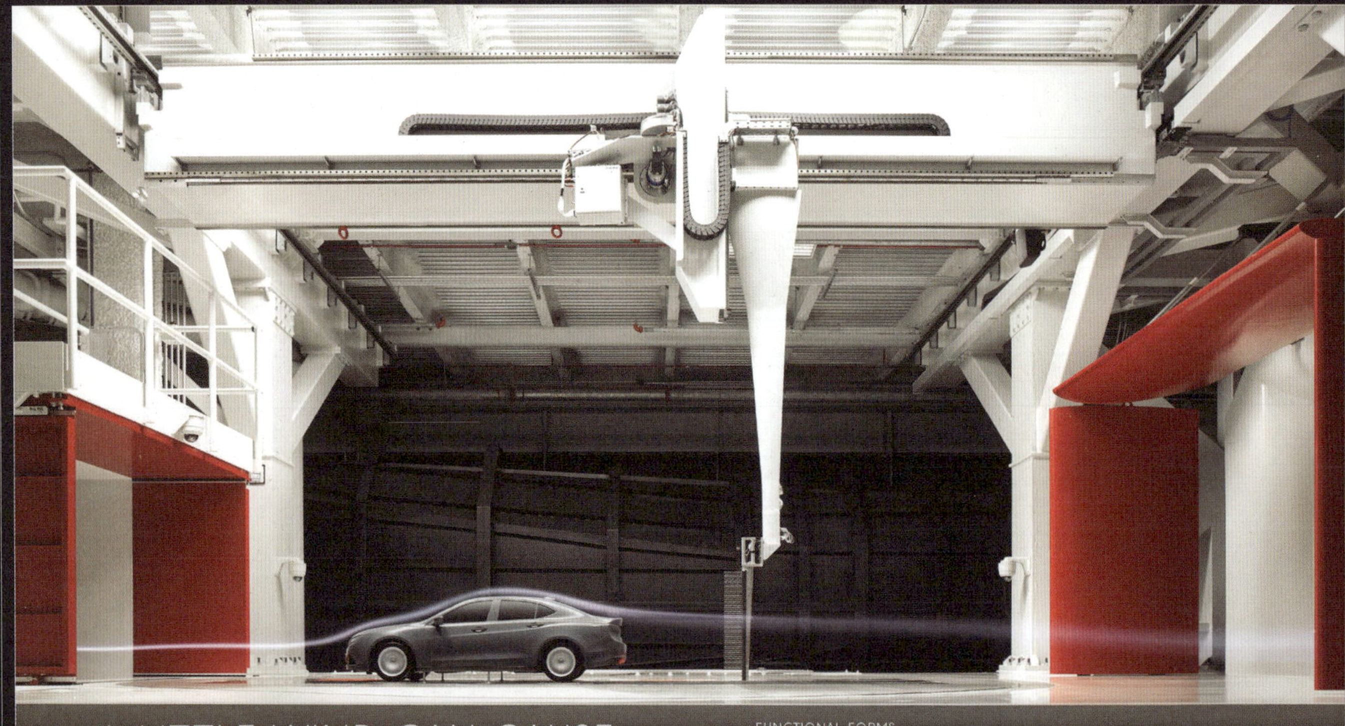

A LITTLE WIND CAN CAUSE A LOT OF CHANGE.

FUNCTIONAL FORMS

Inside our state-of-the-art wind tunnels, every Acura model must master both aerodynamics and aesthetics. After style is first defined—and then refined—performance and efficiency are optimized. And optimized again. The 2014 RLX, for instance, went into the tunnels over 800 times.

IT'S OKAY TO BE CLINGY.

SUPER HANDLING ALL-WHEEL DRIVE

If you're super into high-performance cornering, then look no further than Acura's Super Handling System. Our revolutionary torque-vectoring SH-AWD® continuously directs engine power to each wheel, then actively varies torque side to side between the rear wheels. The result: a level of agility unmatched by conventional all-wheel-drive systems.

Introduction by Dave Damman *EVP/MANAGING DIRECTOR & CCO at The Buntin Group*

Growing up in the world of creativity as an art director, there's nothing I value more than a great writer. I grew up not reading books as much—but wanting to draw them and look at the pictures, not appreciating the words that accompanied them. But it's more than just words. It's having the heart, soul, and passion of crafting an idea with those 26 letter forms of the alphabet. For me, having taken several writing courses of late, it's become clear that writing—great writing—is one of the hardest things to do in the world. It's right up there with hitting a straight tee shot, or a fastball from a major league pitcher. My friend Colin writes very well. He writes more than very well. He's passionate, he's articulate, and he lives in a world of black and white. There is no gray. There is no slight conviction—it's either all or nothing. He's the type of writer that plants a flag and then runs to it. As an art director, that's the writer you want in your corner.

EVERY TIME SOMEONE HAS TRIED TO KILL MY CAREER, I'VE COME BACK EVEN STRONGER.

Colin Corcoran, *Copywriter & Creative Director, The Independent Copywriter*

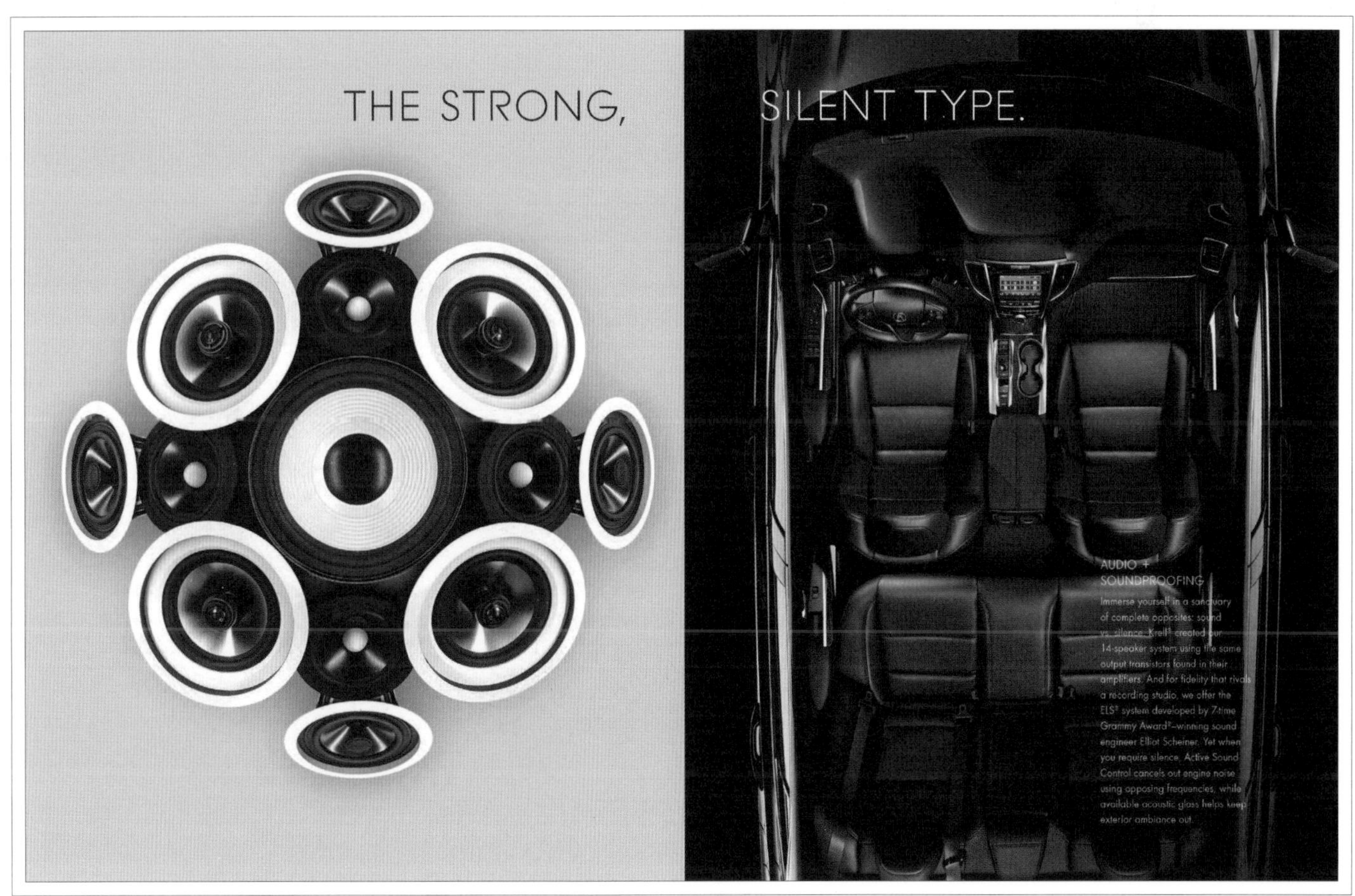

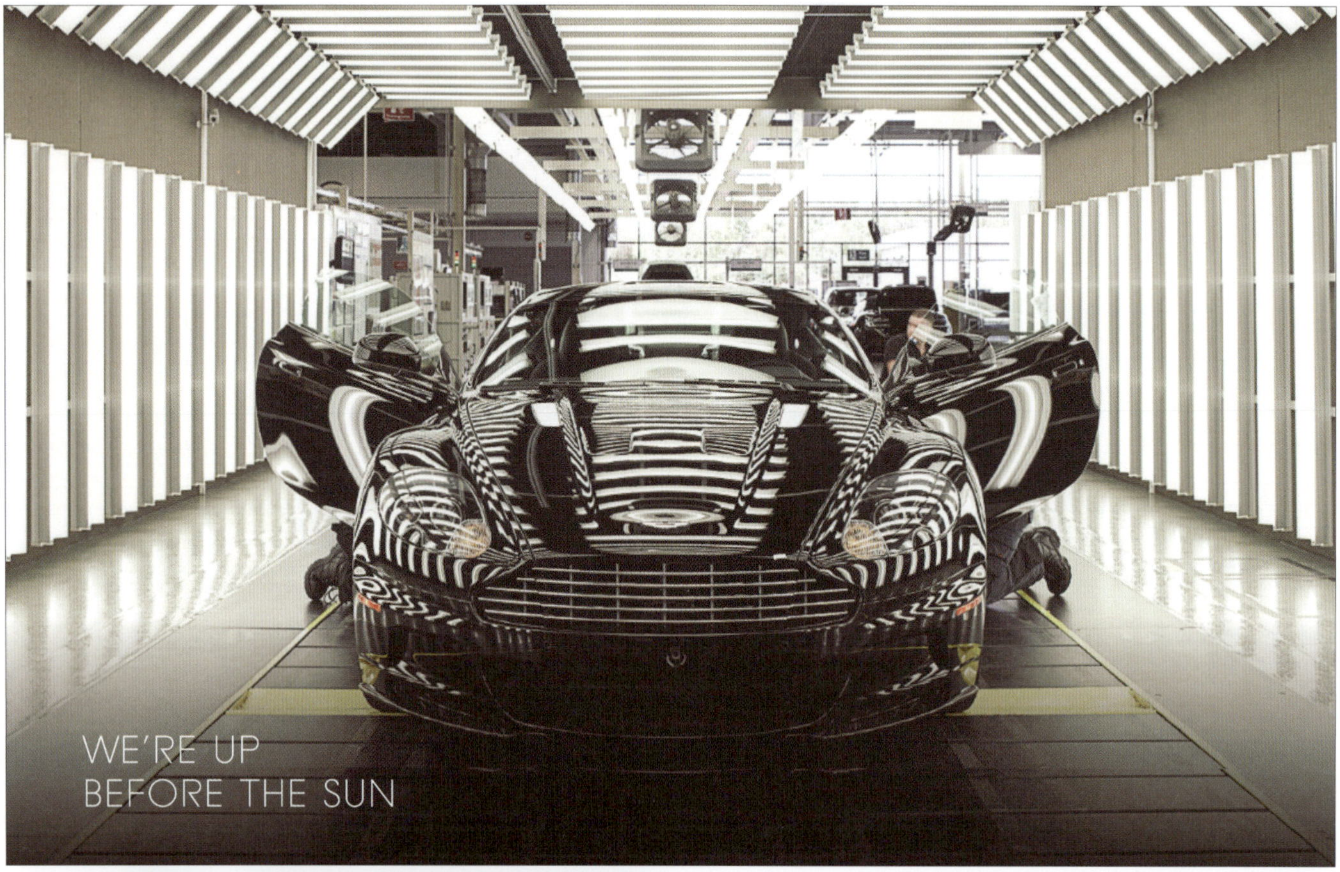

WE'RE UP
BEFORE THE SUN

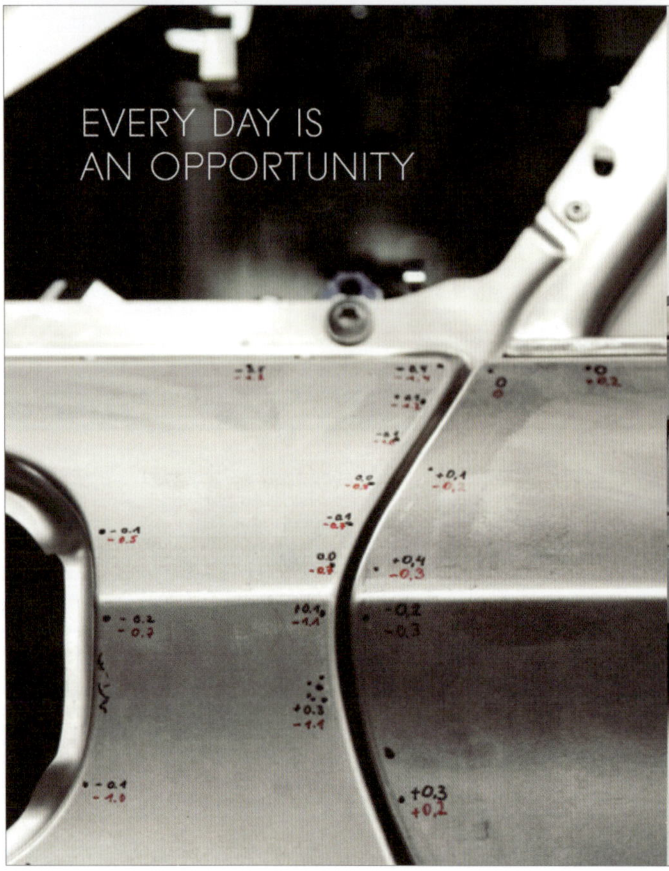

EVERY DAY IS
AN OPPORTUNITY

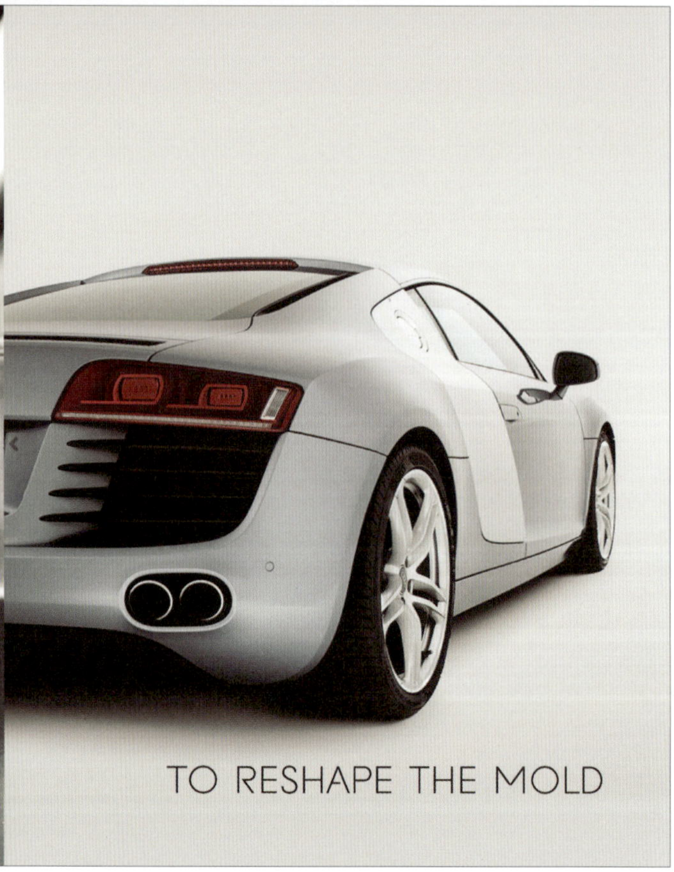

TO RESHAPE THE MOLD

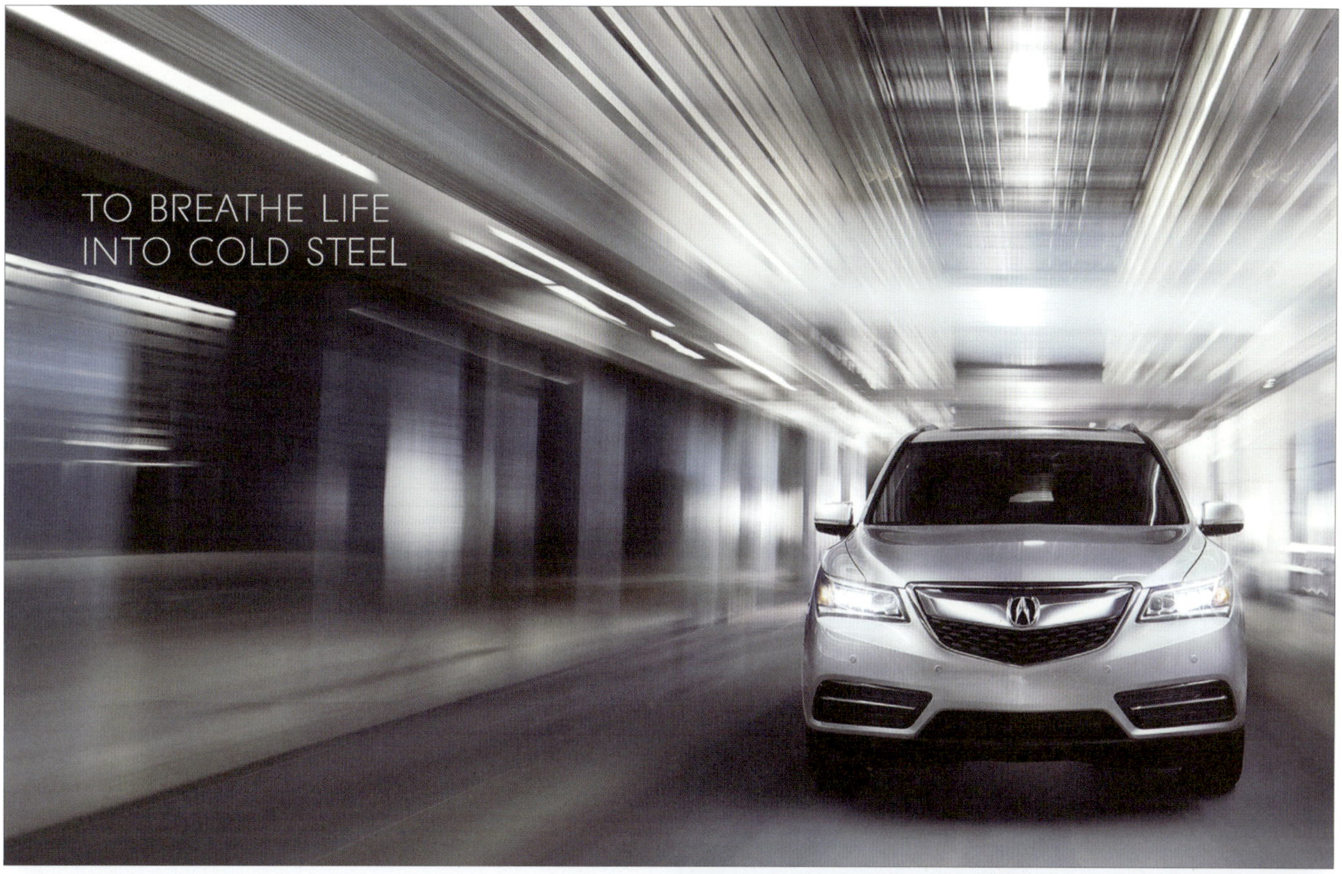

TO BREATHE LIFE
INTO COLD STEEL

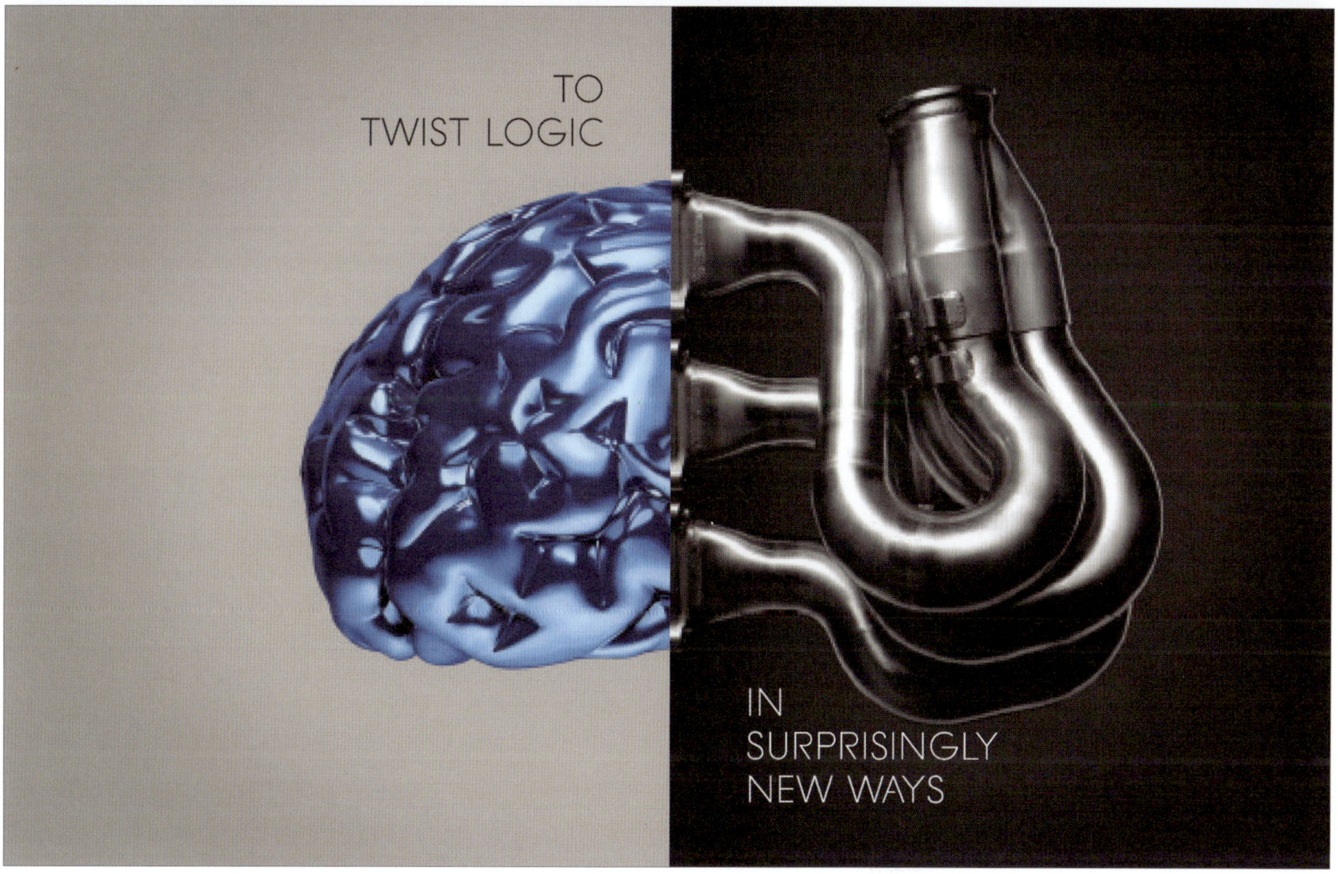

TO
TWIST LOGIC

IN
SURPRISINGLY
NEW WAYS

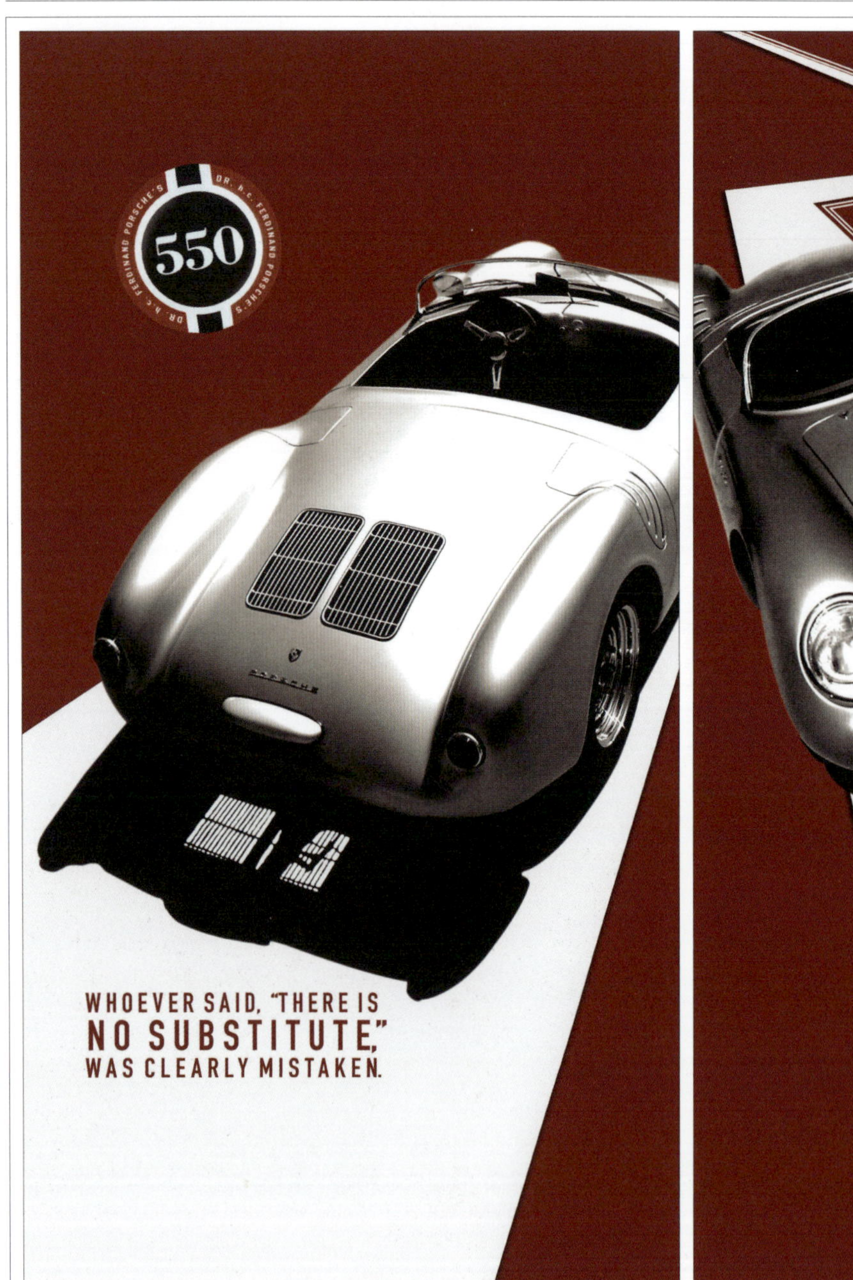

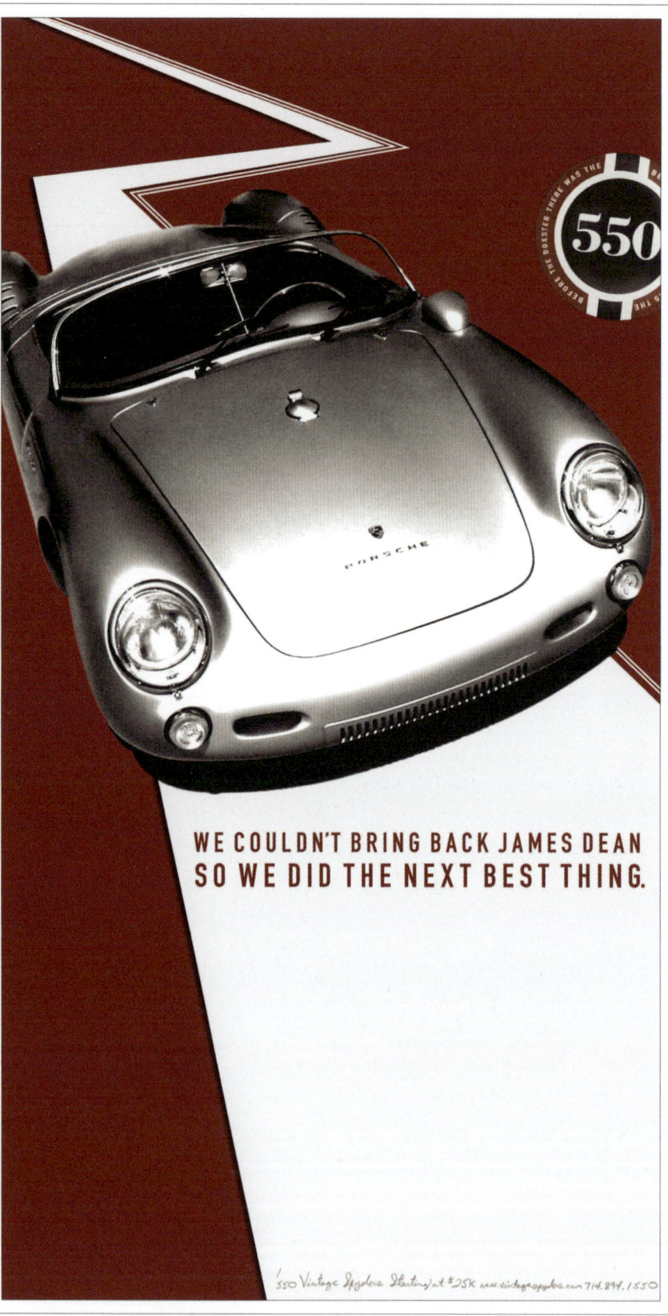

Client: Vintage Porsche Spyder Replicas; Agency: The Blueberry Palace; Creative Director: Colin Corcoran; Art Director: Leena Hashim-Waris; Copywriter: Colin Corcoran

What inspired or motivated you into your career?
Getting fired for being the worst assistant account executive in the world was highly motivating. Being called "Super Tool" by a senior creative team at the time proved to be "super" inspiring.

What is your work philosophy?
It's similar to iconic tattoo artist Sailor Jerry's: "*Good work ain't cheap. Cheap work ain't good.*"

I also have tried to do work over the years that impresses more accomplished creatives than myself, so they can help pull me up, rather than conforming to try to impress peers, or worse, seek the admiration of the generation below me by imitating trends rather than creating them.

What is it about Advertising that you are most passionate about?
The number of brands with different problems to solve and a variety of kinds of people to partner with and learn from.

What prompted you to become The Independent Copywriter?
All of my competitors call themselves the same thing: first name last name, freelance copywriter. Most are really just between jobs or serial full-timers in their respective local markets, working onsite at agencies for 6-24 months at a time. I wanted to create my own unique freelance brand that would also allow me to do a fun self-promotion every year and work remotely the majority of the time. It also didn't hurt that IndependentCopywriter.com was somehow still available in 2010. My goal with The IC brand was to become the most in-demand and consistently awarded freelance copywriter across the country. I am happy to say I've achieved that designation over the past decade, having performed over 600 projects for over 500 ad agencies, design studios, interactive shops, and directly with brand marketers in 36 states, along with London and China. It doesn't mean I think I'm the "best" (there's no such thing) or that I make the most money (I don't, because I prefer to only work approximately half the year). It just means that I have managed to become a tiny, yet trusted brand name within the creative industry.

What do you enjoy most about working independently?
Being able to turn down or walk away from clients and/or projects that suck/aren't worth my time.

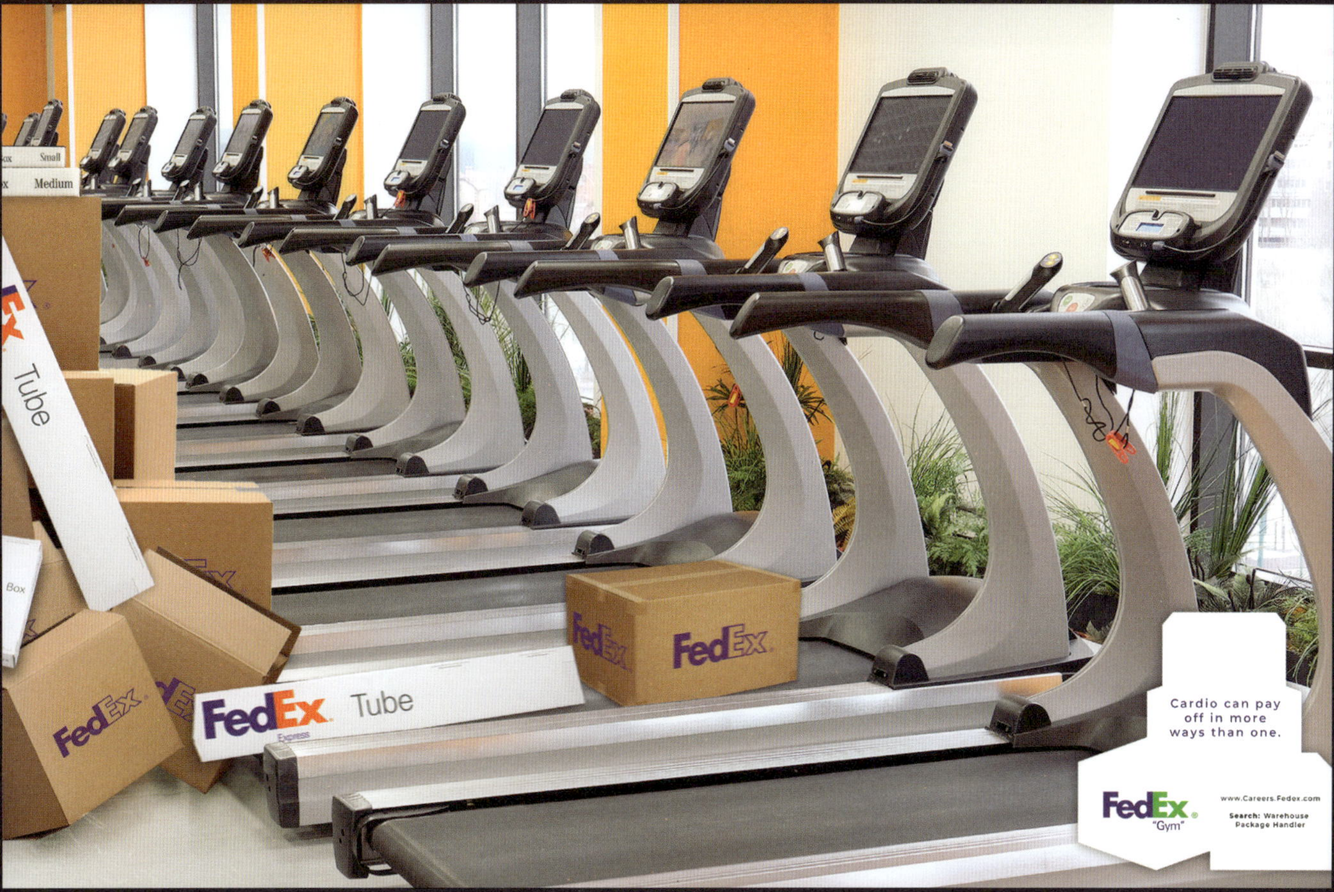

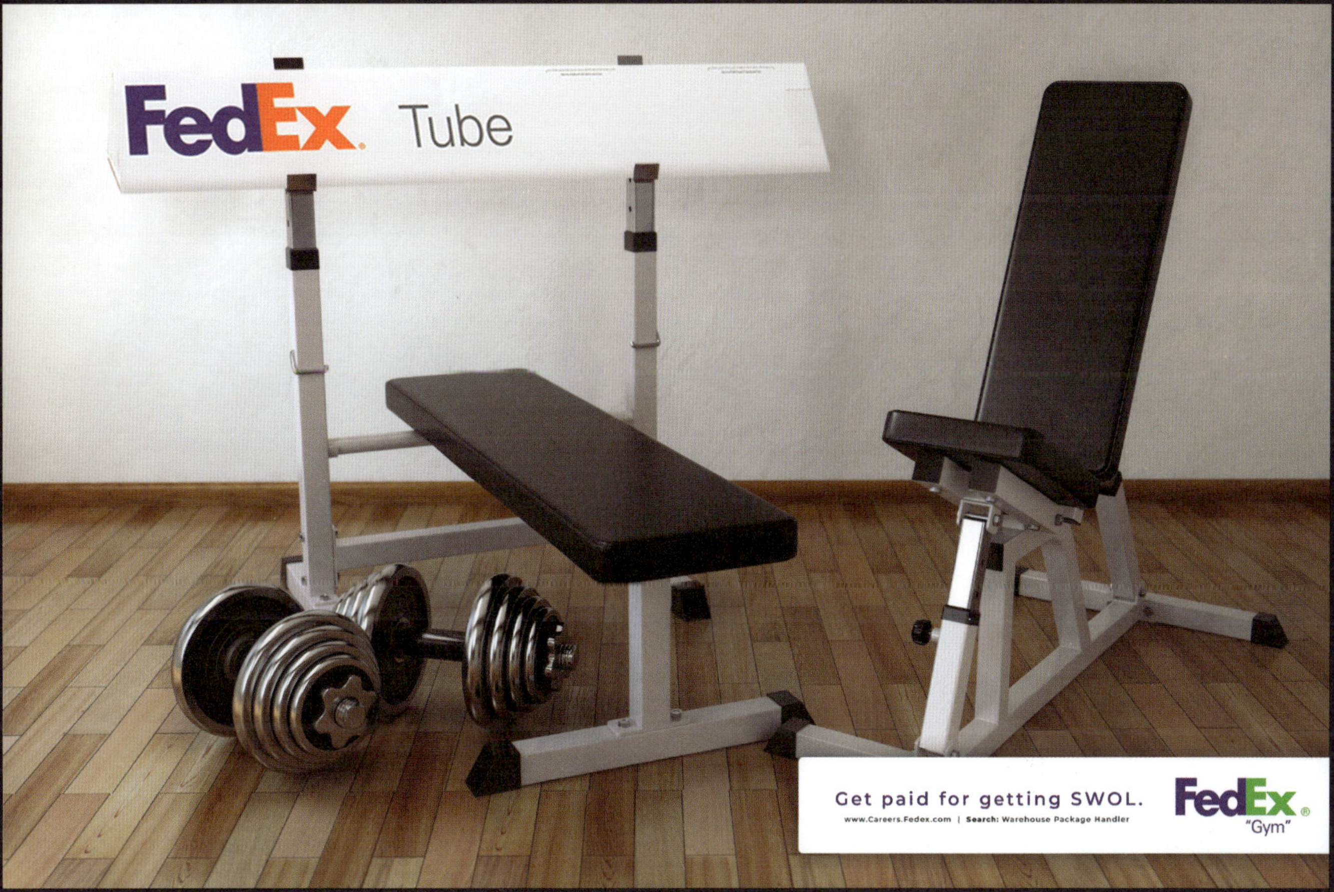

Cardio can pay off in more ways than one.

FedEx "Gym"

www.Careers.Fedex.com

Search: Warehouse Package Handler

FedEx Tube

Get paid for getting SWOL.

www.Careers.Fedex.com | Search: Warehouse Package Handler

FedEx "Gym"

Client: FedEx "Gym" (Recruitment Division); Agency: Colin Corcoran, Independent Copywriter; Executive Creative Director: Colin Corcoran
Art Director: Lindy Taylor; Copywriter: Colin Corcoran; Retoucher: PICS

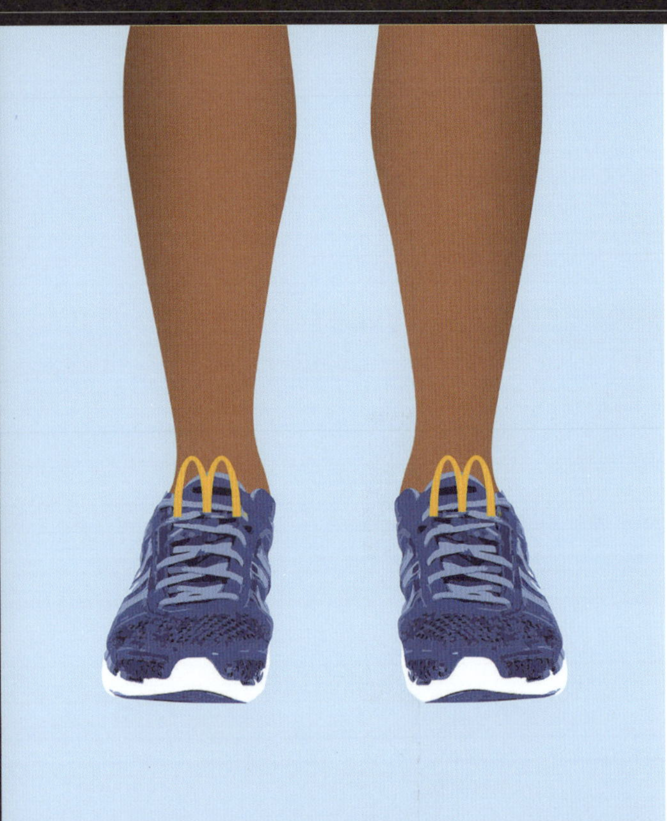

McDELIVERY™
Now in NYC

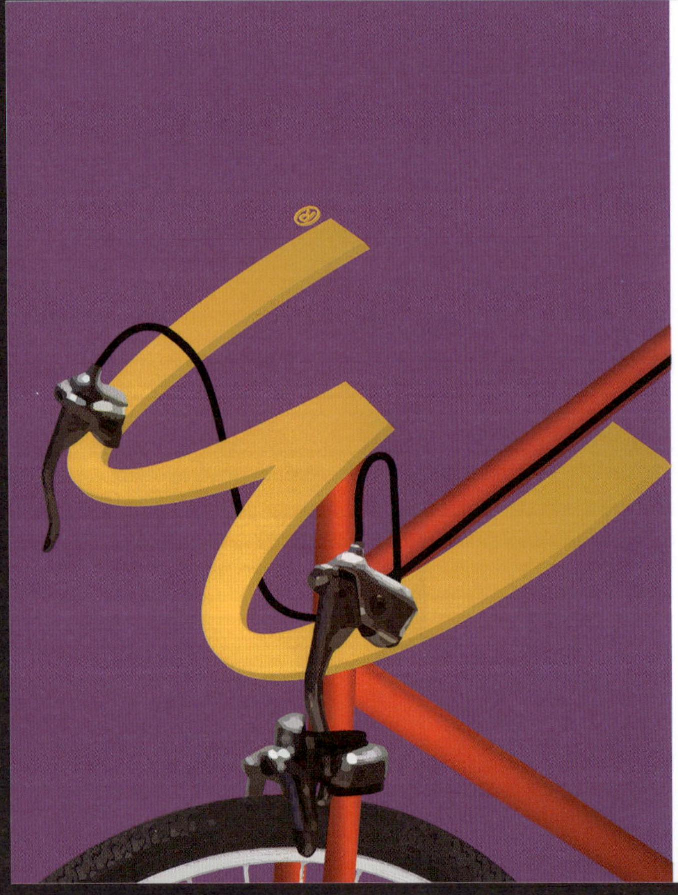

McDELIVERY™
Now in NYC

Client: McDonald's (McDelivery NYC); Agency: DDB Chicago; Creative Director: Colin Corcoran; Art Director: Colin Corcoran; Copywriter: Colin Corcoran

How do you manage the different styles of the advertising agencies you've worked with?
I tend to only work for agencies that don't have a set "house" style. I also have a take it or leave it approach with most agency clients. If you love my style(s) and voices of work, great. If you hire me and don't like anything I did, well then, that's most likely your fault because you knew what to expect with a writer like me and you've already paid me half upfront with your client's money.

How do you balance the work of being a Creative Director and a Copywriter?
As a freelancer, pretty easily. I get paid E/G/CD rates, but usually only do the work of a copywriter since I have zero dog and pony show presentation skills and refuse to be glued to a phone 24/7.

What is your most difficult challenge you've had to overcome?
I've faced plenty of professional challenges, including being fired 4 ½ times, having envious peers try to sabotage my career, having money stolen from me a couple of times by so-called colleagues. But one cool thing about this business is that good work forgives practically all sins. Plus, I have the resilience of Wolverine. Every time someone has tried to kill my career, I've come back even stronger. That's because personally I grew up poor, without a father and with an abusive mother who died an agonizing death from pancreatic cancer five years ago. The ad business is easy in comparison to that in my eyes, because it only makes you suffer adversity in the short-term.

Who is or was your greatest mentor?
Mike Duckworth and Brock Davis. They were a creative team in their early careers while at Martin / Williams, and I was beyond lucky to have both of them as instructors while at Brainco. They are the only two teachers of mine whose careers my own haven't surpassed, and I am glad of this fact because you should always have a mentor no matter how experienced or successful you are.

Who were some of your greatest past influences?
I learned a lot vicariously studying copywriting, with the works of David Abbott, Tim Delaney, Greg Hahn, Kara Goodrich, Dean Buckhorn, Sally Hogshead, Jim Hagar, Tom Thomas, and numerous Wieden + Kennedy and CP+B writers like Evan Fry, Ryan Kutscher, Bob Cianfrone, Rob Strasberg, Janet Champ, Jim Riswold, Ginger Robinson, Jeff Kling, and Stacy Wall.

Who among your contemporaries today do you most admire?
Heath Pochucha and Doug Pedersen were a senior creative team on Harley-Davidson a decade ago and both have gone onto to even bigger and better things. I admire that they too don't have just one set voice or style. They are also both legitimately good, humble, and kind human beings.

Who have been some of your favorite people or clients you have worked with?
People: I'd rather keep them all to myself because it's very rare to work with truly talented and good folks, so I don't want to share them with the rest of the world. Besides, they know who they are. Clients: The past few years ad agency Eleven, design studio Turner Duckworth, and Chinese Smartphone maker OPPO have all placed a high value on the kind of work I do and our working relationship is more of a partnership. Doing great, award-winning work and getting paid well for it is really the sweet spot for all us creatives. After 16 years in the biz, I have found my white whales.

What is your greatest professional achievement?
The creative industry is cool in that you don't have to wait until the very end of your career to win an award or to receive long overdue acknowledgement of your talent. There are 200+ professional achievements I'm proud of, but they all boil down to having been the result of impressing and gaining the respect of many industry heroes of mine, either in the form of a hard to win award or them telling me they like my work in person or over email.

What are the most important ingredients you require from a client to do successful work?
A creative is only as good as their client's creative vision, risk tolerance, and trust.

What would be your dream assignment?
Working for/with Diesel or U2. The closest I've come to that level of creativity is pitching an idea of big dogs walking naked Millennials to Hush Puppies, which met every requirement of the brief.

What is the greatest satisfaction you get from your work?
Working in an industry where I simultaneously can care too much about creative standards, but also not giving a fuck at the same time if a client, creative director, or partner likes my ideas or not.

What part of your work do you find most demanding?
Phone calls with clients who possess zero imagination, personality and/or communication skills. Also, married couples who own an agency or a start-up can be the absolute most demanding and worst people to work for because everything about their business becomes personal to them.

What advice would you have for students starting out today?
Social media has quickly become the junk food of advertising by devolving into low-cost, quantity over quality. If you choose to work for a brand that makes minimally viable products and/or an agency that does minimally viable advertising in the form of vanilla, vapid non-idea social posts, then you will have a minimally viable career as a glorified production artist making barely more than minimum wage. On a related note: work for someone whose work you actually admire. Not just some agency that happens to be hiring and has a foosball or ping-pong table. I only have the career I do today because of where I first started out: Fallon | Minneapolis (which was arguably the best agency in the world at the time back in 2003). And then Hunt Adkins right after that.

What interests do you have outside of your work?
Cycling. Tennis. Basketball. Video Gaming. Art Collecting. Fine Dining. Travel. Theatre. Cinema.

What do you value most?
It is said that time is the only true luxury. In that regard, I value the freedom I have to do what I want, when I want, how I want and with whom I want, without having to ask for permission first.

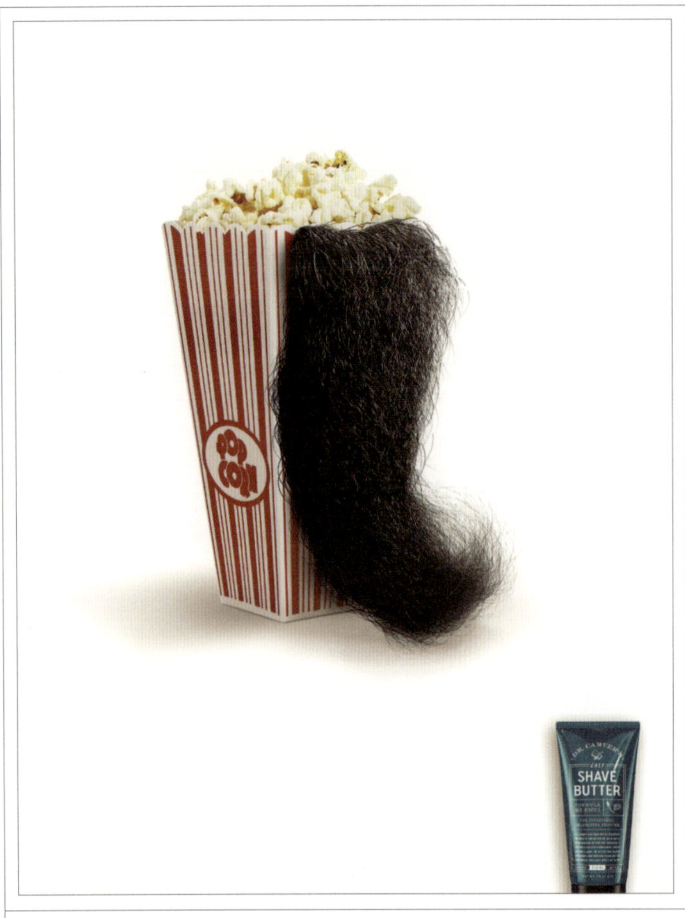

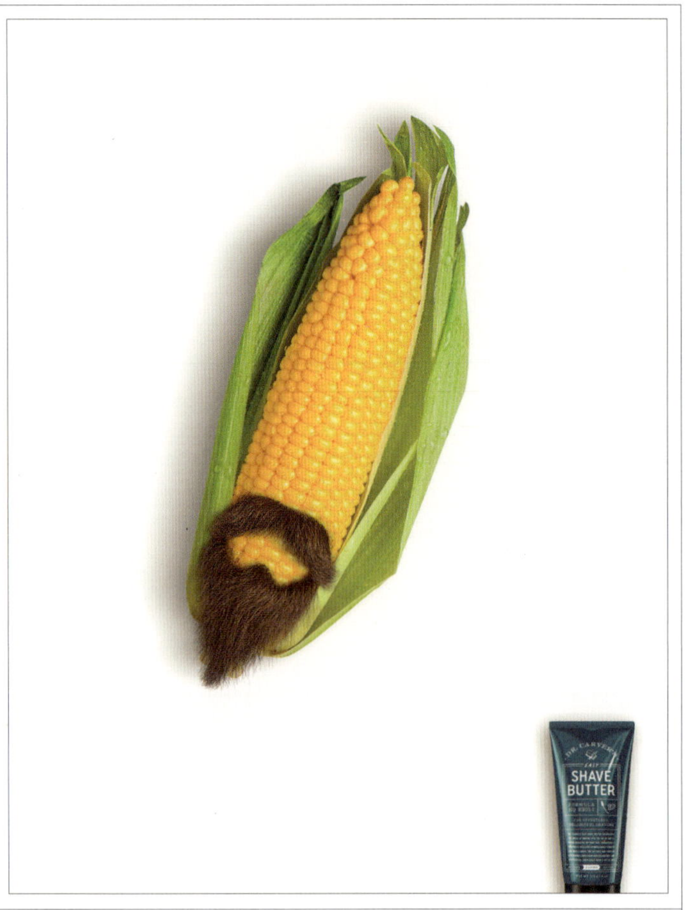

Client: Dollar Shave Club; Agency: DSC (in-house agency); Creative Director: Alex Brownstein; Art Director: Colin Corcoran; Retoucher: Giannini Creative

What would you change if you had to do it all over again?
Welp, I was asked by both Wieden + Kennedy and CP+B if I was interested in full-time back in 2007 and 2008, respectively. Most people will probably think I was crazy for politely declining each inquiry. But I had just bought a house, just started freelancing and just launched a website and printed business cards. With 2009 being around the corner, who knows what would have happened if I had uprooted my entire life to move to Portland or Boulder right before the great recession.

In hindsight, the only thing I truly wish I could take a mulligan on was the decision to turn down a 3+ month, $100k+ freelance gig (with Commonwealth in Detroit on Chevy) that would have also involved traveling for free to Japan, Dubai, and Mexico for film shoots. Their recruiter who inquired about my availability and interest never mentioned the fact that I was referred for the job by a close industry friend who also happened to be serving as interim CCO of the agency at the time. That info would have been very useful in helping me make a more informed, better decision. Ugh.

Where do you seek inspiration?
I try to put a little bit of my personal life into each piece of work whenever I can, instead of just putting something out. It can be something that's happened to me, or the exact opposite. It can be something that happened to a friend or something they said. My life is in most of my ads.

The brand and/or product has also always provided me with plenty enough inspiration if I do a bit of digging into its history, and experience the product or service first-hand. I believe if you have a general knowledge of a brand and some of its past advertising, you really don't need a brief.

How do you define success?
"Success without integrity is failure."—Anonymous. In that sense, I've been successful in never lying to folks. Not stiffing people out of money they are owed for their time and talent. Not throwing anyone under the bus to get ahead or cover up a mistake of mine. Not taking credit for work I had no part in or putting another writer's stuff in my book. I'm especially proud of myself for not succumbing to common industry pitfalls like alcoholism, drug abuse, or sexual harassment.
My own definition of success is achieving my own personal set of goals, not what everyone else's are. I've never wanted to be a CCO, let alone a creative director, but that tends to be most people's professional desire in this industry. Ironically, over the years, multiple CCOs and ECDs and have all told me the same thing: "I wish I could do what you do."

Where do you see yourself in the future?
Early-retired ad copywriter, semi-retired design writer and business owner (either a new restaurant chain concept founder, toy inventor and/or comic book franchise creator). Let's just say I've had several potential exit strategies in mind.

What's a great piece of advice you've received?
I didn't want to hear it early on in my career. And it took me a decade to start aspiring beyond the Midwest "make everything by hand" mindset. But the fact is, doing great work on small brands will only get you so far in your career. So I've moved away from screwing on a bolt, gluing on a piece of yarn and stamping a forest critter on stuff, and onto creative work for major companies that win major awards and pay major amounts of money. I don't consider it as "selling out" now. I think of it as not selling myself short anymore.

Colin Corcoran www.independentcopywriter.com
See his Graphis Master Portfolio on graphis.com.

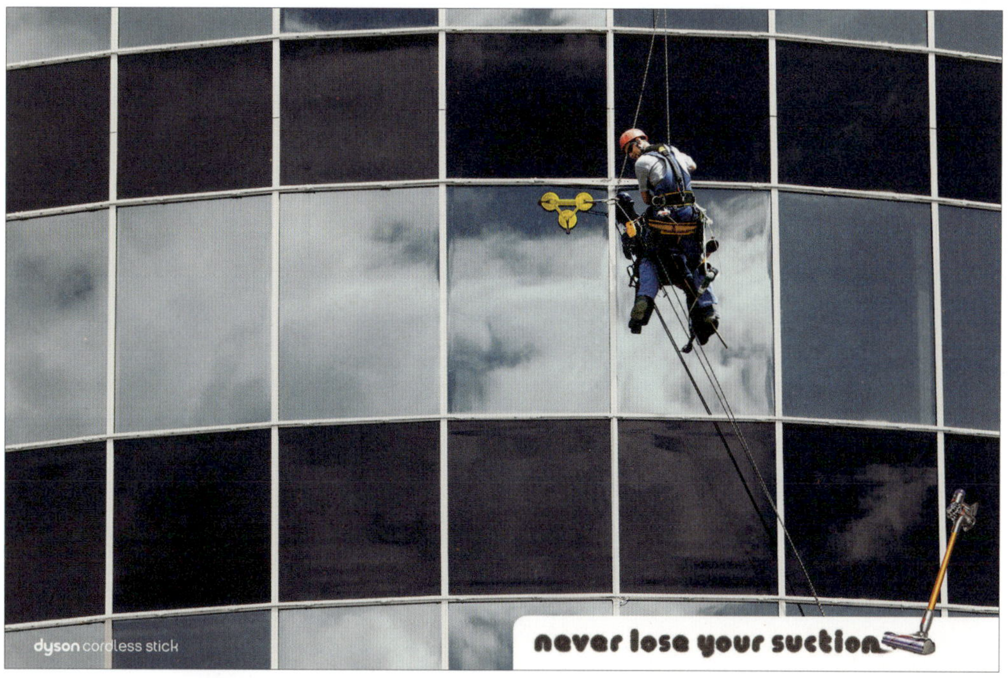

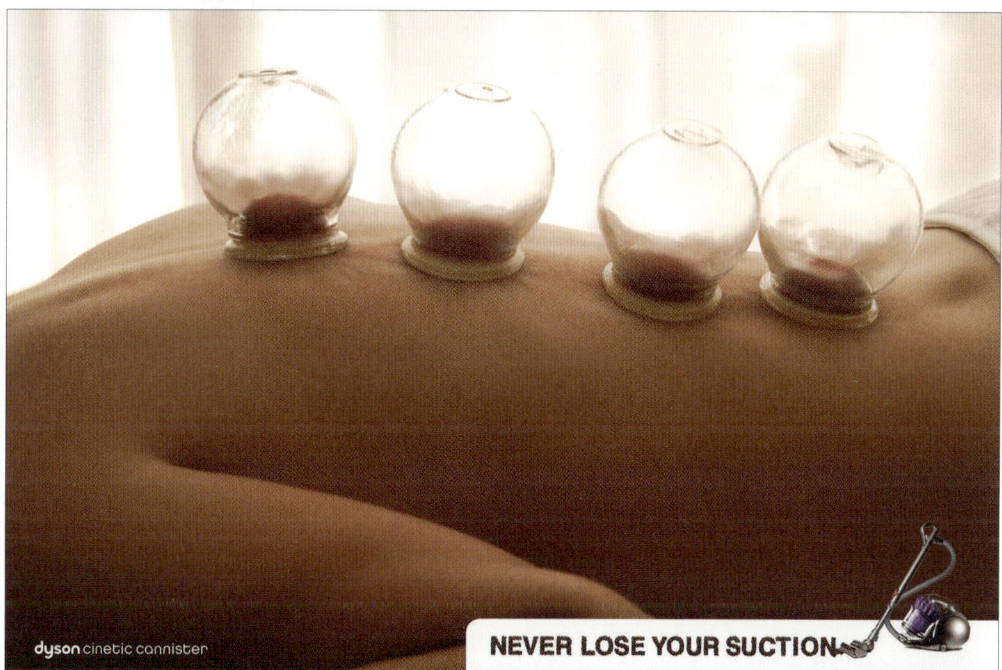

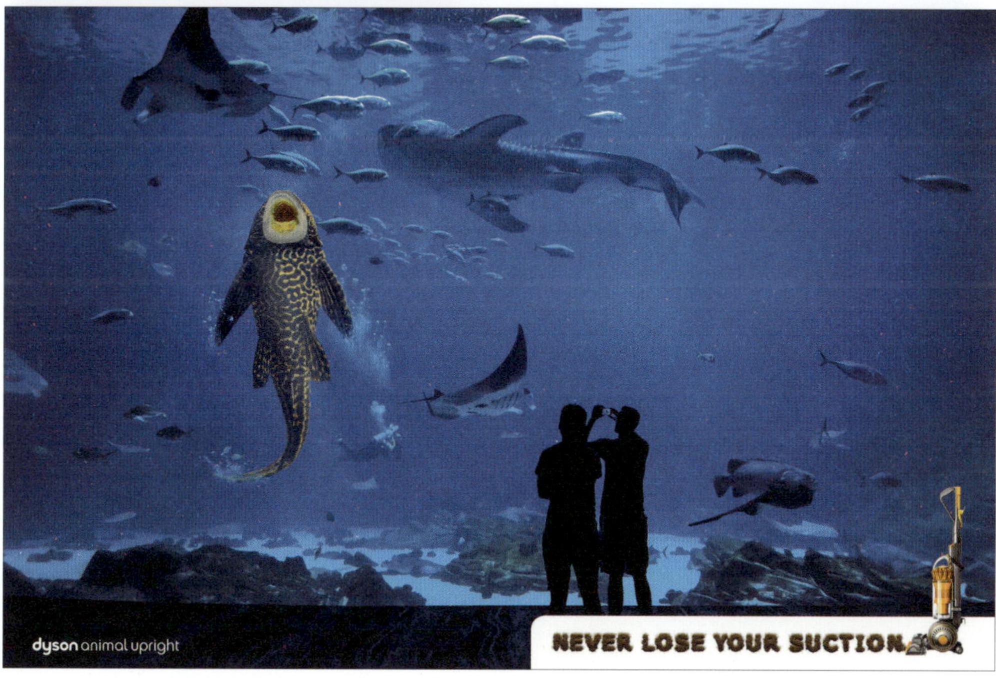

Client: Dyson Vacuums; Agency: Colin Corcoran, Independent Copywriter; Executive Creative Director: Colin Corcoran
Art Director: Colin Corcoran; Copywriter: Colin Corcoran; Typographer: Graham Clifford; Retoucher: PICS

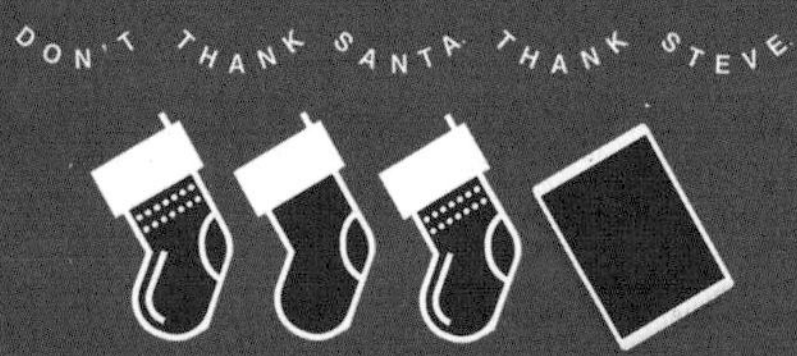

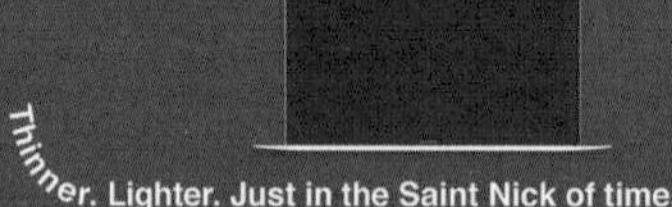

Client: Apple Computer (2010 winter holiday in-store signage); Agency: Apple (in-house); Art Director: Vidur Raswant; Copywriter: Colin Corcoran

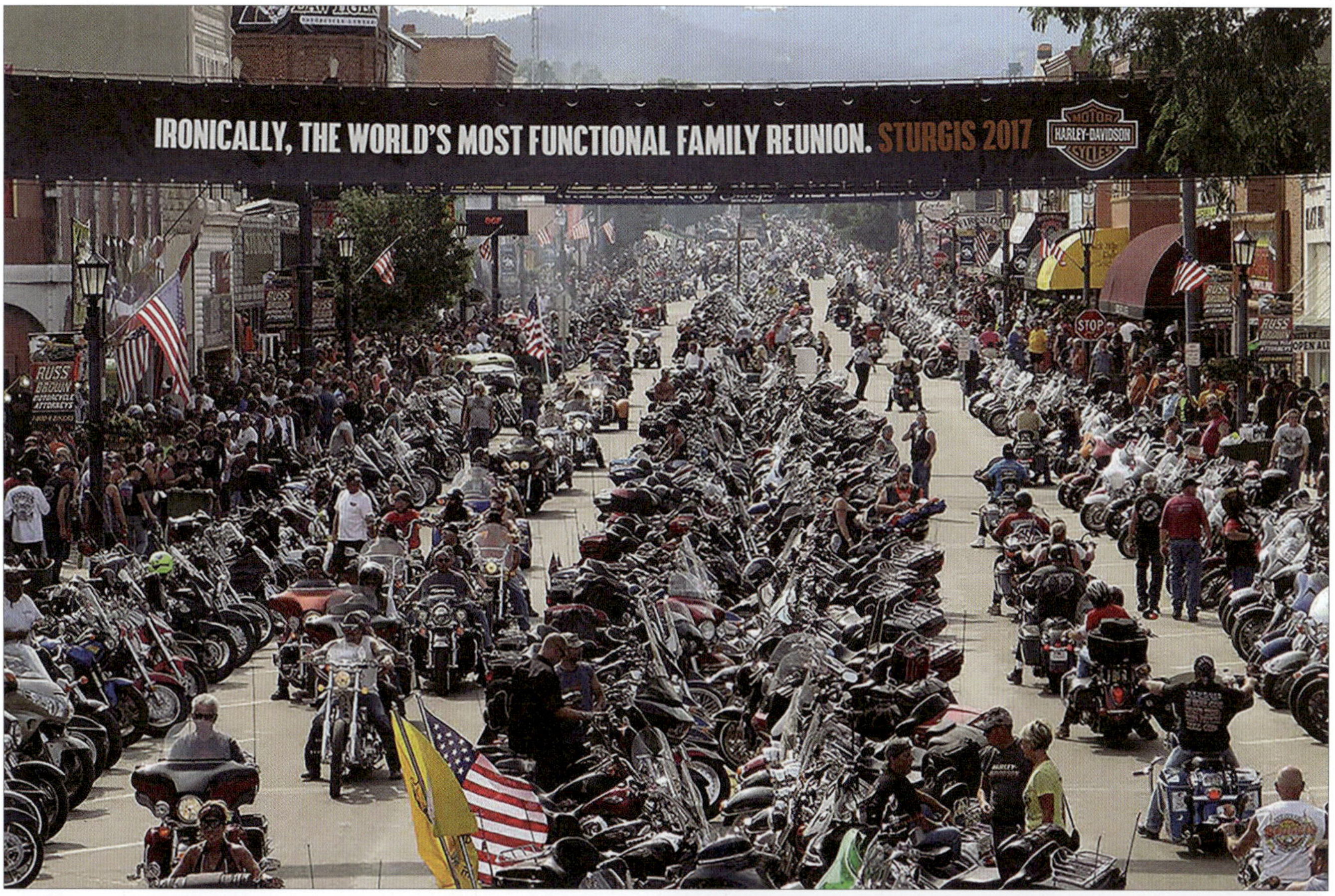

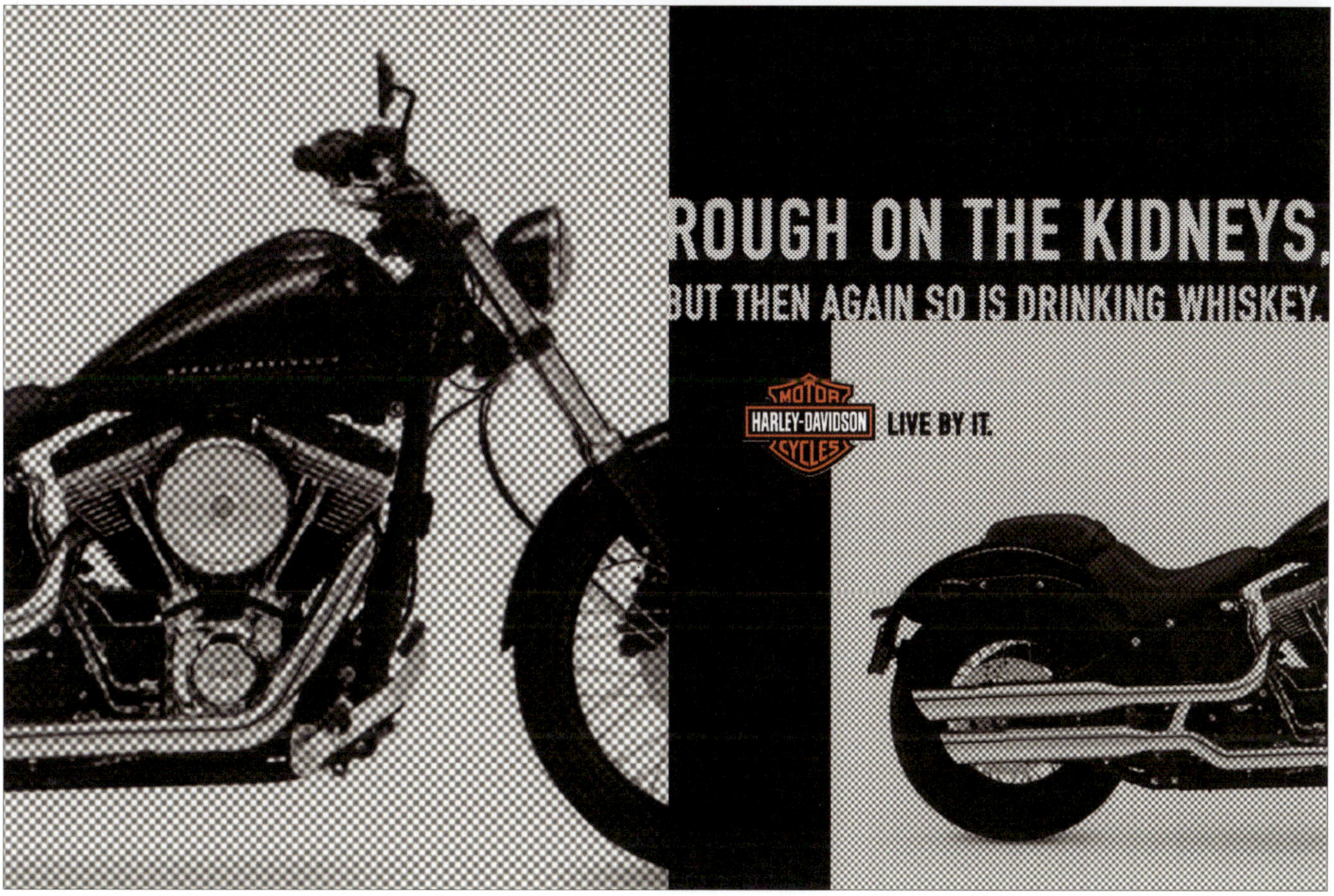

IRONICALLY, THE WORLD'S MOST FUNCTIONAL FAMILY REUNION. STURGIS 2017

MOTOR HARLEY-DAVIDSON CYCLES

ROUGH ON THE KIDNEYS,

BUT THEN AGAIN SO IS DRINKING WHISKEY.

MOTOR HARLEY-DAVIDSON CYCLES LIVE BY IT.

(Top) Client: Harley-Davidson (Sturgis Welcome Banner); Agency: Camp3; Creative Director: Tom Riddle; Copywriter: Colin Corcoran
(Bottom) Client: Harley-Davidson; Agency: Victors & Spoils; Art Director: Name Withheld; Copywriter: Colin Corcoran

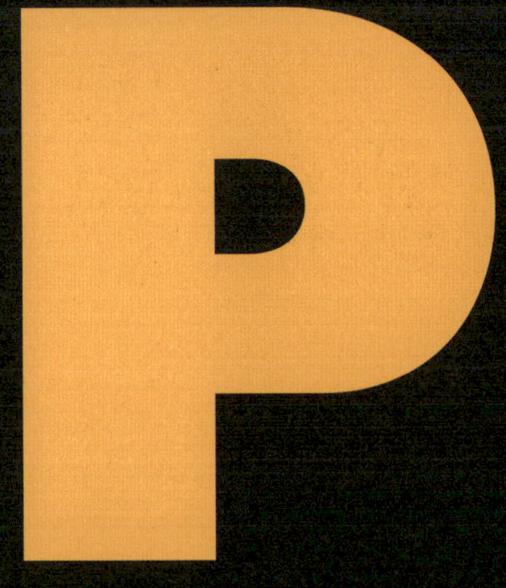

PHOTOGRAPHY

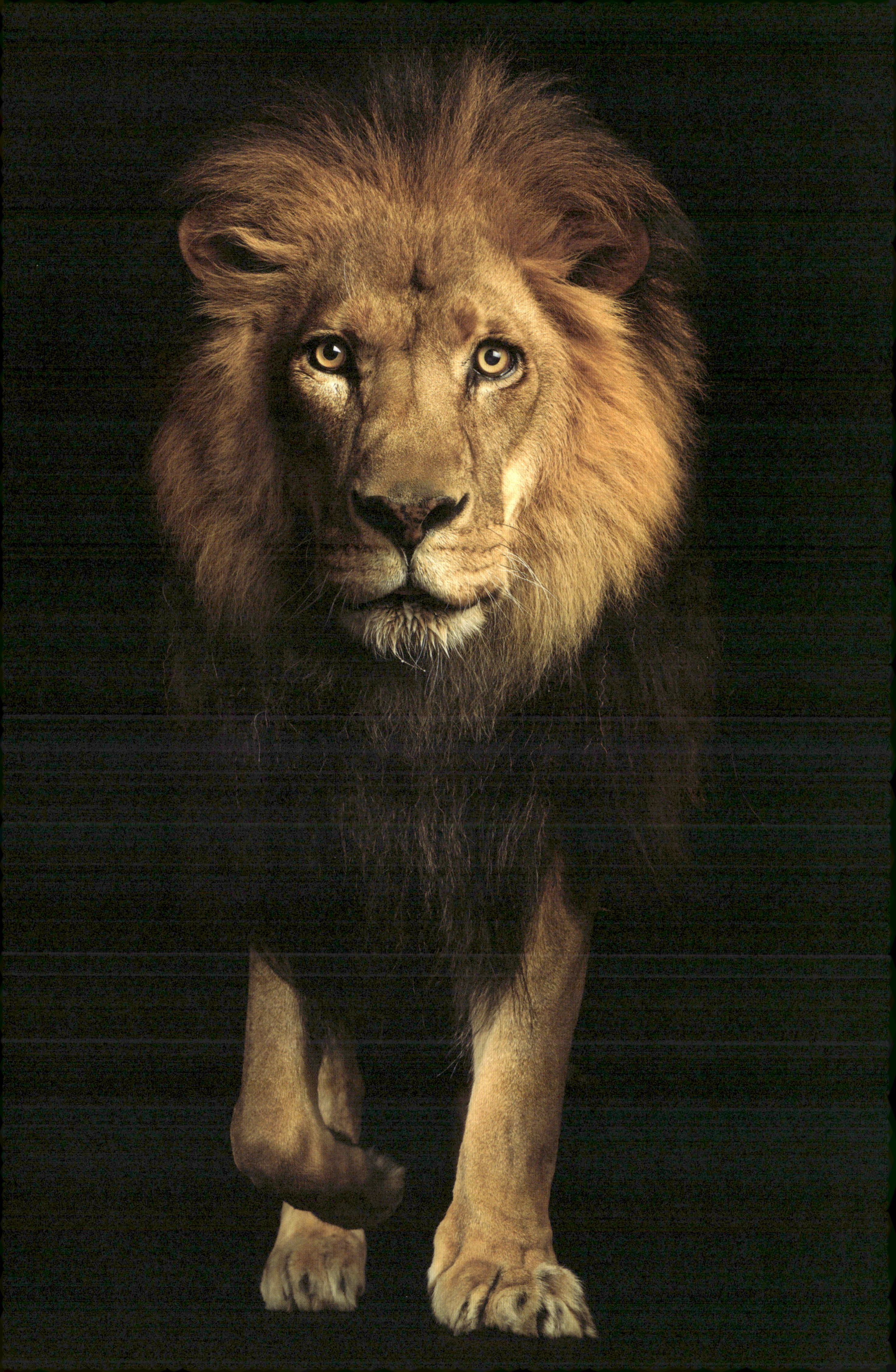

AUDACITY IS A FUNDAMENTAL INGREDIENT IN CREATING MAGIC. TO BE AN ARTIST WHO DOESN'T CREATE MAGIC IS LIKE BEING A DOCTOR WHO DOESN'T ACTUALLY HELP ANYONE BECOME HEALTHY.

Mark Laita, *Photographer*

I HAVE FOLLOWED MARK LAITA'S CAREER FOR SOMETIME AND HAVE ALWAYS ENJOYED HIS VISUALLY COMPELLING WORK!

Lennette Newell, *Photographer (Graphis Master)*

THE PHOTOS OF SNAKES, STUFFED BIRDS AND WILD LIFE THAT MARK LAITA PRESENTS TO US IS VISUALLY STUNNING. MANY DESERVE TO BE PRINTED LARGE, FRAMED AND HUNG ON OUR WALLS.

B. Martin Pedersen, *Publisher & Creative Director, Graphis Inc.*

MARK HAS A NATURAL INSTINCT FOR SHAPES AND FORMS. HE DEMONSTRATES A SENSE OF LINE AND DYNAMICS, WITH HIS SUBJECTS FREQUENTLY VIVID IN COLOUR AND EMERGING FROM A DARK VOID.

Tim Flach, *British Photographer, Tim Flach Photography Ltd.*

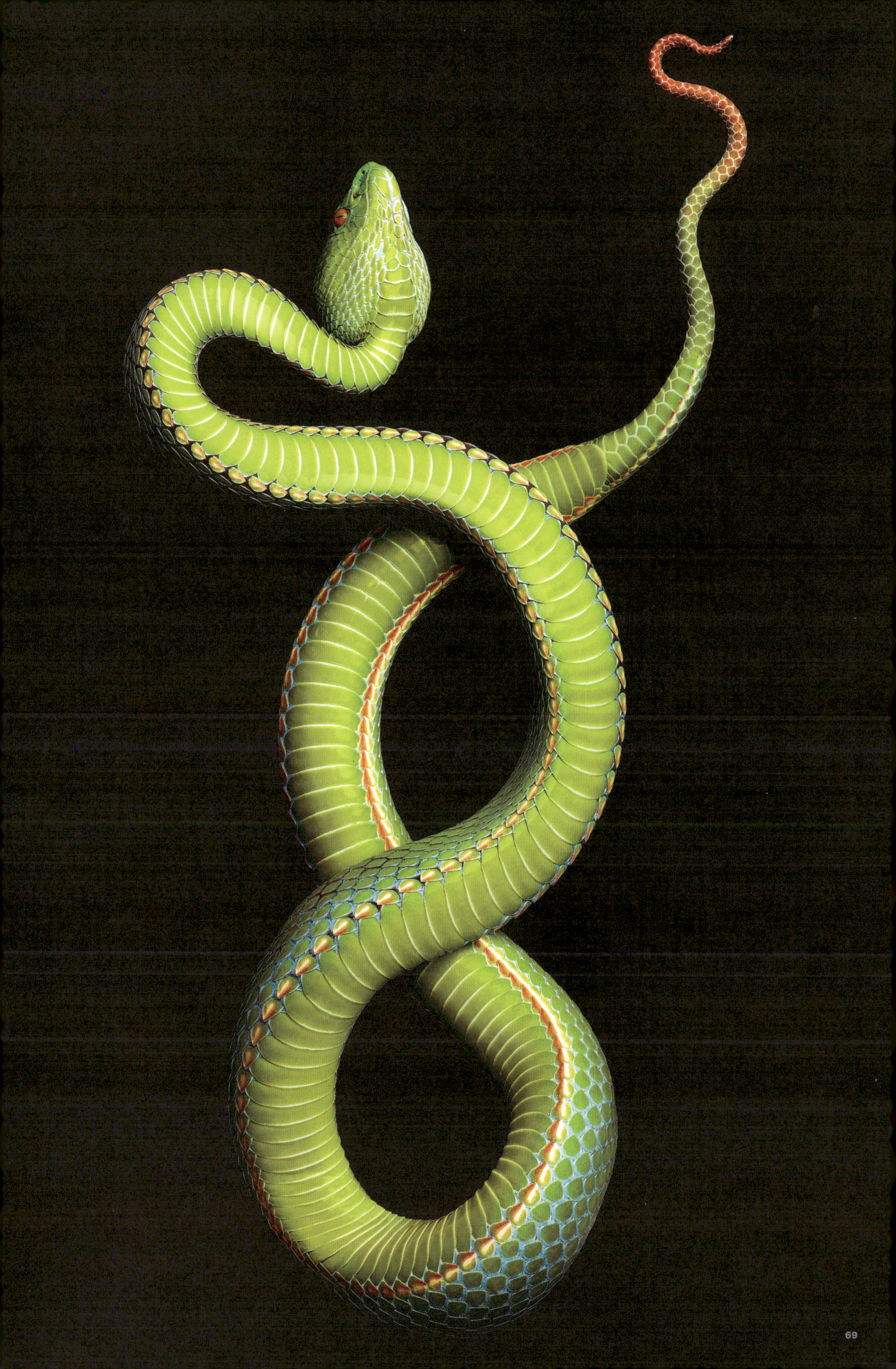

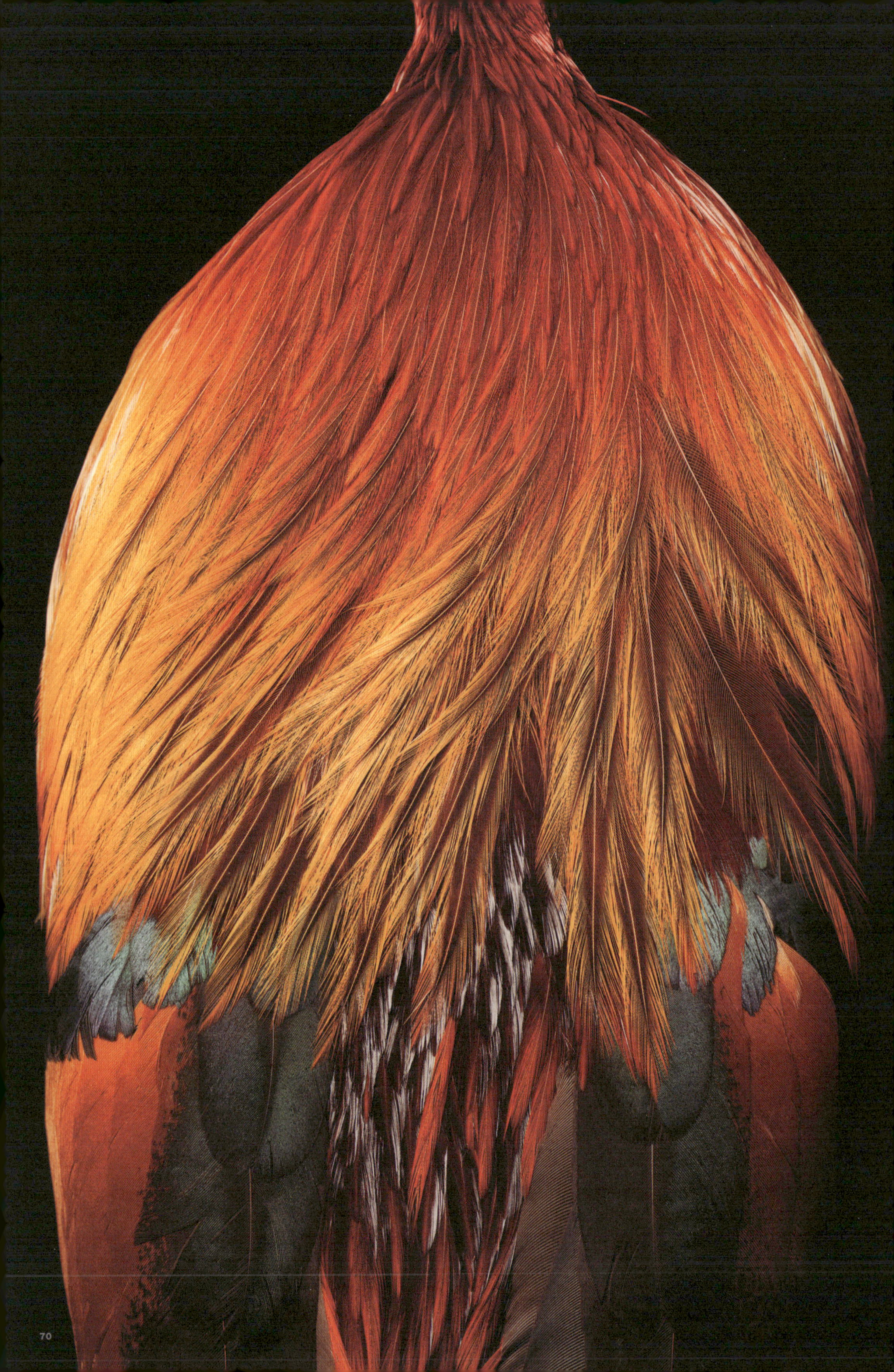

Introduction by Adam Voorhes *Photographer at The Voorhes*

I idolized Mark Laita when I was a student and sent him letters begging to work for him. They included photos of toilet brushes in toilets and brooms with dustpans. His studio manager did have me come into his Culver City studio for a couple of days, but it was just two weeks before I moved to New York. ■ Laita's work has been an inspiration and a high water mark for Robin and I to look up to from the beginning of our career. From the simplicity of light raking over soft folds of fabric, to complex conceptual composites, Laita paved the way from classic to contemporary still life photography. His work can be simultaneously timeless and timely, and endlessly inspiring.

PHOTOGRAPHER MARK LAITA HAS A CAREER THAT SPANS OVER 20 YEARS, WITH HIS CLEAN, GRAPHIC IMAGERY USED BY CLIENTS SUCH AS APPLE AND BMW.

Jessica Stewart, *Mymodernmet.com*

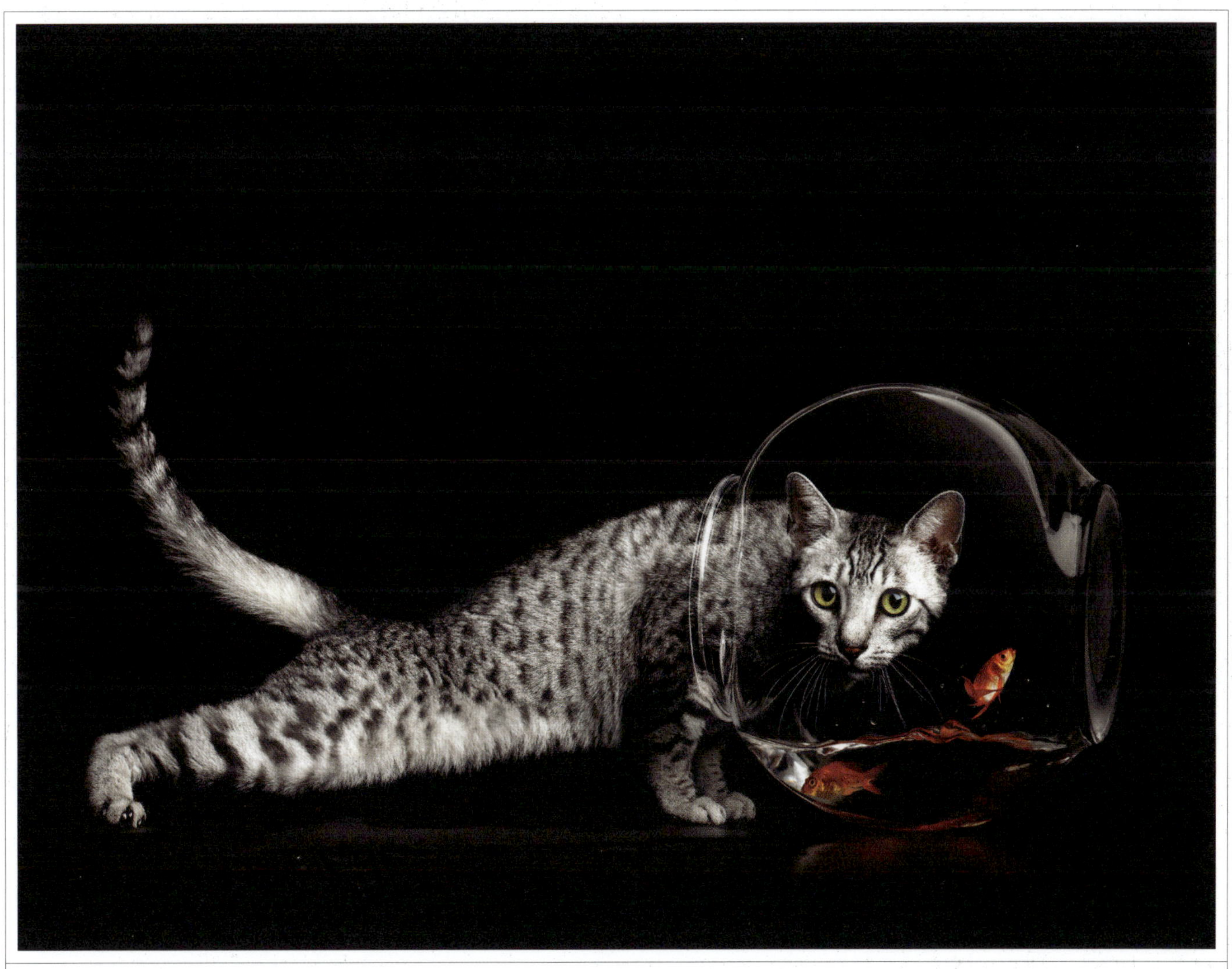

(Page 67) Lion C / (Page 69) Vogel's Pit Viper Playing Dead / (Opposite page) Red Junglefowl / (Above) Cat with Fish Bowl / (Page 72-73) Elephant Profile

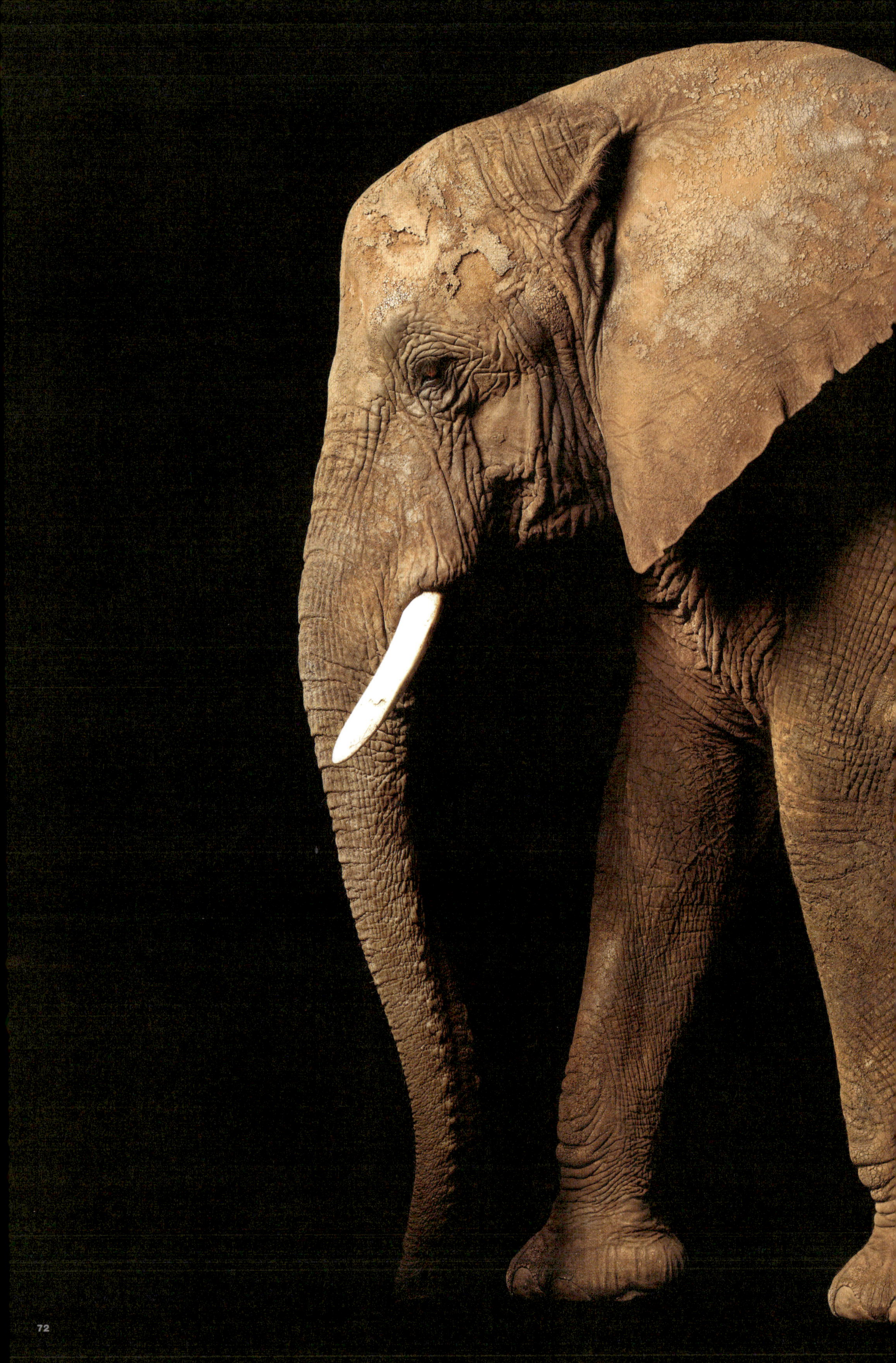

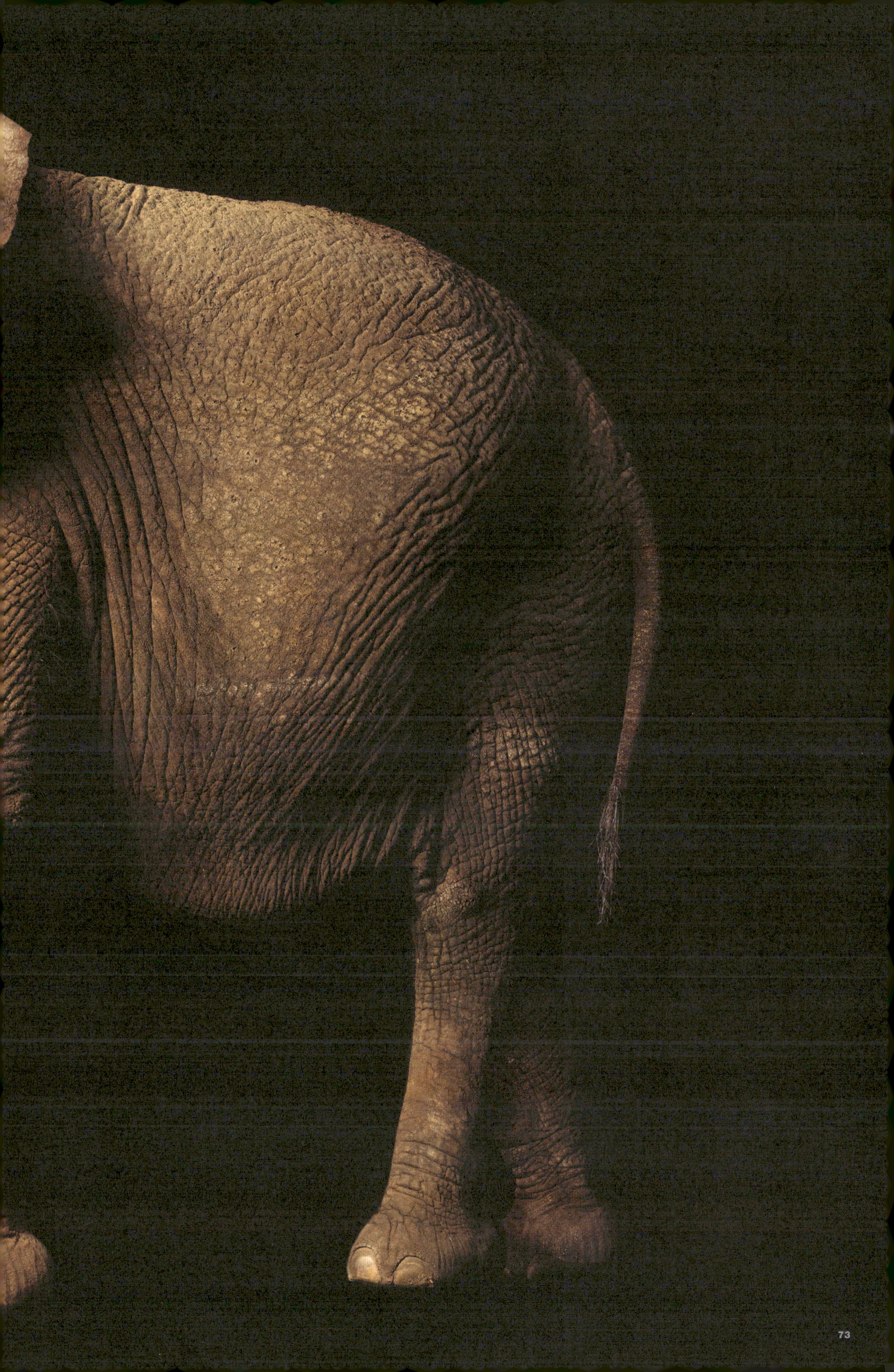

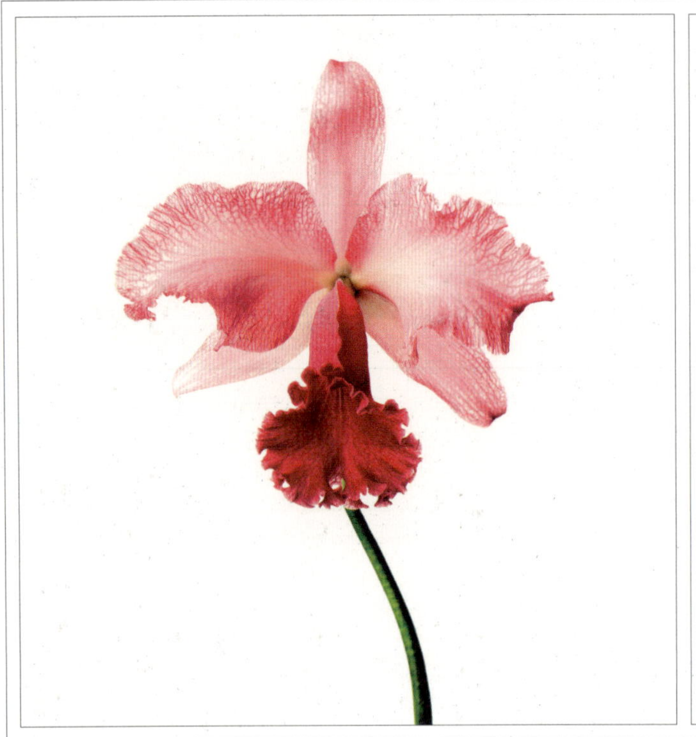

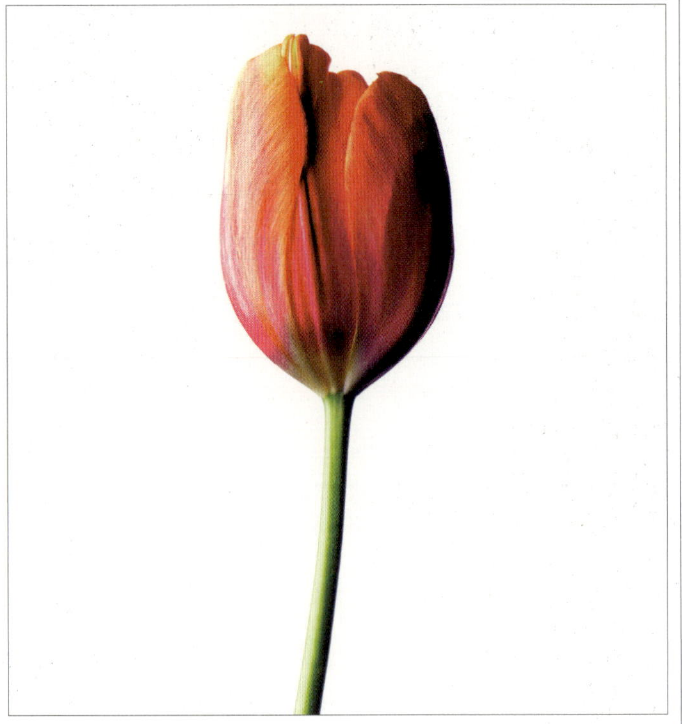

(Left) Cattleya Orchid / (Right) Tulip 'Couleur Cardinal'

What inspired or motivated you into your career?
As a child I was always drawing and painting. At fourteen I picked up my dad's camera and fell in love with photography's ability to be both scientific evidence and artistic at the same time. Now that we have digital manipulation, photography's integrity as a representation of the truth is compromised, but I avoid image manipulation with my personal work.

What is your work philosophy?
I've found that if I'm working on a personal project that has meaning to me, I'm much more able to deal with all the demands that come with commercial work. Ad work supports my personal projects financially and my personal work makes me a better commercial photographer.

Where do you seek inspiration?
I find I get inspired by nature more than anything else. Incredibly passionate people who have made incredible sacrifices make me crazy as well.

Who is or was your greatest mentor?
I worked with Richard Avedon many years ago and while artists like he, Irving Penn or Dennis Manarchy certainly had some influence over my work, I would say that people like Curtis Kulp, who I assisted early in my career or my father, who was not a photographer, were mentors that taught me how to simply work my ass off and shut up about it, how to focus fully on what I'm doing, to make dependability my first priority when I'm working on a project for a client. These are things a great mentor teaches by example. I was very lucky to have been around these kinds of people.

Who among your contemporaries today do you most admire?
I don't really pay attention to other photographers anymore. When I was starting my career I admired the magnificent work of Dennis Manarchy in Chicago. In my opinion, there has never been an advertising photographer whose commercial work looked like inspired personal work, except for Dennis Manarchy. Whether he was shooting products, food or people, you could always recognize Manarchy's work. His amazing aesthetic, his desire to push the limits of what he was willing to do for his art and his unwavering belief in himself truly expanded my mind of what was possible. Dennis Manarchy was a magician and a genius. Probably still is.

What aspect of photography do you most enjoy?
Truth. I know that photography no longer represents the truth as it once did because of all the digital retouching around now, but there are still ways to use the camera as a tool for getting to the truth.

What is your most difficult challenge you've had to overcome?
Challenges just make you stronger, which makes you better. I'm always looking for challenges. The biggest regret we'll have later on is not facing big challenges in our lives. I've learned that chasing them is the best thing I can do for my fulfillment and I find it positively effects my attitude in everything I do.

How would you describe your process?
Figure out what it is that I want, then do whatever it takes to make it happen and never listen to anyone except myself. I've been this way since I was a kid, so it isn't a process for me as much as it's just how I'm built. Whether that's a personality defect or trait depends on your tolerance for obsessive behavior. When I was younger I thought my extreme focus and drive were things I needed to fix, but once I accepted that it's just how I am, I became okay with it. Now I nurture it, but keep it from getting out of control.

What are the most important ingredients you require from a client to do successful work?
One art director can come to my studio and direct me to shoot his ad five different ways, just to cover his ass when his CD back at the office sees the work. Another art director will show up and tell me he's always loved my work and asks that I just do what I think is cool. One of these behaviors inspires me to win an award with the ad and make the AD very glad he decided to shoot with me, and the other behavior gets me to

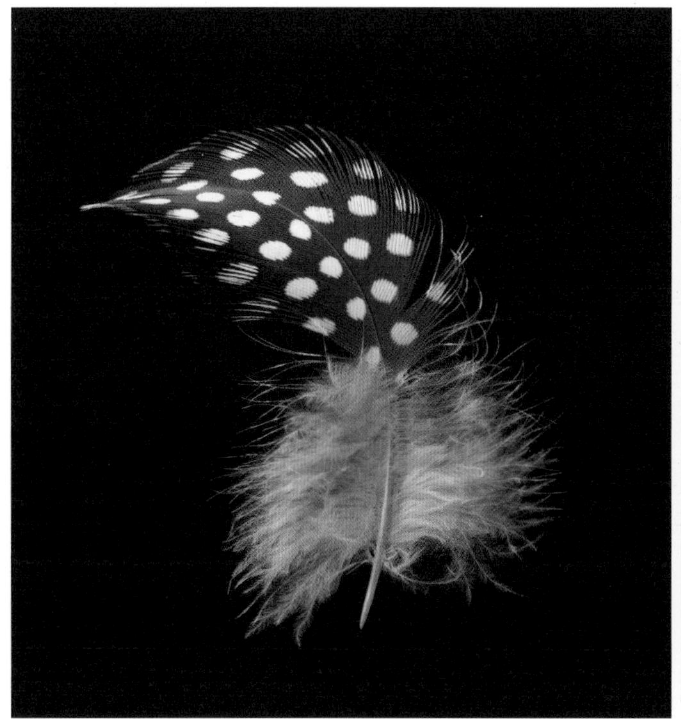

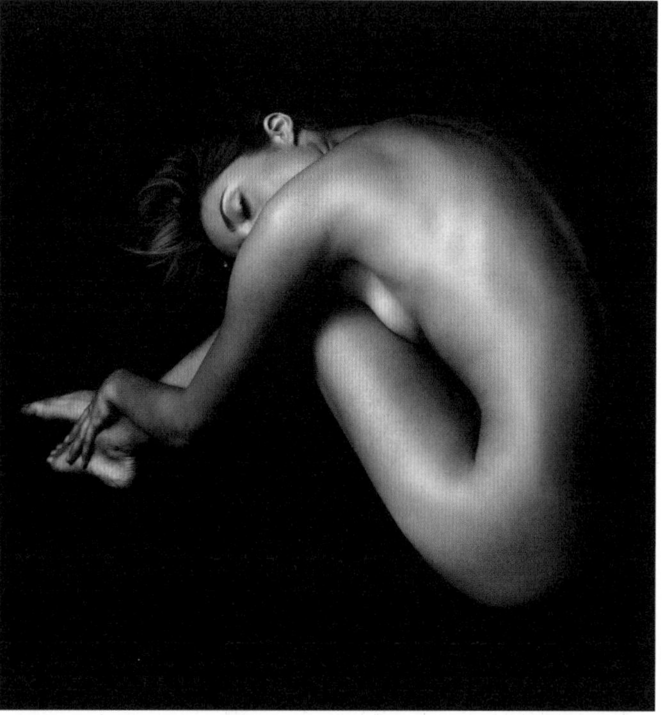

Feather-Katie

work my ass off to make sure his boss doesn't fire him. One behavior produces magic. The other behavior produces really good work. Magic is what I live for, not safety.

What is your greatest professional achievement?
I guess Created Equal since it took about nine years and was my obsession for a decade. I don't look back much so it's not something I think about. I don't think I've looked at that book once since it was published. 100% of my attention is on the next project, never the past.

Who have been some of your favorite people or clients you have worked with?
There's a long list of great clients and art directors I've worked with. I've been truly lucky.

Your work was used in several Apple campaigns. What was it like working with this tech giant?
Apple wasn't a giant in 1999 when I shot the first iMac. At that time Apple was faltering, but Steve Jobs had just returned and that was the beginning of their resurrection. I shot pretty much all their ads for about ten years. In the beginning it was honest, simple and beautifully effective advertising. By the end, a lot of the things that come with great success became part of the process.

What is the greatest satisfaction you get from your work?
When my absolute belief in an idea or project, despite all kinds of obstacles and signs that I'm probably wrong, turns out just as I'd hoped. Audacity is a fundamental ingredient in creating magic. To be an artist who doesn't create magic is like being a doctor who doesn't actually help anyone become healthy.

What part of your work do you find most demanding?
If you're truly an artist, the best realization you can make is that you need to constantly grow and push your limits of what you're capable of creating. If you stop you'll start to self destruct. With both work or life, only great courage and enduring discomfort lead to fulfillment. Fear is a compass to tell you exactly what you should do next.

What would be your dream assignment?
I create dream assignments for myself. That's what I've always done. As for my commercial work, I love how I get these projects sometimes that require I shoot something I'd never choose to shoot, but it turns out to be really fun and interesting. I was asked recently to photograph a bottle using a handheld light source to "paint" the bottle with light. This isn't something I'd ever do on my own, but it was a blast and turned out great.

What would you change if you had to do it all over again?
After Created Equal I should have bitten off something even bigger. I rested for several years which an artist should never do. I've learned from that mistake.

You have three books out now: Created Equal (2010), Sea (2011) and Serpentine (2013). How did the creation of these books differ and do you plan on releasing a new book in the future?
Created Equal cost me $400K and took years off my life. It beat me up, wore me out, and was the best thing I ever did. It really forced me to grow emotionally. Imagine going to the Hell's Angels Oakland headquarters and waking them up at 9am, taking them to breakfast and then getting them to allow me to photograph them. You're not the same person after that. I did things like that so many times for Created Equal.

Sea and Serpentine are just eye candy. Cool eye candy, but pretty meaningless stuff. Those kinds of projects are fun distractions from the heavier projects I take on. I'm not satisfied with any of my projects. I'm still chasing something, though. I never talk about what I'm currently working on. I find it dissipates my focus.

Where do you see yourself in the future?
Pushing to create something that matters in this world.

What advice would you have for young photographers starting out today? Be your own hero.

Mark Laita www.marklaita.com
See his Graphis Master Portfolio on graphis.com.

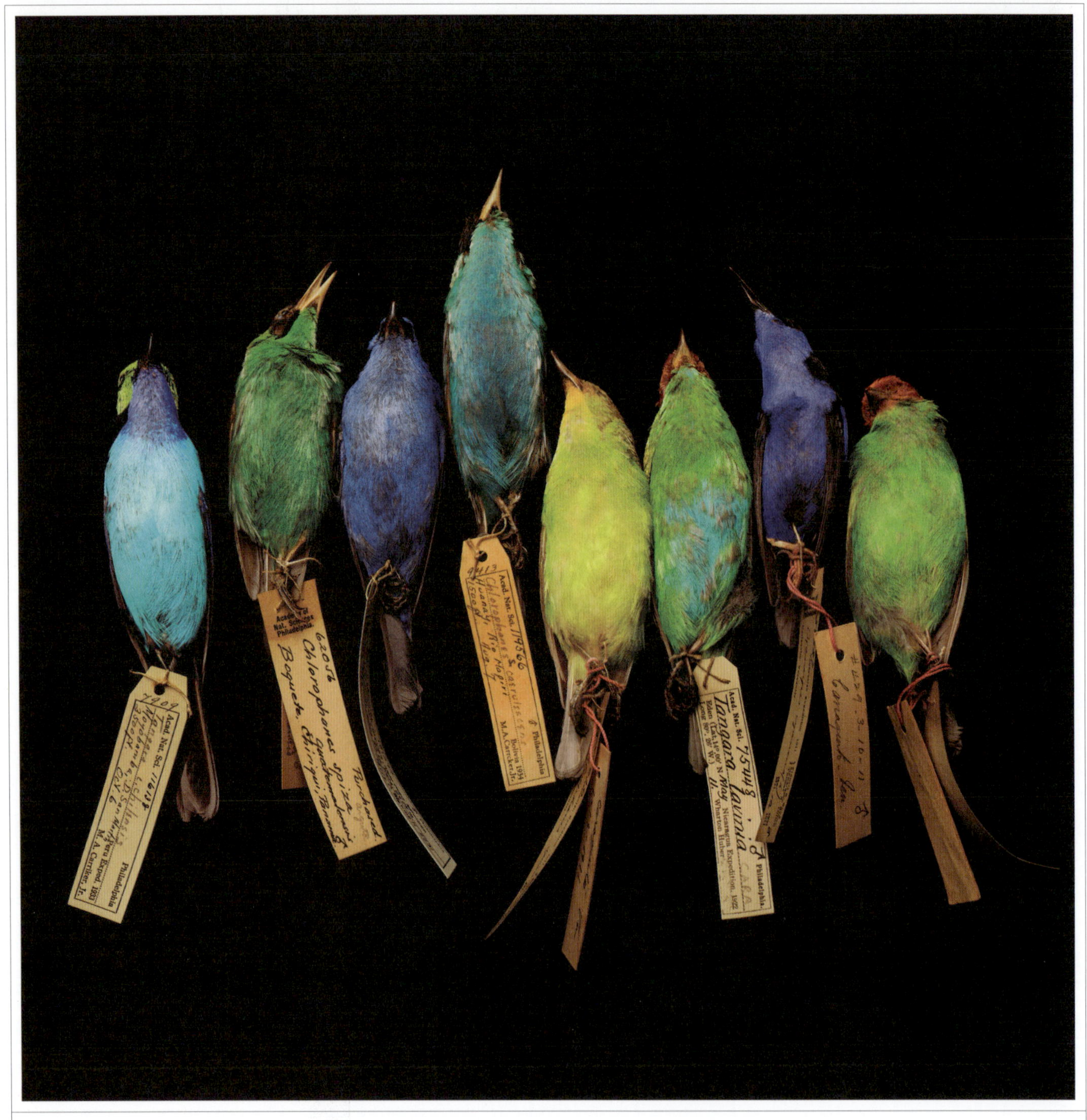

(Above) Tanagers & Honeycreepers / (Opposite page) Hanna Goby

YOU CAN CATCH A MOMENT AND TELL GREAT STORIES WITH ONLY ONE VISUAL.

A PICTURE IS A STAGE, AND NO MATTER WHAT YOU TAKE, YOU GIVE THE PERSON, THE OBJECT OR THE SCENE A UNIQUE CHARACTER.

Mark Laita, *Photographer*

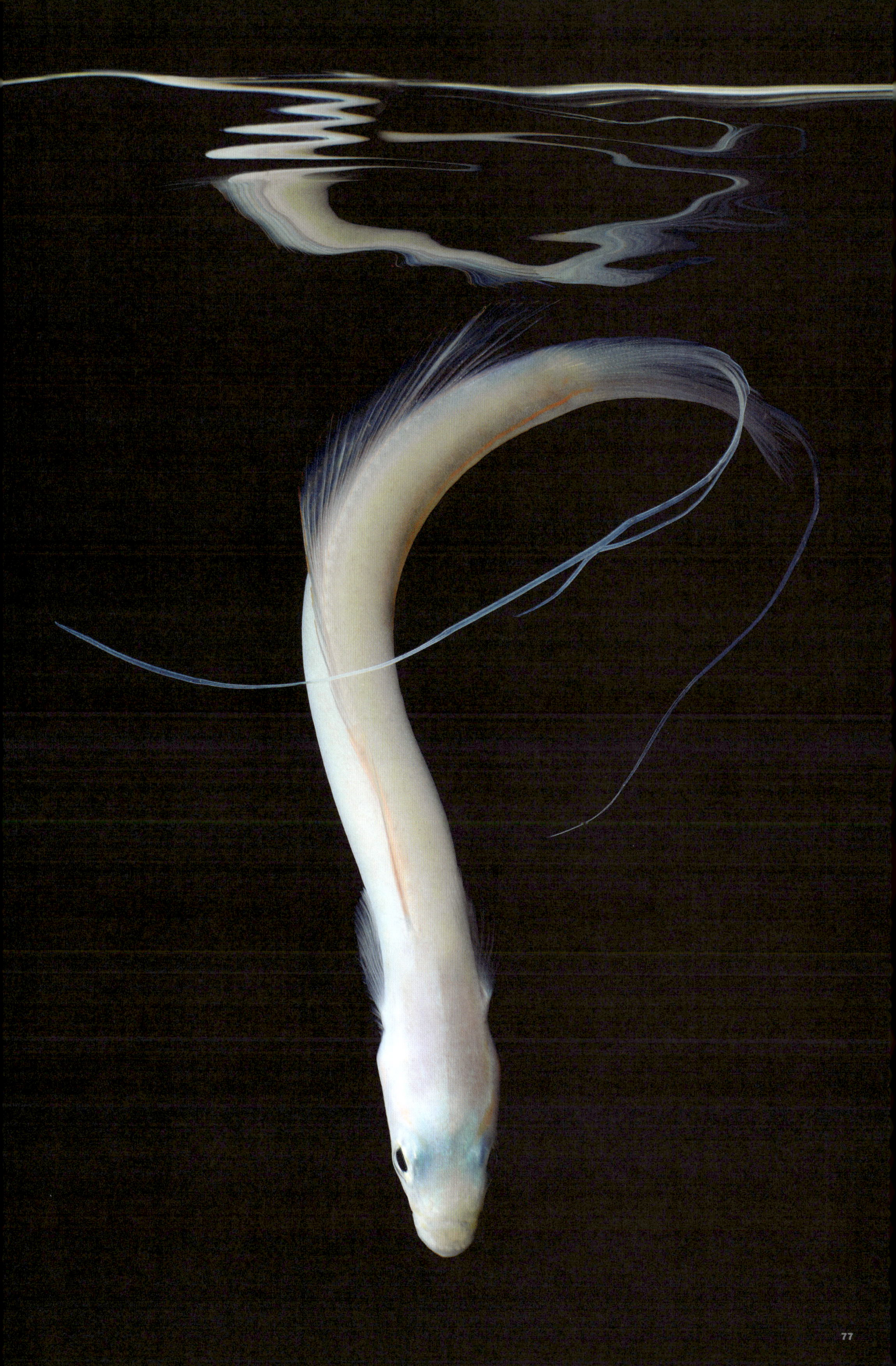

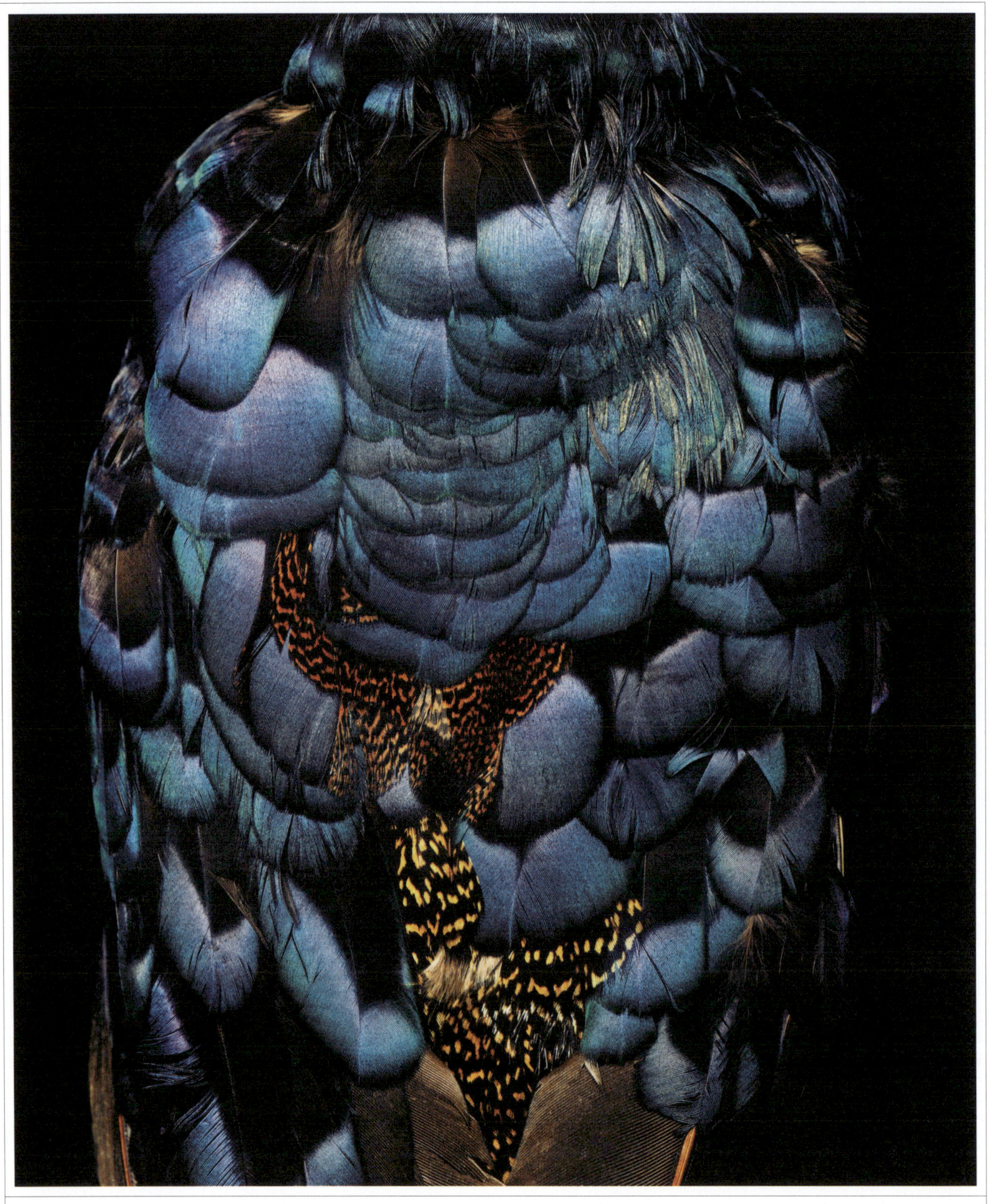

Palawan Peacock-Pheasant 1

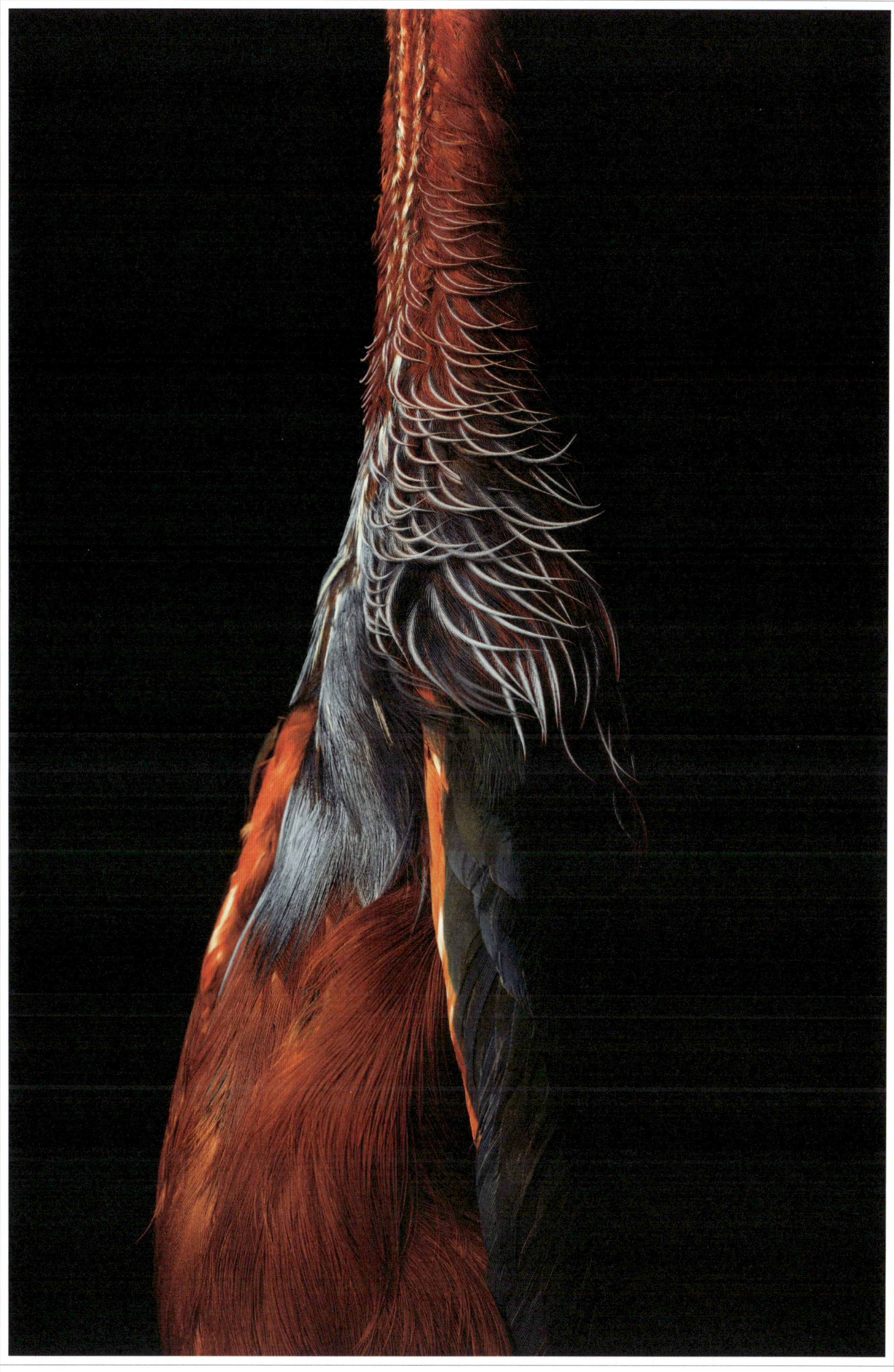

Agami Heron

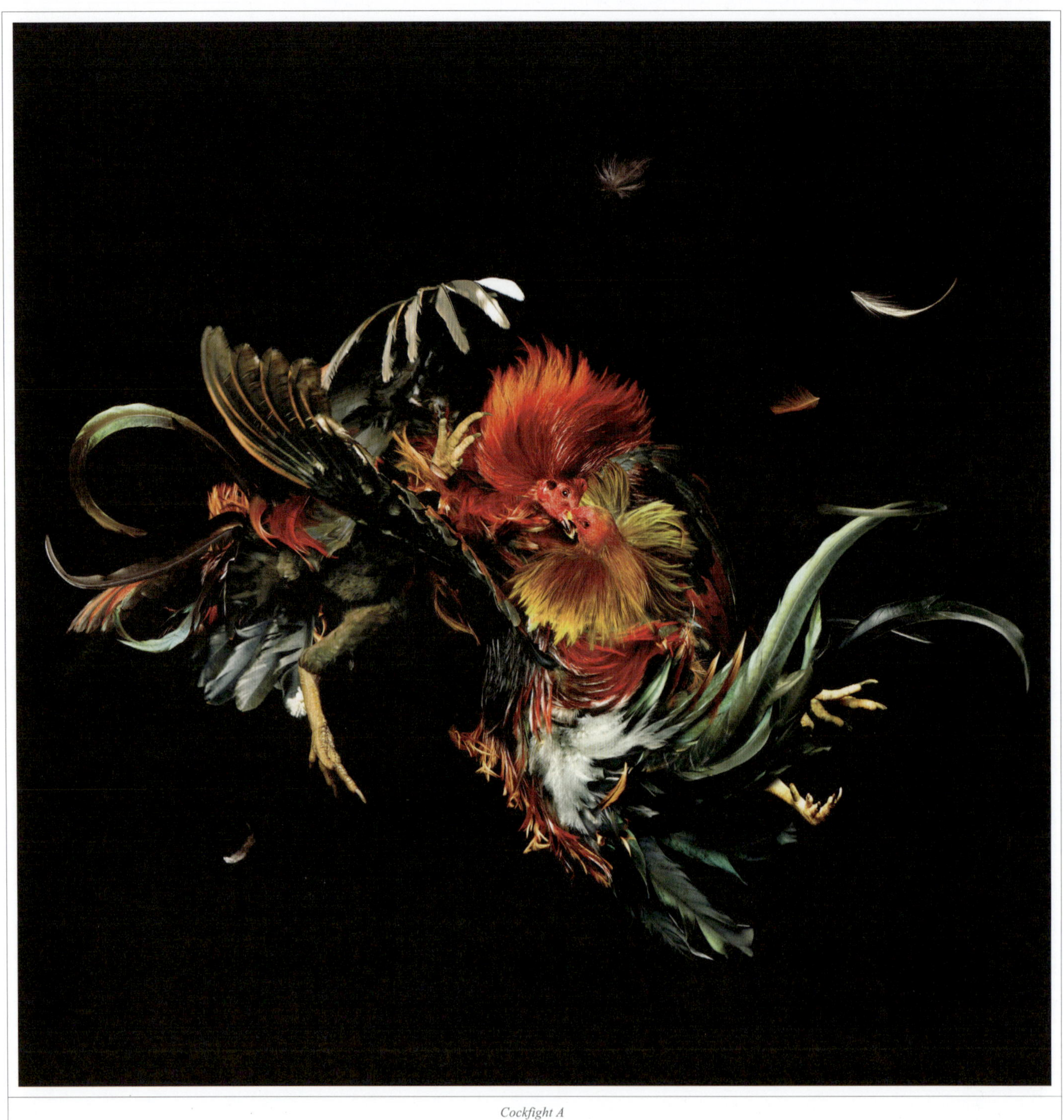

Cockfight A

IF YOU'RE TRULY AN ARTIST, THE BEST REALIZATION YOU CAN MAKE IS THAT YOU NEED TO CONSTANTLY GROW AND PUSH YOUR LIMITS OF WHAT YOU'RE CAPABLE OF CREATING.

Mark Laita, *Photographer*

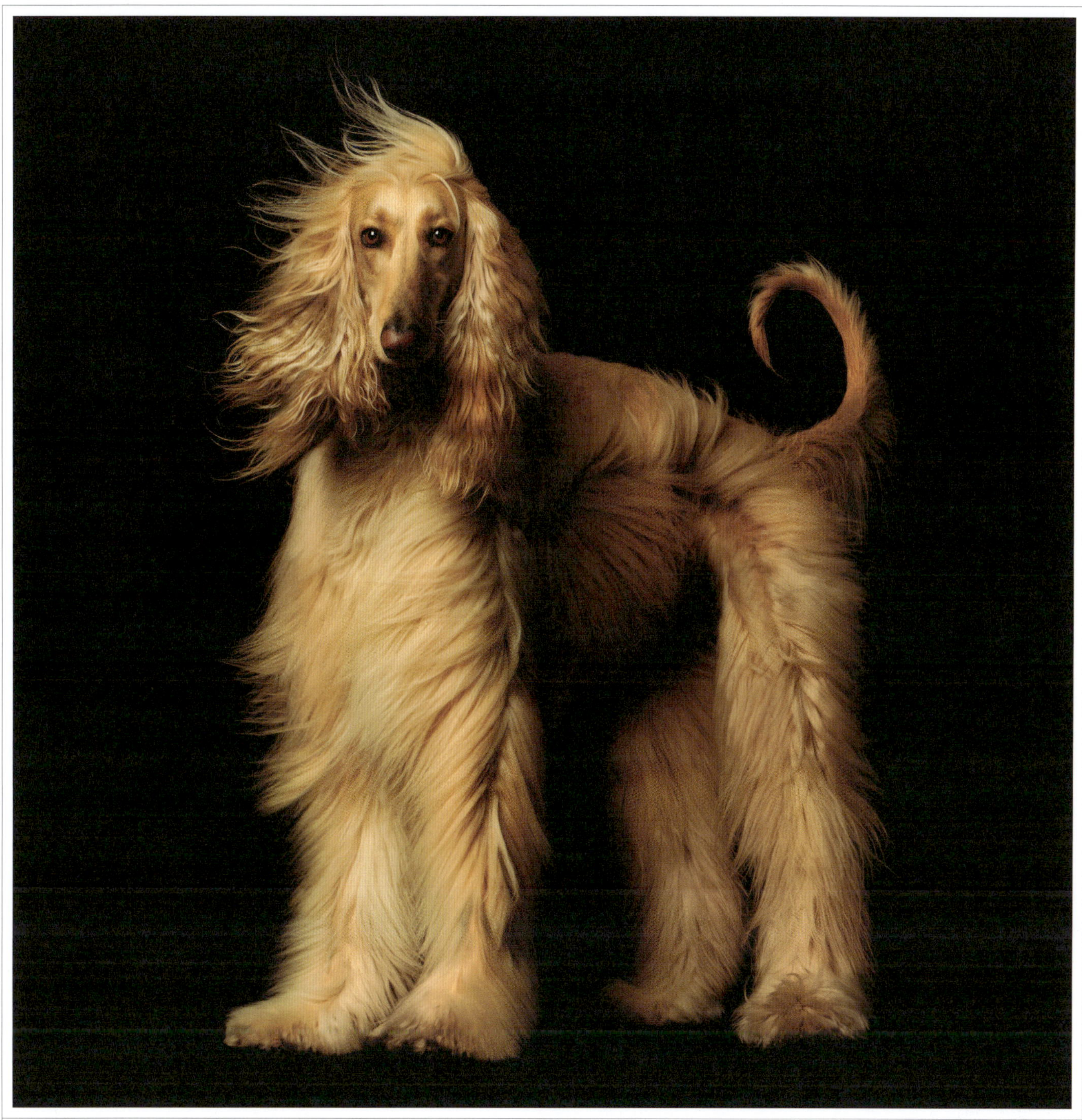

Afgan

WORKING WITH STEVE ON THE 99TH FLOOR PHOTO SHOOT WAS AN INCREDIBLE EXPERIENCE. HE CAPTURED WHAT WE DO IN BEAUTIFUL, RICH TONES. HE IS A METICULOUS PHOTOGRAPHER AND A VISIONARY.

Doug Cohen, *Co-Founder of 99th Floor NYC*

HE STANDS OUT AMONG MANY PHOTOGRAPHERS IN PROVIDING HIS CLIENT AN EXPERIENCE THAT MEETS HIGH STANDARDS; HIS IMAGES ARE CREATED WITH MEANING AND PURPOSE.

Kristine Ramezani, *VIS Manager at Coca-Cola Canada Ltd.*

I REALLY LOOK FORWARD TO SHOOT DAYS WITH STEVE AND HIS TEAM. HE ABSOLUTELY NEVER SETTLES. HE ISN'T SATISFIED UNTIL YOU HAVE WHAT YOU NEED AND YOU'RE EXCITED ABOUT THE WORK. PLUS, HE IS AS HOSPITABLE AS HE IS TALENTED!

Jenna Anderson, *Creative Director, Cossette*

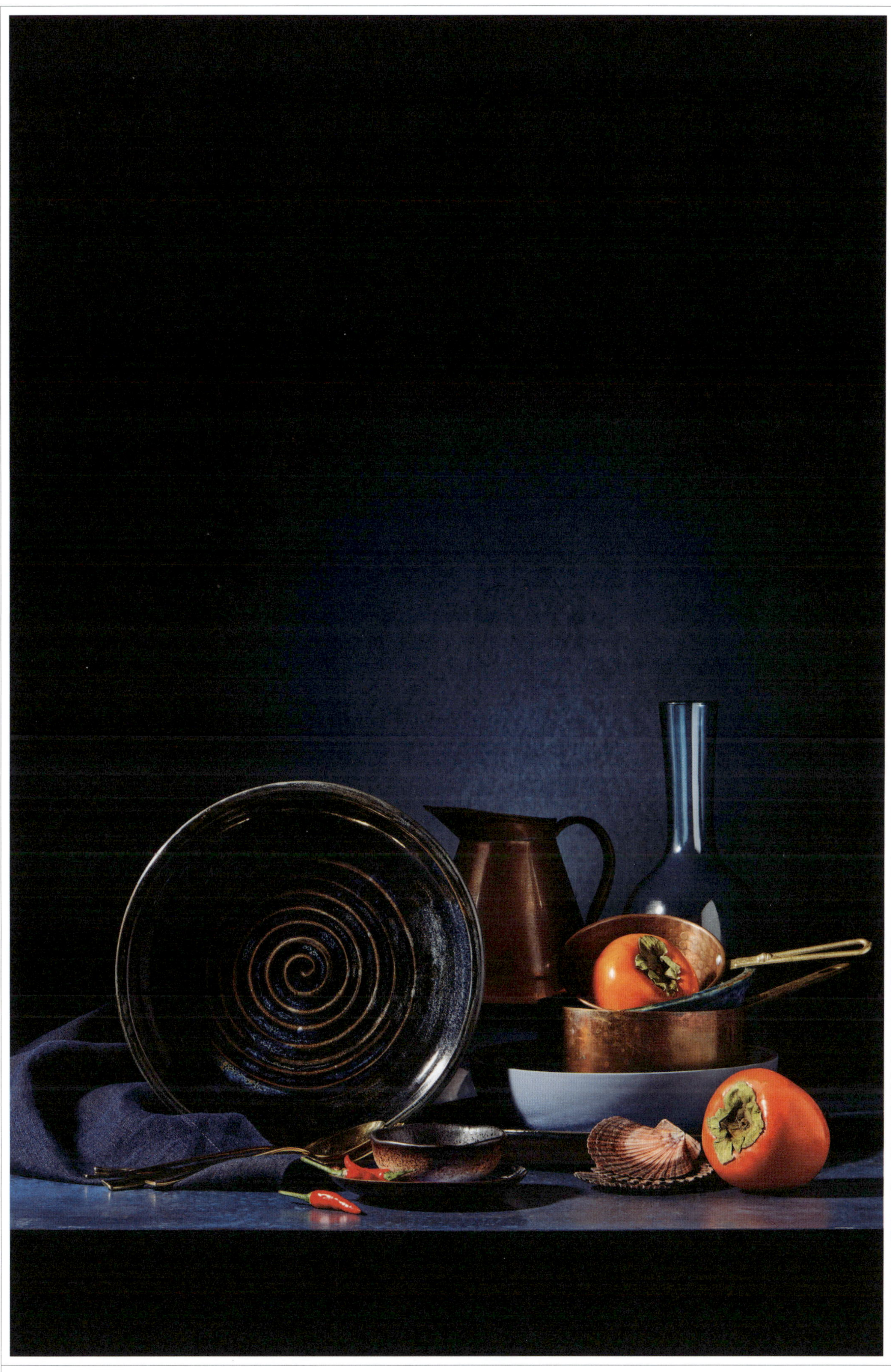

City of Toronto - Winterlicious

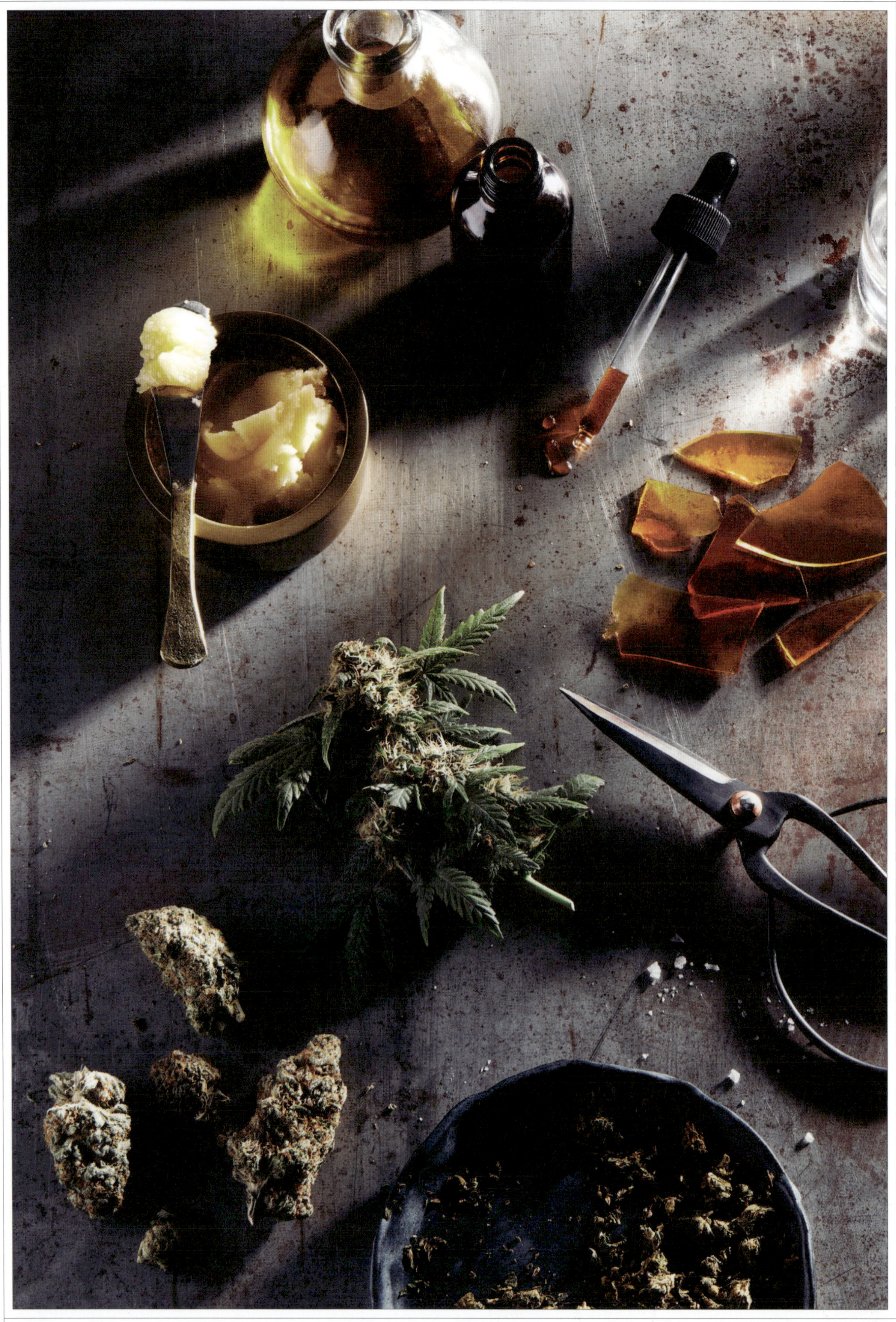

Krug Sessions - 99th Floor NYC

Introduction by Rob Fiocca *Photographer and Director, Fiocca Studio*

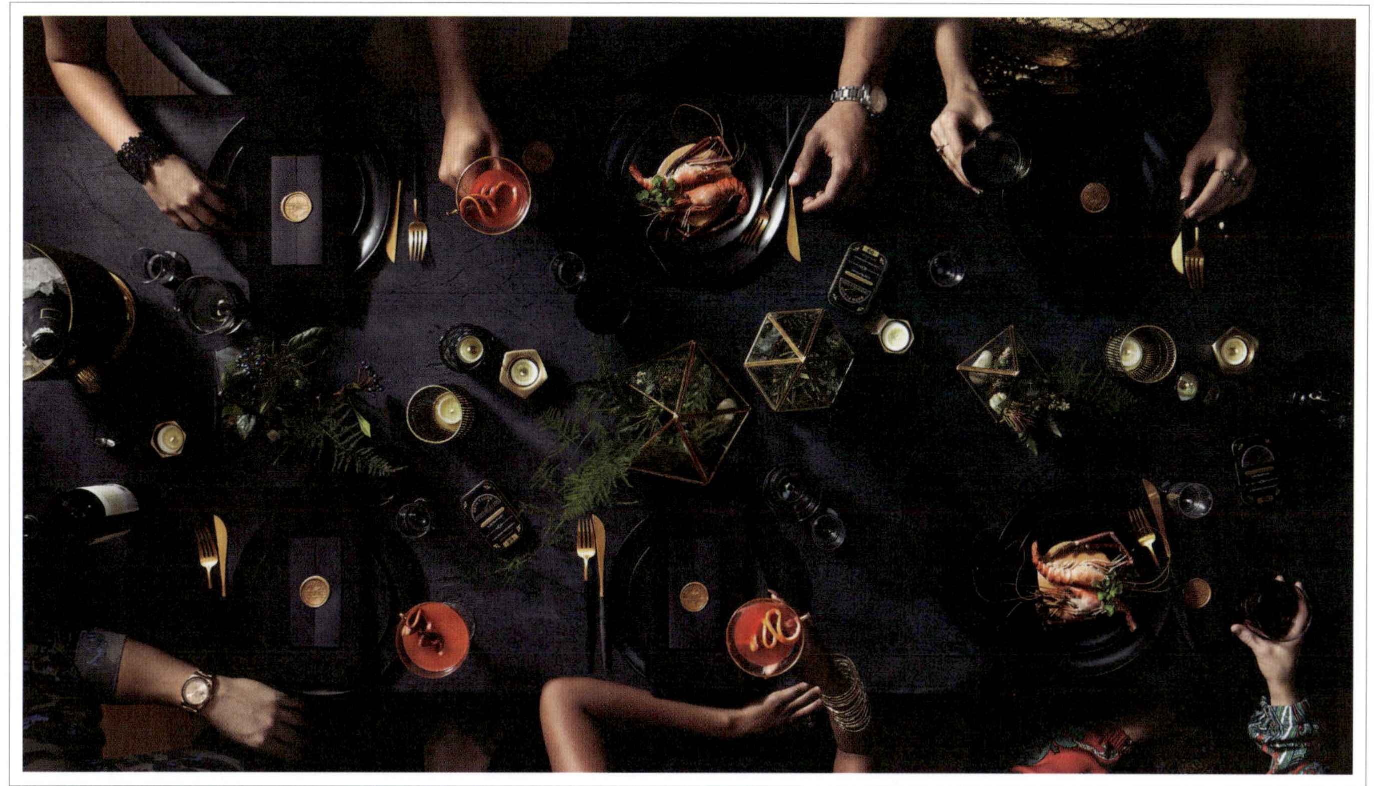

(Above) Krug Sessions - 99th Floor NYC / (Page 87) City of Toronto - Winterlicious

Several years ago, I hired Steve Krug to assist me on an advertising shoot on location in Toronto. Having never worked with him before, he came recommended by another reliable assistant. On that shoot he was so intuitive, detailed, energetic and smart, and always a step ahead of me. After that shoot I knew he was someone special with a bright future ahead of him. He became my first assistant from that day forward. Steve was unconditionally dedicated to my studio. He put in countless hours improving our infrastructure, our photographic process, pushing me, my creativity and my people to do better. He was relentless and uncompromising in his quest to assist in making Fiocca Studio the best it could be. Fiocca Studio was always a busy studio but with Steve by my side we became on fire. Traveling on assignments to the US, Europe, and literally around the world, bigger and better jobs came our way. This went on for several years, and not only did we do great work together, we both had wonderful times as friends and professionals. Eventually it was time for Steve to take the next step and become an independent photographer and fly from the nest. Our relationship was so strong that neither one of us wanted it to end, so our reps at the time, Fuze Reps, put him on the roster and well, the rest is history. Despite all of his accolades and accomplishments to date, he still to this day, works so hard on making his work, his people and studio the best it can be. His client list has grown and grown to the point of now being one of the most sought-after photographers in Canada. He still is relentless in his creativity, tenacious in his goal of becoming the best. It gives me great satisfaction to know that I have been a part of his soaring career as a photographer. Side note: for those people that haven't had the pleasure of working with Steve at his studio, he and his team make the best Sourdough bread around, it's become legendary!!

What inspired or motivated you into your career?
I was always fascinated by the way light could change an everyday object so dramatically. And then, once I traveled to Africa, with the landscape's textures and colors, I knew that I wanted a career that would fulfill my desire to explore, whether that be far flung locations, cooking experiments, technology, new subject matter, whatever. It was the freedom to explore the world that drove me.

What is your work philosophy?
Prepare for the worst, expect the best.

Who is or was your greatest mentor?
That would be Rob Fiocca. Before going out on my own, I worked closely with Rob for six years and learned a lot. What stuck with me most, and what's played the biggest role in my success, was his approach to building teams and how to get the best out of each contributor. This extends to how I work with clients, too. Rob solidified the notion of building something bigger than yourself and it's been invaluable.

What has been your most memorable Photography project?
In early 2017 I shot an editorial-style promotion that allowed me to marry two of my greatest passions – fine dining and cannabis. In collaboration with 99th Floor NYC, we created a stunning visual storyline of an elevated private dining experience featuring infused gourmet food prepared by Chef Miguel Trinidad. We had a blast creating this piece with them and it brought in a lot of new business – it dropped at the dawn of legalization in Canada.

Who among your contemporaries today do you most admire?
Peter Beard's work continues to amaze me, as does James Nachtwey. I'm also super intrigued by the work Neri Oxman is doing with the MIT Media Lab, around art and architecture that combines design, biology and materials engineering.

What are the most important ingredients you require from a client to do successful work?
A clear brief with stated goals, trust and honesty with a dash of risk taking.

What is the greatest satisfaction you get from your work?
Providing an extraordinary client experience, part of which includes making fresh baked homemade bread every morning in our studio. There's nothing better than when a client tells me that coming to the studio is the best part of their week.

Who have been some of your favorite people or clients you have worked with?
That's like asking me to choose a favourite child! Truthfully, I've made it a priority to work with people and clients who I genuinely enjoy spending the day with. Not every relationship is a perfect match, but I've been exceedingly fortunate to be connected to, and have success with, a large group of excellent human beings.

What professional goals do you still have for yourself?
Well, I started working in motion last year and it's been a huge learning curve but super rewarding. I've got a lot to learn, but so far, it's been fun and I'm motivated to practice, experiment and explore how far I can push myself in this new direction.

What advice would you have for students starting out today?
Practice listening, actually hear your clients and stop at nothing to deliver an exceptional experience from the first meeting through to final delivery of images.

What interests do you have outside of your work?
Well, my two young kids keep me pretty busy. I love cooking with them and watching them discover things or seeing the expression on their face when they experience an "aha" moment. It's beautiful to watch them grow and be a part of that experience.

What do you value most?
Integrity. Doing what you say you will.

How do you define success?
Years-long, fruitful relationships with clients.

Where do you see yourself in the future?
Continuing to deliver on the service aspect of commercial photography and providing solutions for my clients that make their work effortless.

Steve Krug www.krugstudios.com

HE WILL PUSH HIMSELF UNTIL THE DESIRED SHOT IS ACHIEVED. I HAD THE WONDERFUL OPPORTUNITY TO WORK WITH HIM FOR OVER 10 YEARS ON A WIDE VARIETY OF PROJECTS. NOT MANY LIKE STEVE!

Kristine Ramezani, *VIS Manager at Coca-Cola Canada Ltd.*

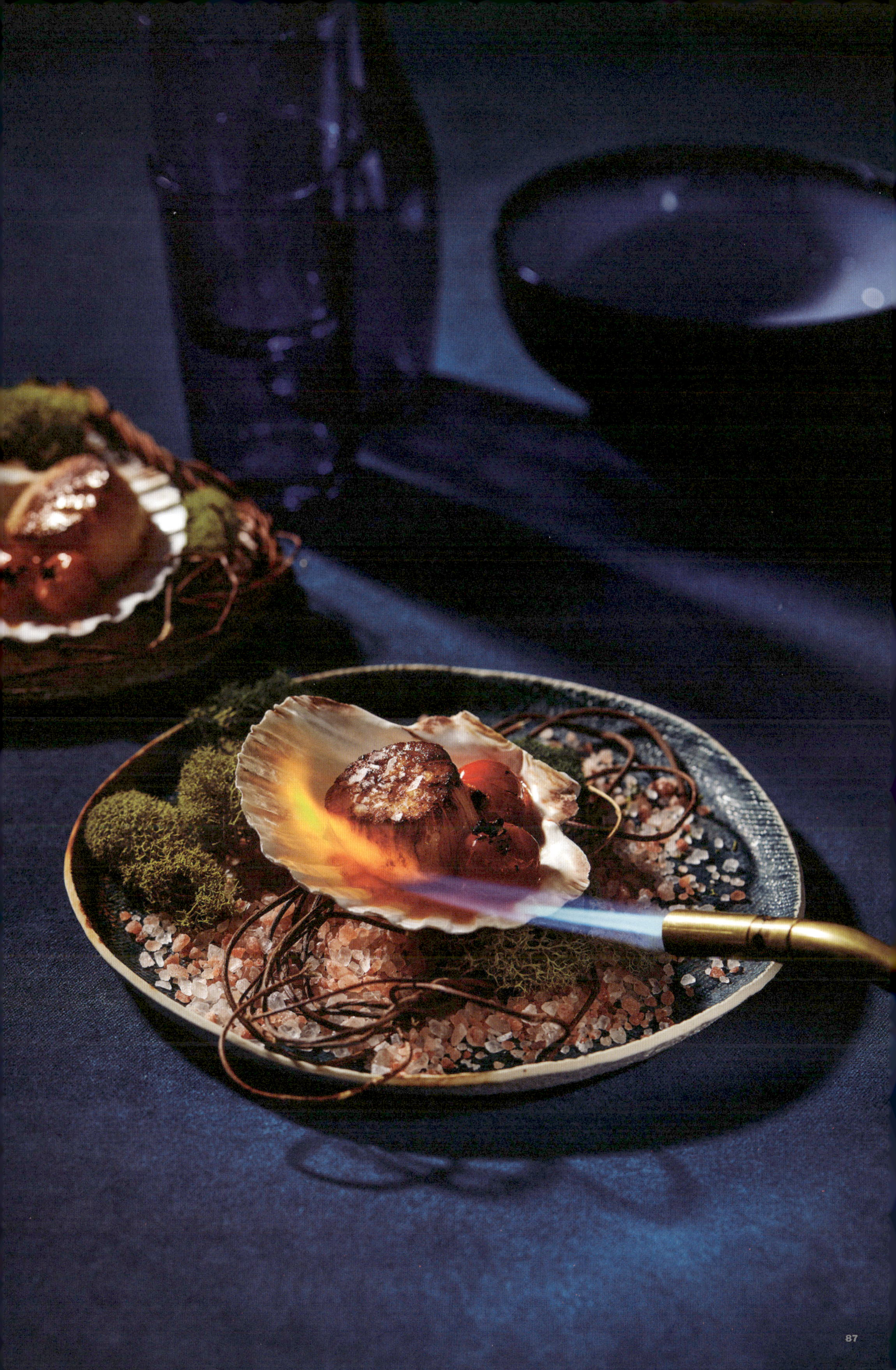

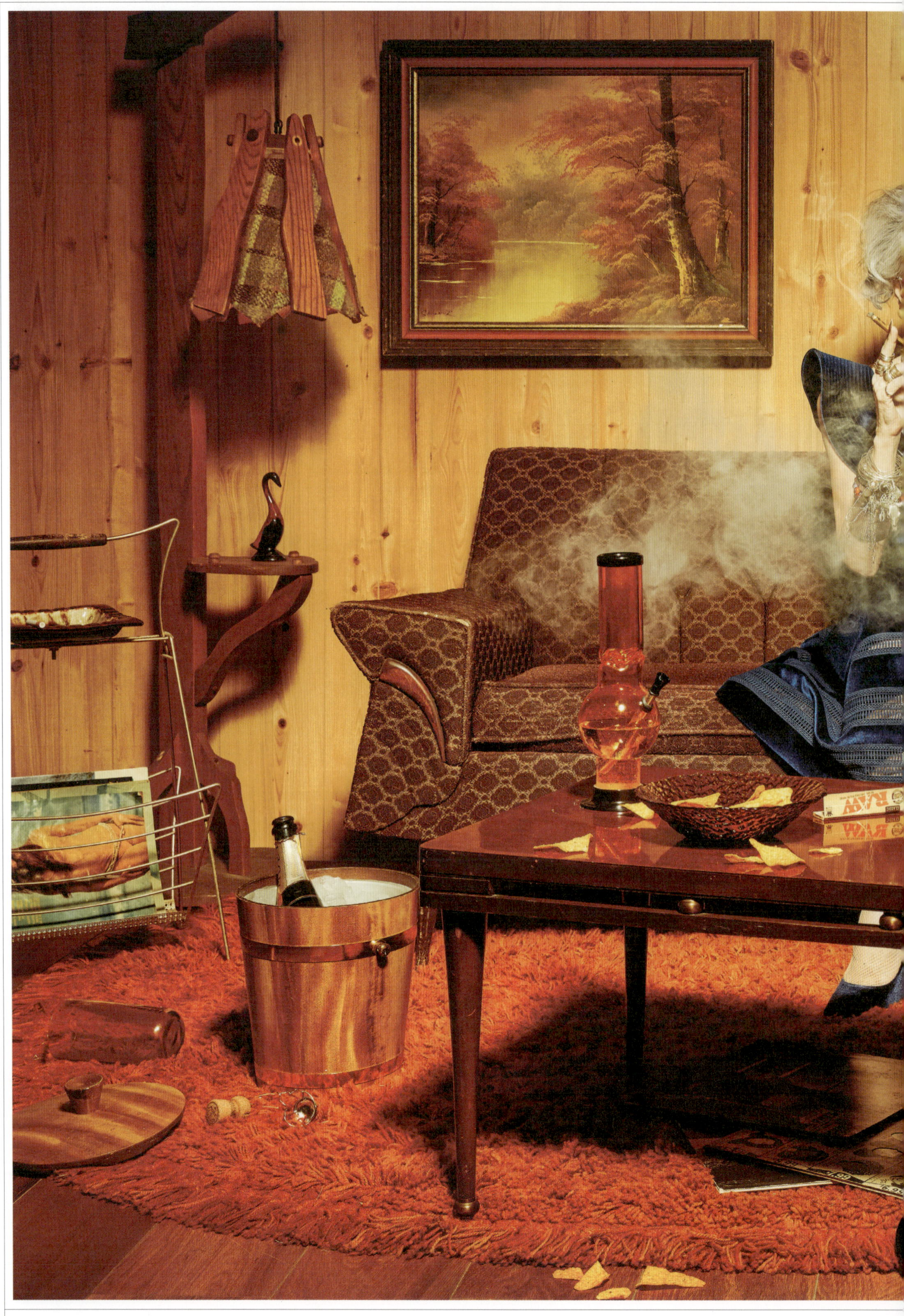
RAW

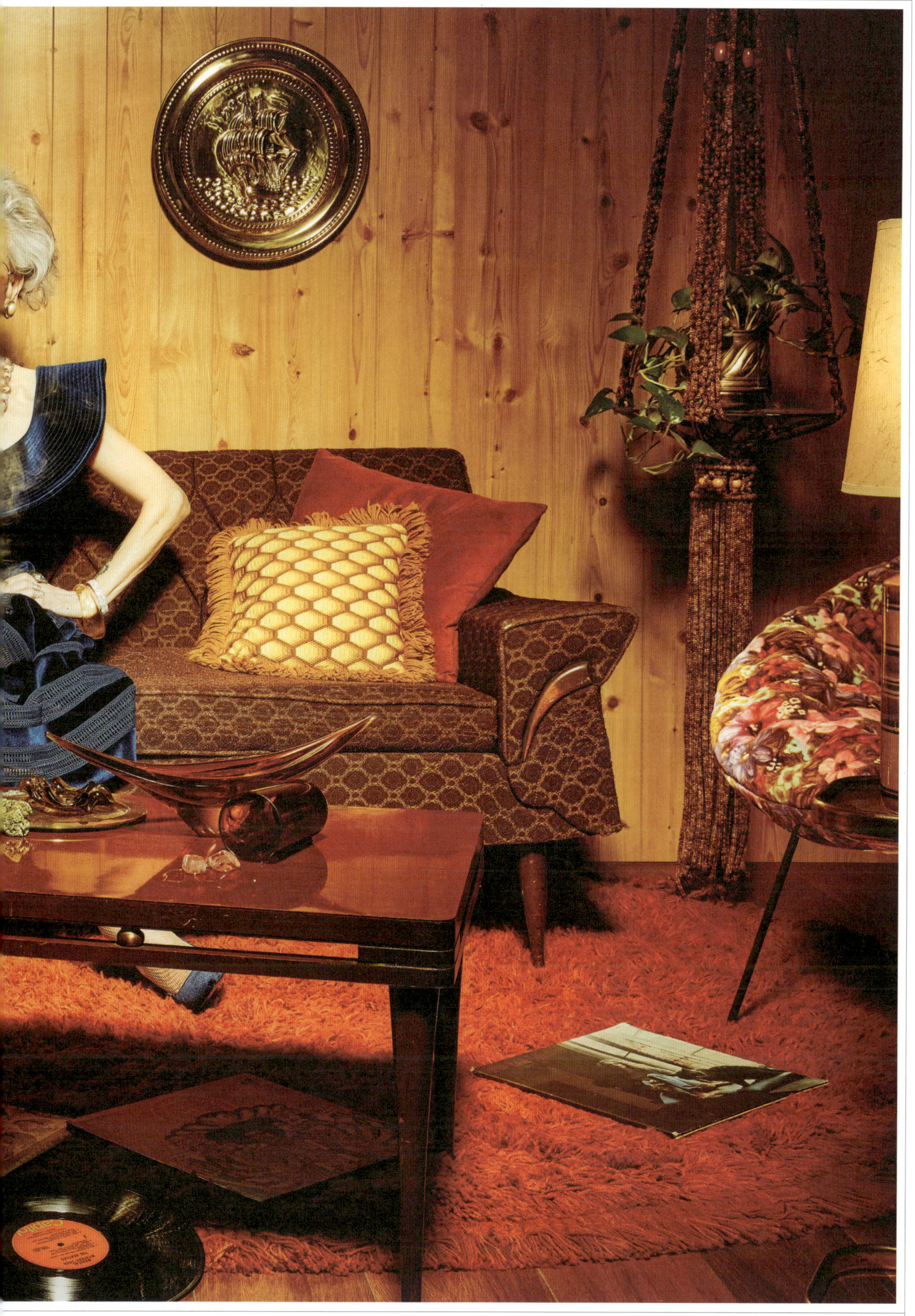

Judith's House Party

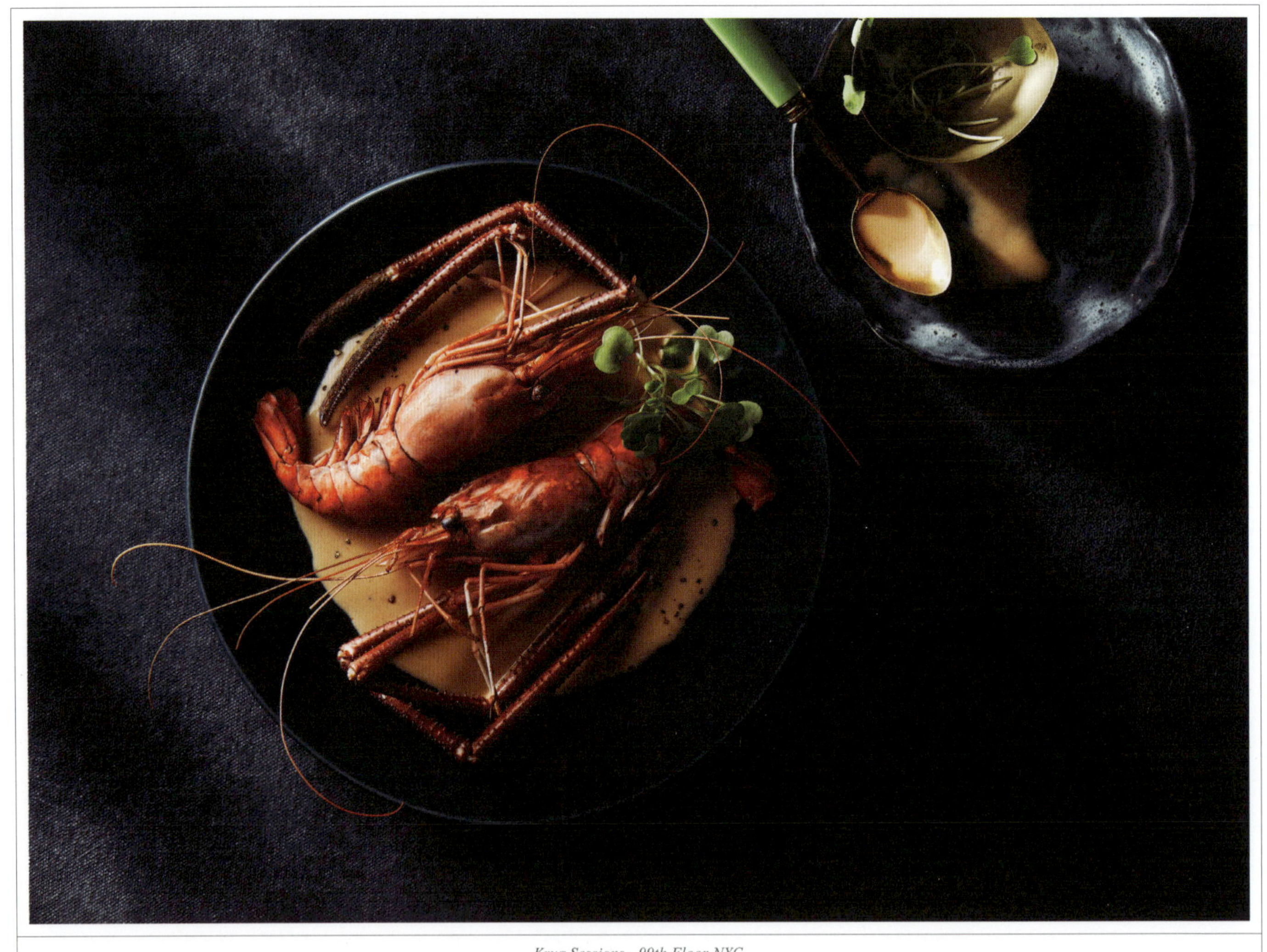

Krug Sessions - 99th Floor NYC

NOTHING'S BETTER THAN WHEN A CLIENT TELLS ME THAT COMING TO MY STUDIO IS THE BEST PART OF THEIR WORK WEEK.

Steve Krug, *Photographer, Krug Studios*

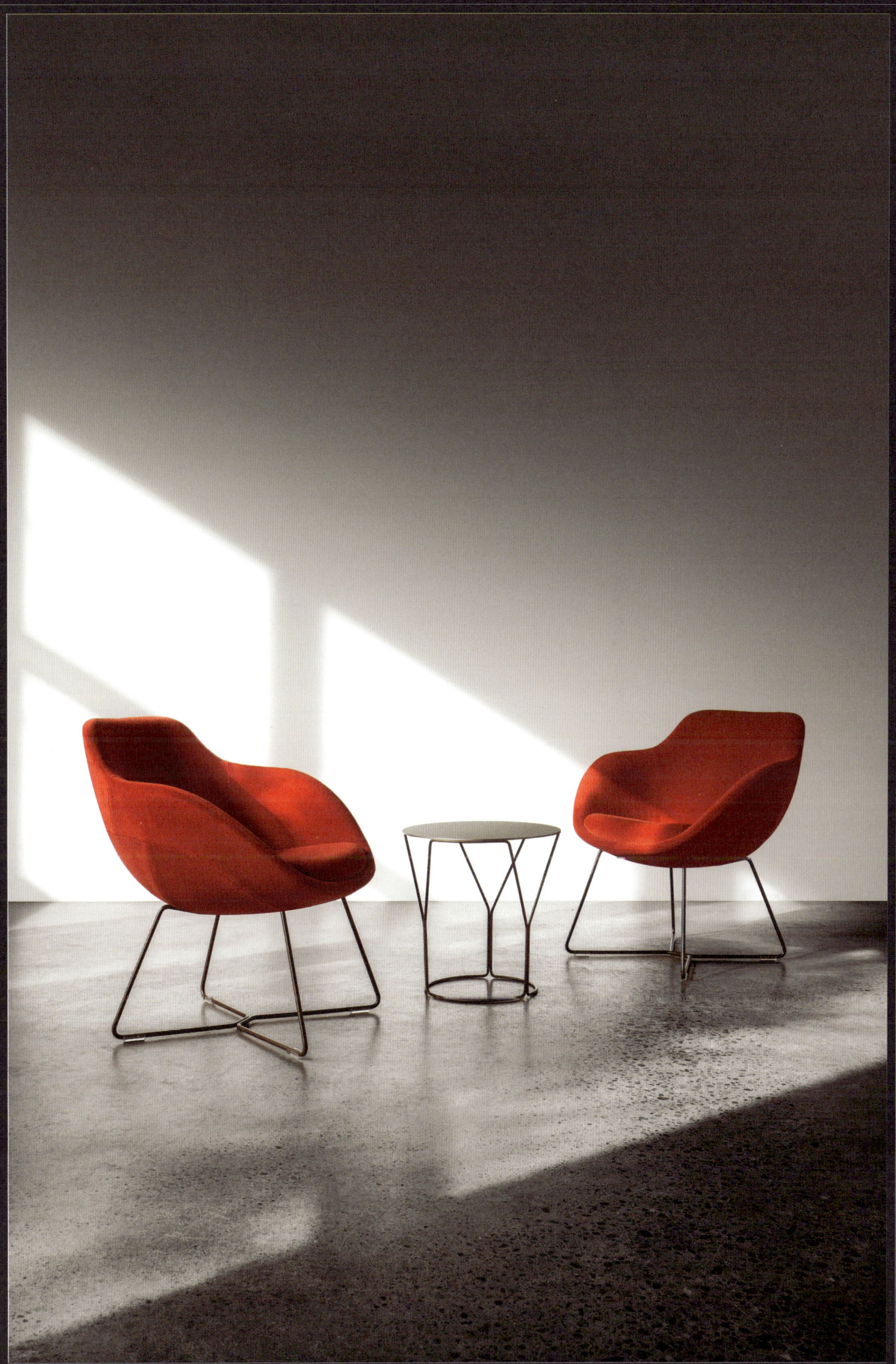

Keilhauer

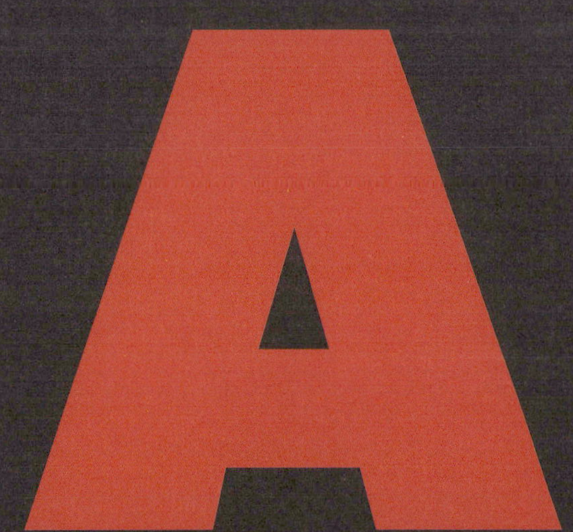

ART/ILLUSTRATION

94 BRALDT BRALDS / USA & NETHERLANDS

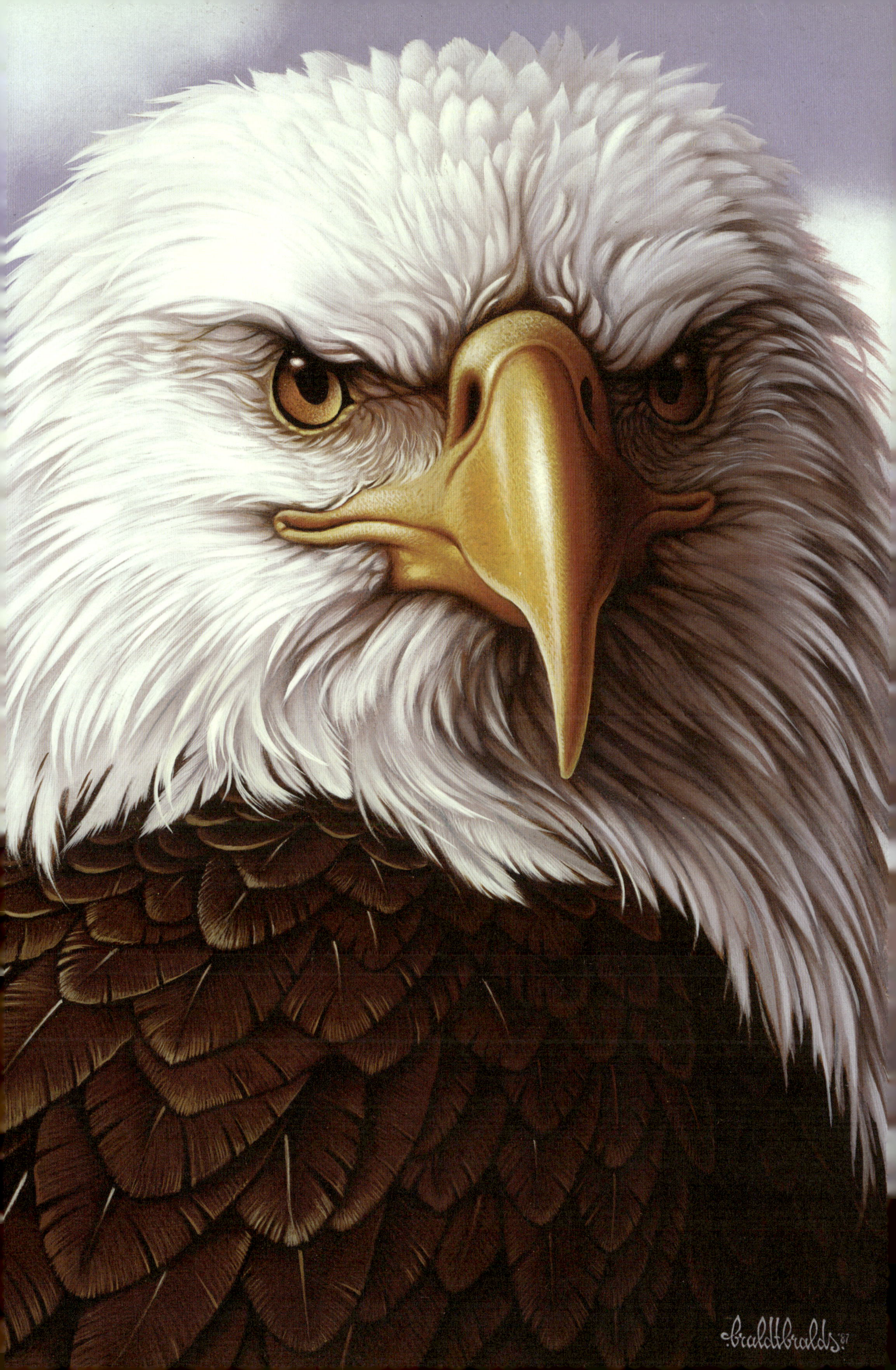
braldtbralds '87

WHEN I WAS A YOUNG ILLUSTRATION STUDENT, I SEARCHED FOR ARTISTS WHO HAD ELEGANT IDEAS, SHOWING TASTE WITH THEIR WORK. BRALDT BRALDS CAPTURED IT ALL. HE IS A MASTER OF HIS CRAFT, AND I'M PROUD TO NOW CALL HIM A FRIEND.

Tim O'Brien, *Illustrator & President of the Society of Illustrators NY, Graphis Master*

ONE ONLY HAS TO LOOK AT BRALDS' ILLUSTRATIONS TO RECOGNIZE AND APPRECIATE HIS TALENT AND SKILLS AS AN ARTIST. HIS PAINTINGS ARE ALWAYS BEYOND THE ORDINARY.

Robert Giusti, *Illustrator*

I FIRST BECAME AWARE OF HIS WORK IN THE '80S, AND MARVELED AT HIS SOPHISTICATED IDEAS AND BEAUTIFULLY RENDERED PAINTINGS. TO TOP IT ALL OFF, HE'S SUCH A KIND, HUMBLE PERSON. ONE OF THE GREATS. HE IS A LEGEND.

Anita Kunz, *Canadian Artist and Illustrator*

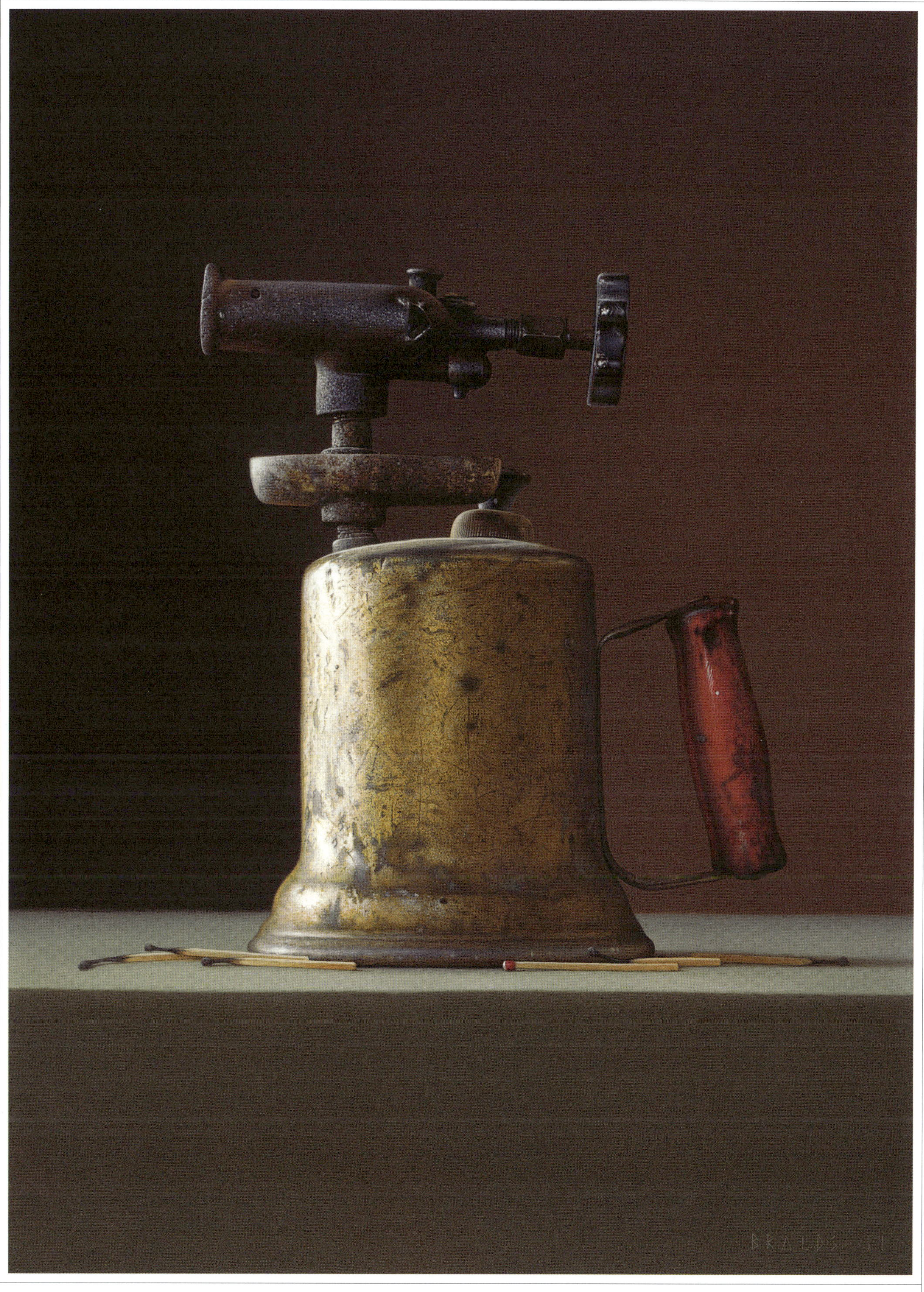

(Page 93) "American Icon" (from collegiate poster series, commissioned by Anheuser Busch, 1982.) / (Above) "One More Shot", 2011

Introduction by Robert Rodriguez *Illustrator, Graphis Master*

Several years ago, at ArtCenter College of Design, I remember Braldt telling students he wasn't a better artist than anyone else, he just worked harder. I knew at the time it was exactly what they needed to hear, even though it wasn't completely accurate. The fact is, Braldt is better than anyone else. His paintings could easily fall into just being about technique, but they never do. There is an emotional calmness that always makes them more than that. His work is so personal, though the influence of the early Dutch masters is evident, it's filtered through Braldt's personality, with all his sensitivity and humor. ■ I saw a recent painting of his from across the room and I immediately knew the artist. The colors and atmosphere read from 15 feet away, even before I got close enough to see the perfection in the brushwork.

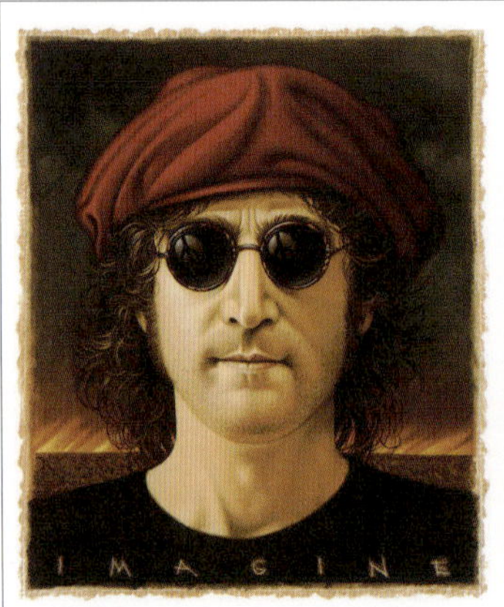

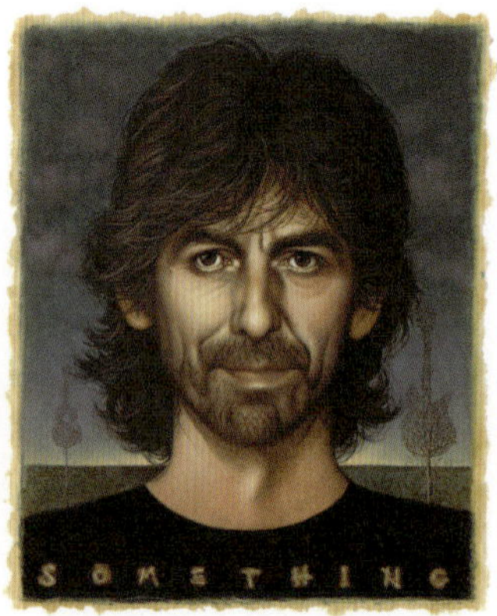

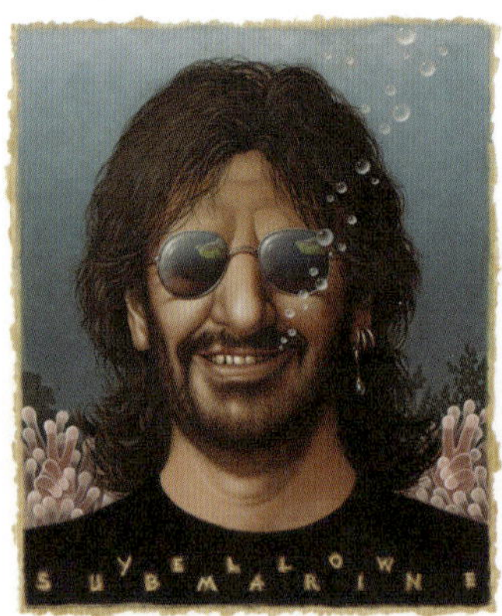

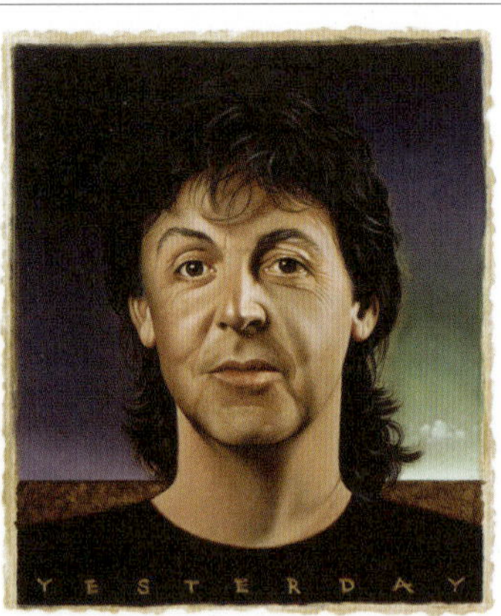

(Above) "Imagine" (Lennon) Rolling Stone Magazine, 25th Anniversary issue, 1992. "Something" (Harrison), "Yellow Submarine" (Ringo), "Yesterday" (McCartney)
(Opposite page) "Why She Smiles" (Germany's Postal Service, 1993).For Ad campaign promoting their new shipping boxes. "She had found the perfect sized box"

I PERSISTENTLY PURSUED MY PATH
BY MY OWN MEANS, TEACHING MYSELF
HOW TO DRAW AND PAINT.

Braldt Bralds, *Illustrator & Fine Art Painter*

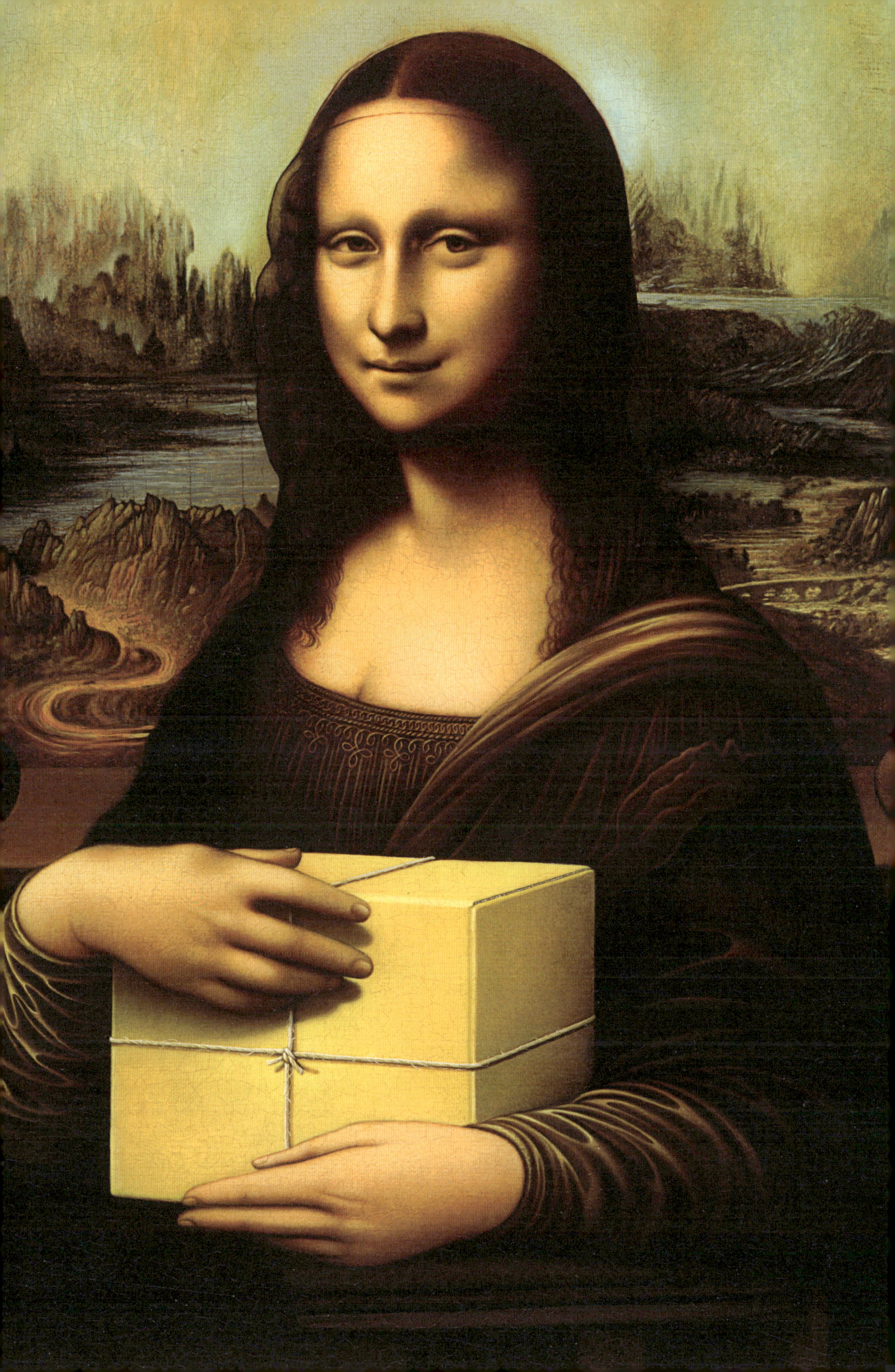

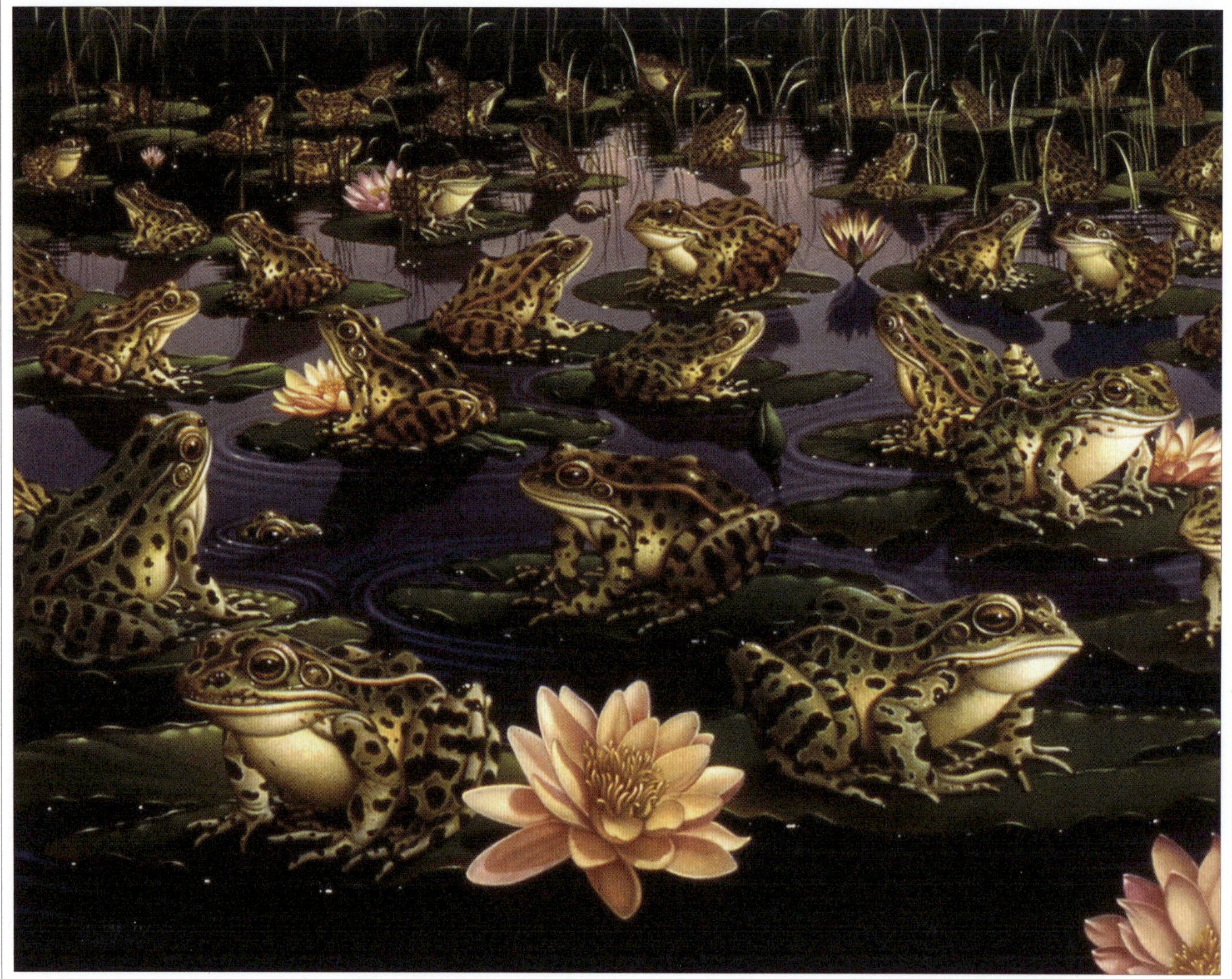

"Frogs" (London Times, 1992). Ad for English brokerage firm. Headline: "If You've Kissed As Many Frogs As We Have, You Become Pretty Good At Spotting Princes"

Who were some of your greatest past influences?
Before I ever came to the United States, the top American illustration artists were my art heroes. As a child, through American magazines and illustrated books I was fascinated by Norman Rockwell's work, as well as Maxfield Parrish, Joseph Leyendecker and N.C. Wyeth. In my late teens and early 20s, the contemporary illustration luminaries solidified my decision to become an illustrator.

What is your most difficult challenge you've had to overcome?
During the span of my career as an illustrator, whenever I encountered a problematic moment with an assignment - which was often - I always blamed it on the fact that I wasn't properly trained. Despite my successes, this "not being good enough" has remained in my system.

Through the years my eyesight has diminished, due to a rare eye disorder. My ability to paint became an increasing challenge, and five years ago my sight took a major 'nosedive' when I lost the ability to focus in my central vision zone. Painting came to a halt. This was probably the biggest challenge I've ever had to overcome; yet in this last year, after numerous attempts, I have once again picked up paint and brushes, and am giving it a go with my peripheral vision. So far, so good.

Who is or was your greatest mentor?
The Old Dutch Masters, along with the other European Renaissance artists were, and continue to be, my silent teachers. Growing up, I spent countless hours in Holland's museums, standing nose to nose with their masterpieces, studying their paint strokes and how they accomplished a sense of light and shadow.

A contemporary painter that I became aware of when I was twelve years old, was Rene Magritte. His paintings were difficult to understand but I was totally mesmerized by the strangeness of them. Magritte has inspired me many times when I have been in search of a concept. (See image "Why He Never Called Back") In a way, my father was my mentor as well. As with

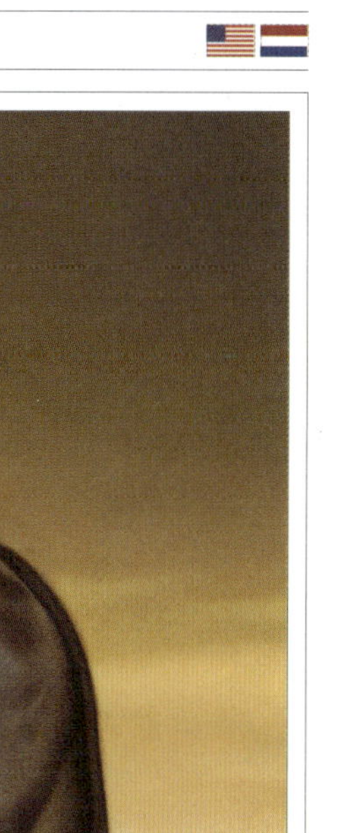

"Angus", 1988

many parents at the time, choosing a career in art seemed a risky choice, and he discouraged that path. But since the age of ten I was solid in my decision, and even though he refused to send me to the Art Academy, I persistently pursued my path by my own means, teaching myself how to draw and paint.

Who have been some of your favorite people or clients you have worked with?
Some of my top editorial clients have been *Time Magazine*, *Newsweek*, *Rolling Stone*, *Der Spiegel*, and *Texas Monthly*, to name a few.

When I worked with advertising clients such as Grand Marnier and Pirelli, I had the greatest pleasure working with amazing art directors, who gave me 'carte blanche' to come up with my own concepts or solutions. Those were dream jobs.

Book cover work afforded me a similar freedom. *Mists of Avalon* and *Sea Beggars* remain two of my most treasured paintings. On three occasions I was honored by the United Nations Postal Administration to create stamp issues for their environmental division.

In conclusion, I do have to mention, that all of this was made possible due to my brilliant representative, Milton Newborn. I could not have done it without him!

Who among your contemporaries today do you most admire?
While still living in Holland, I eagerly followed the works of Richard Hess, Paul Davis, Roy Carruthers, Wilson McClean, Robert Giusti, and many others whose works I found on the editorial pages of top American and European magazines. Eventually I had the great fortune to become a friend and colleague with several of these top artists.

Braldt Brald Studio www.braldtbraldsstudio.com
See his Graphis Master Portfolio on graphis.com.

THE CONTEMPORARY ILLUSTRATION LUMINARIES SOLIDIFIED MY DECISION TO BECOME AN ILLUSTRATOR.

Braldt Bralds, *Illustrator & Fine Art Painter*

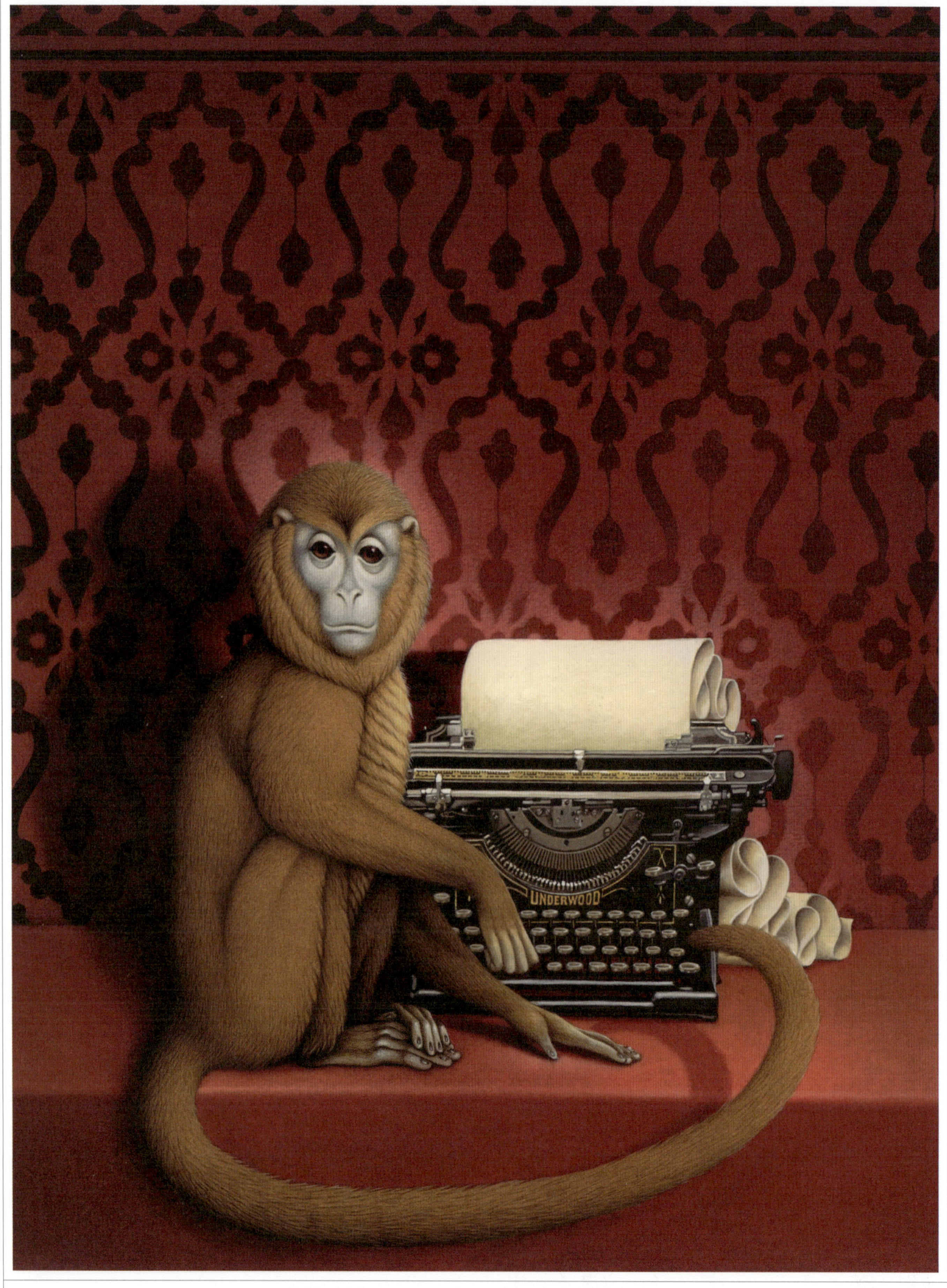

"Red Earth & Pouring Rain" (Book cover for Little Brown publishers, 1994).

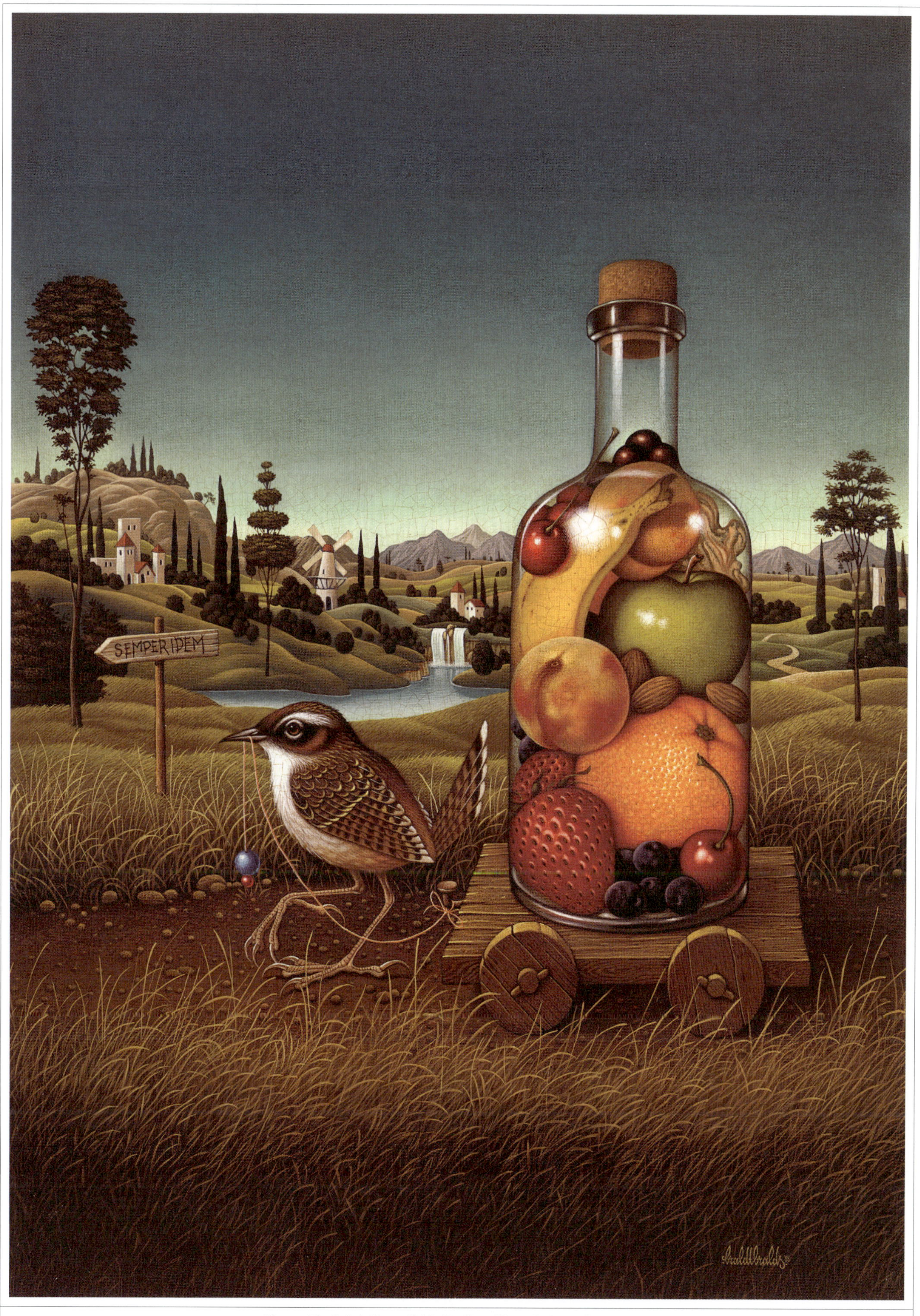

"Semper Idem" (Bols Liquor, 1986). Headline: "Tastes From A Different World."
Advertising 12 new fruit liqueurs, as denoted in bottle. Semper Idem - Bols' quality is 'always the same.'

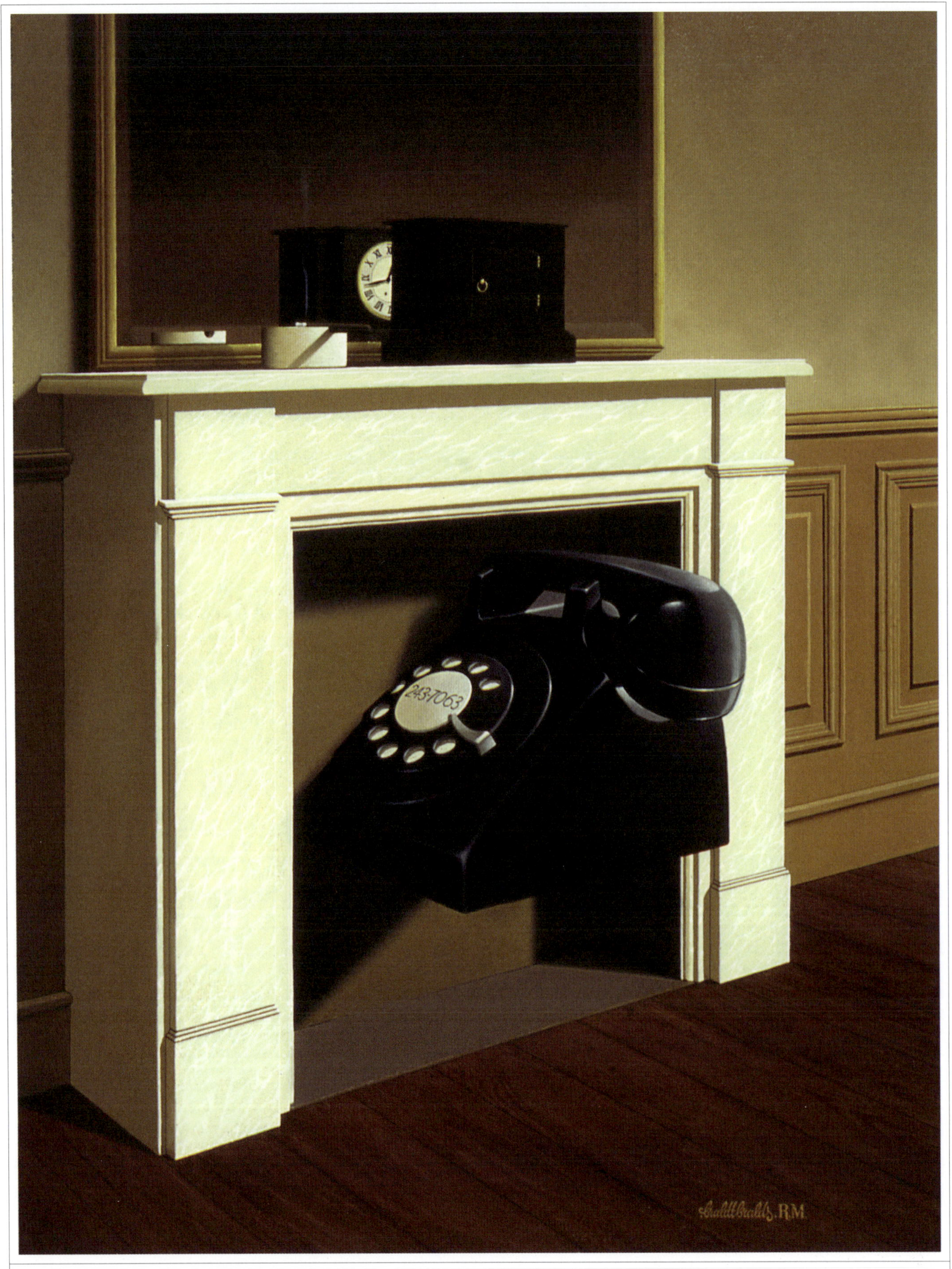

"Why He Never Called Back" (Oui Magazine, 1981) Article concerning new 'single bars' phenomenon, leading to one-night stands.

I HAVE ONCE AGAIN PICKED UP PAINT AND BRUSHES, AND AM GIVING IT A GO WITH MY PERIPHERAL VISION. SO FAR, SO GOOD

Braldt Bralds, *Illustrator & Fine Art Painter*

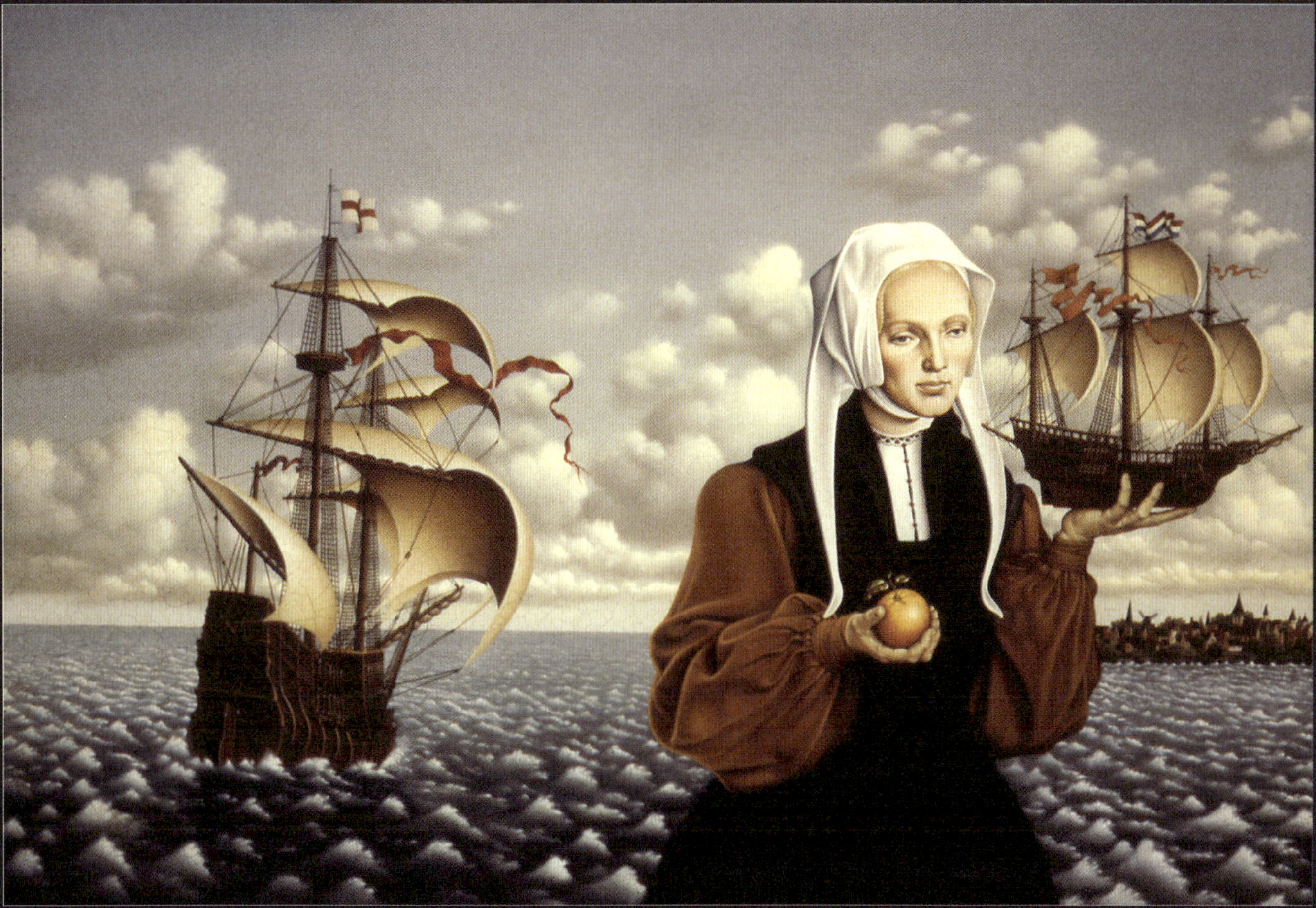

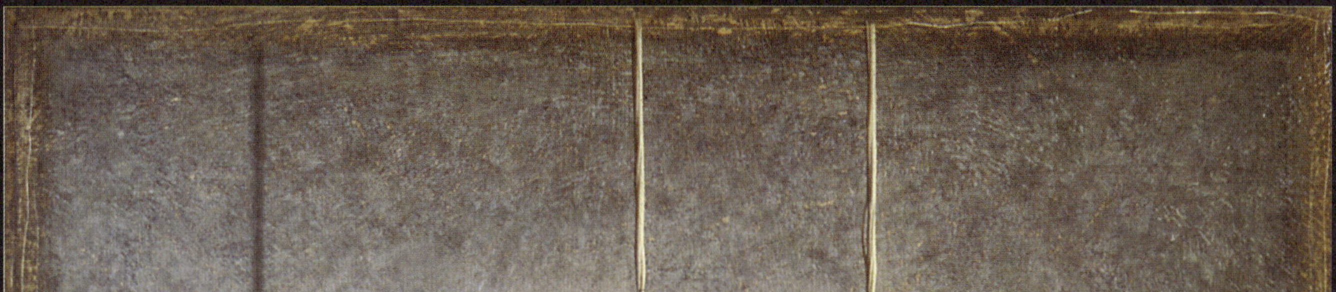

(Top) "Sea Beggars" (Book cover for Albert A. Knopf publishers, 1982) / (Bottom) "Riverstone", 2000

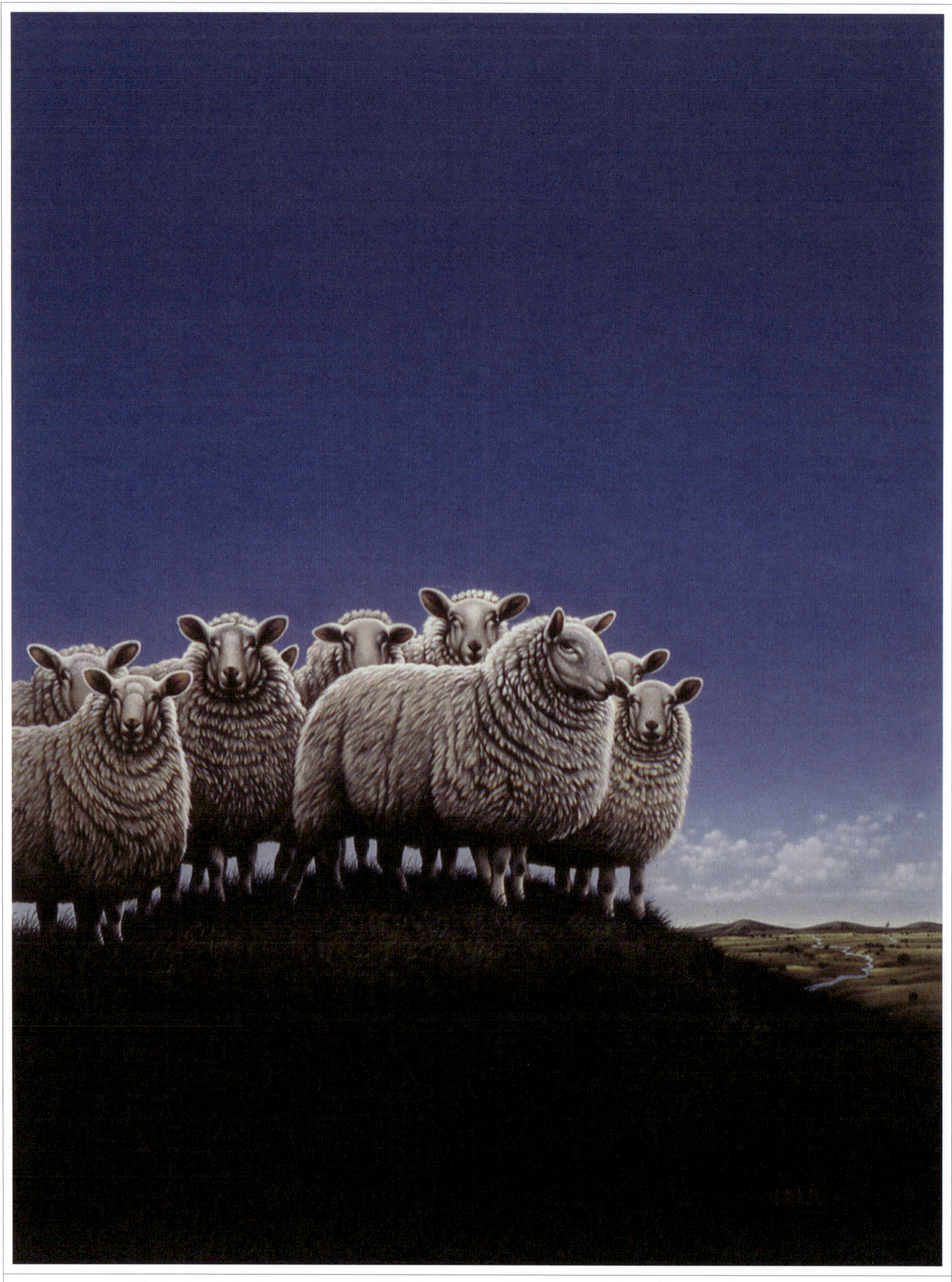

"Counting Sheep" (Control Data trade magazine, 1986). Message cautioned shoppers not to be 'led around like sheep' with other companies.

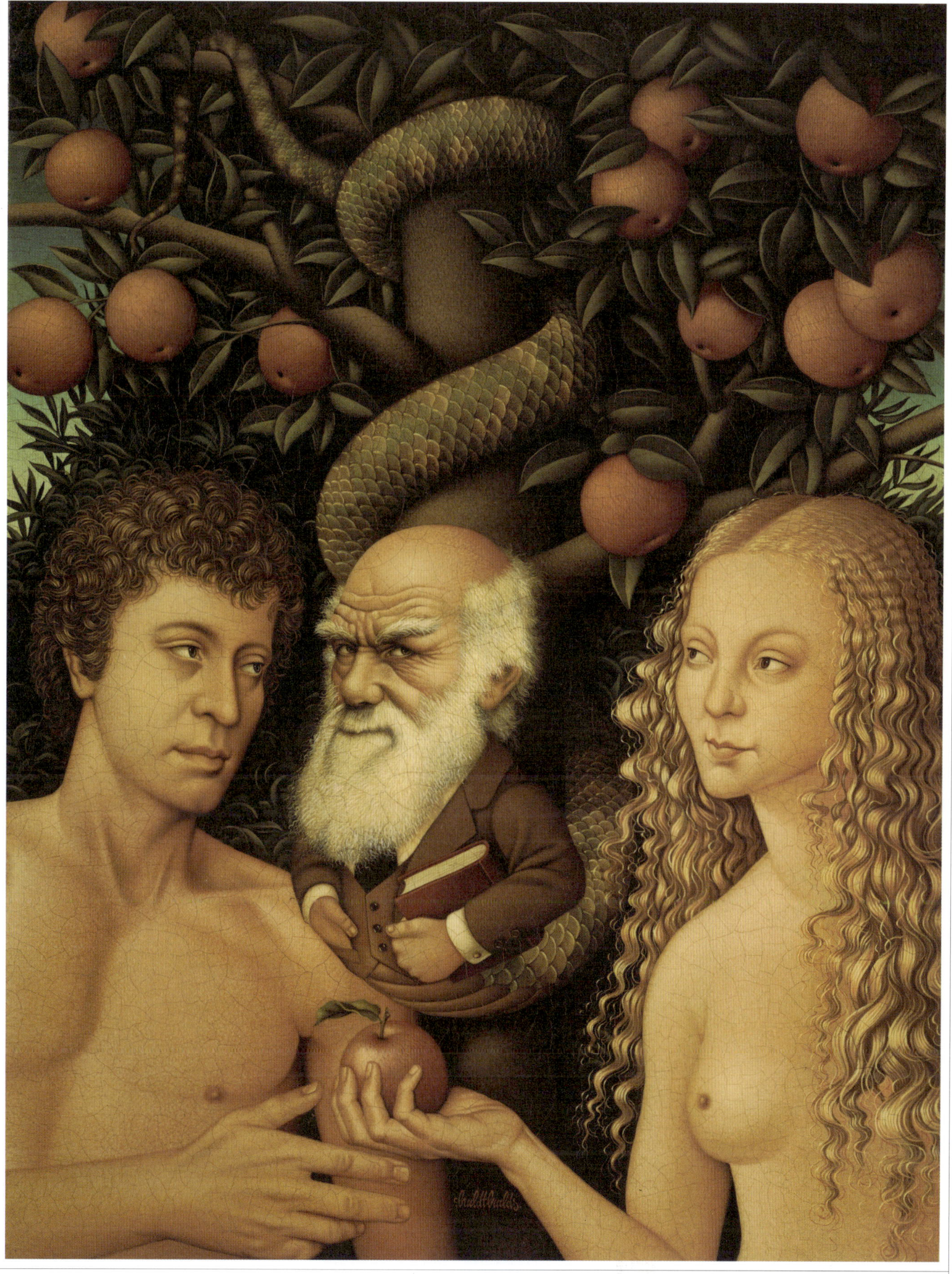

"Adam & Eve Versus Darwin" (created in 1982 for Time Magazine, never published). Used as cover for Der Spiegel Magazine's Christmas issue in 2005.

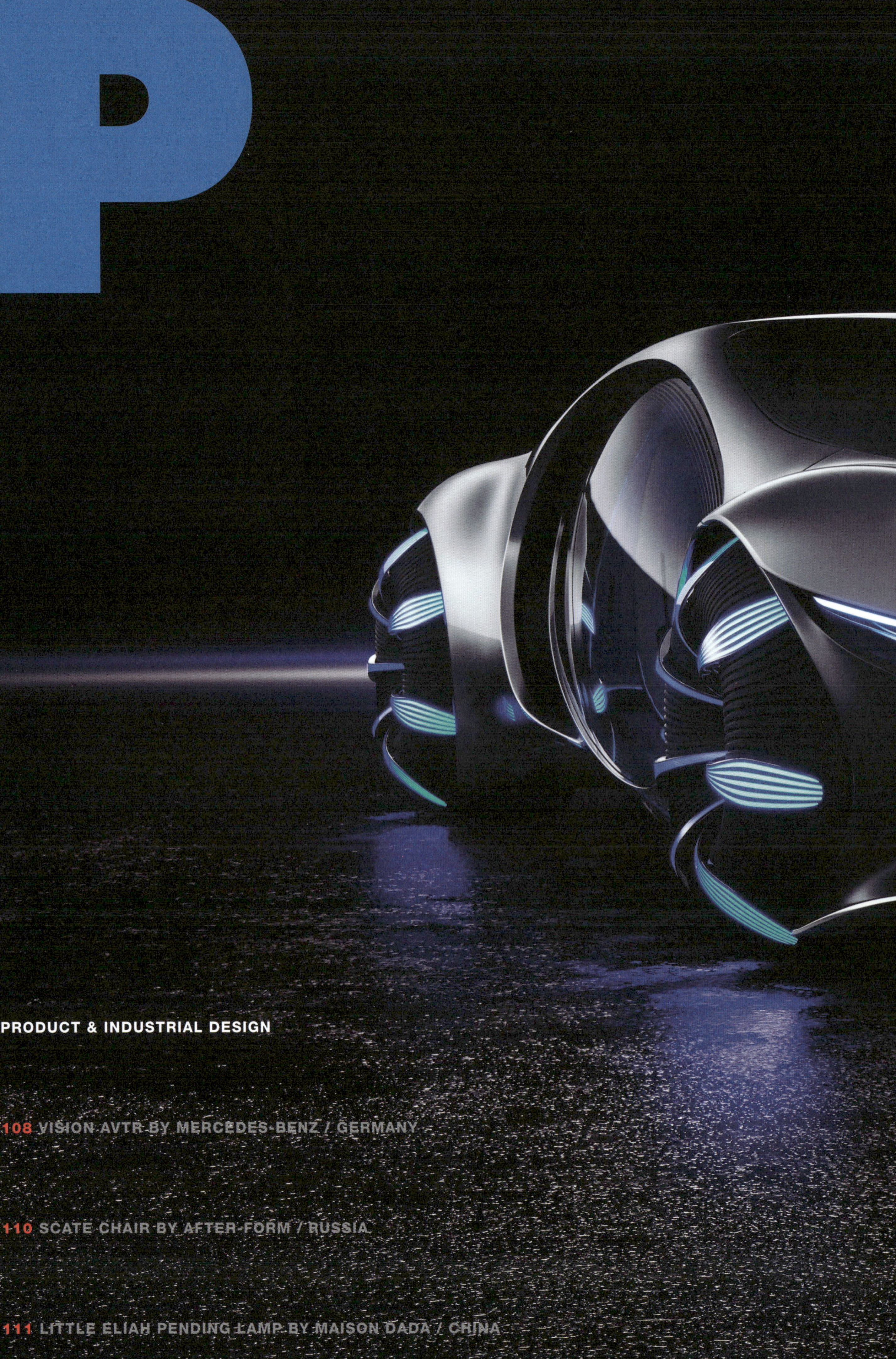
P
PRODUCT & INDUSTRIAL DESIGN

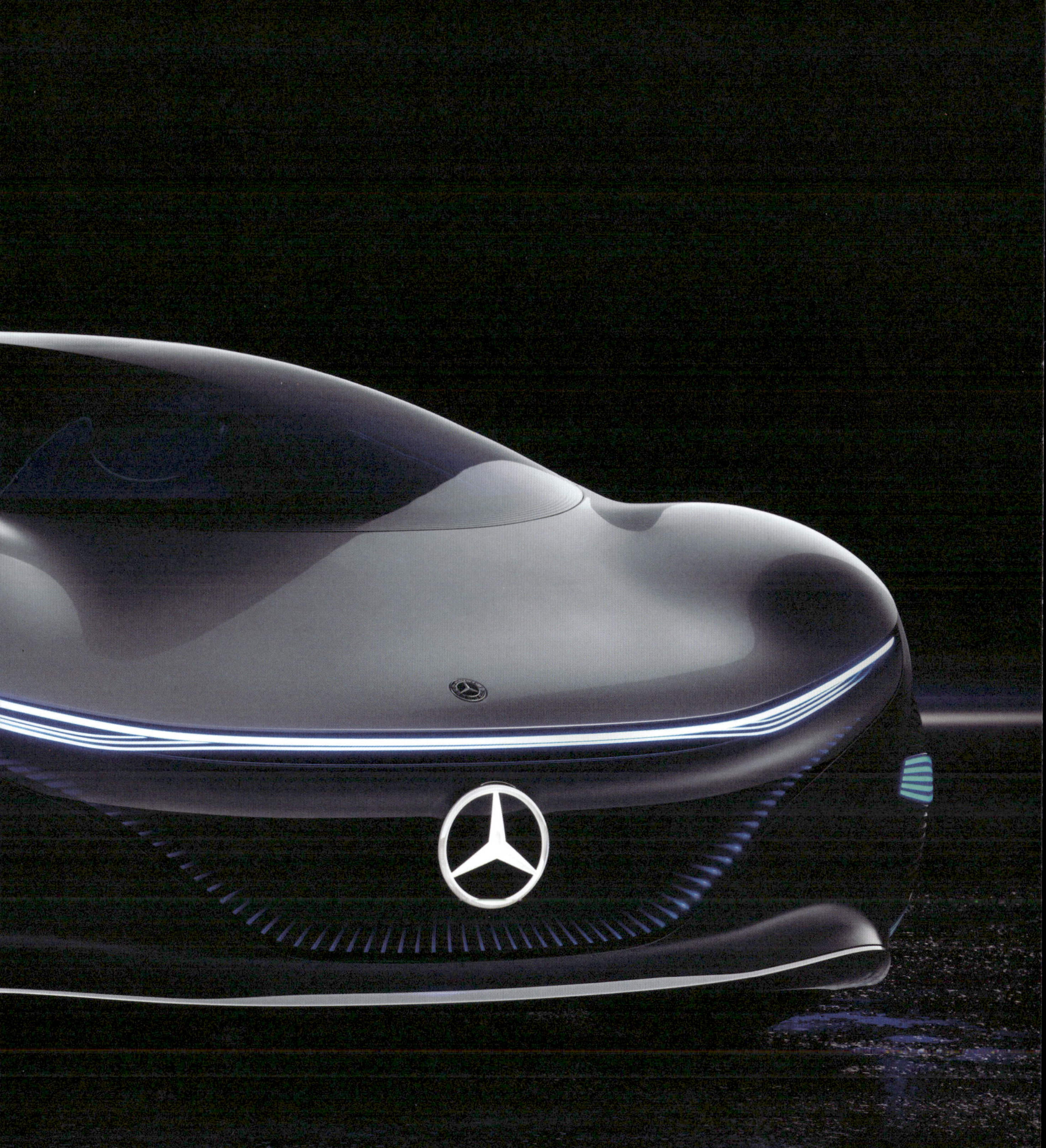

The Mercedes-Benz VISION AVTR is an exhilarating collaboration between two titans - the skills of both the Mercedes-Benz brand and the Avatar film production team have come together to create a car that demonstrates the future of driving. The lush visuals of Avatar combined with the luxury inherent in the Mercedes-Benz brand create a gorgeous aesthetic, both futuristic and current.

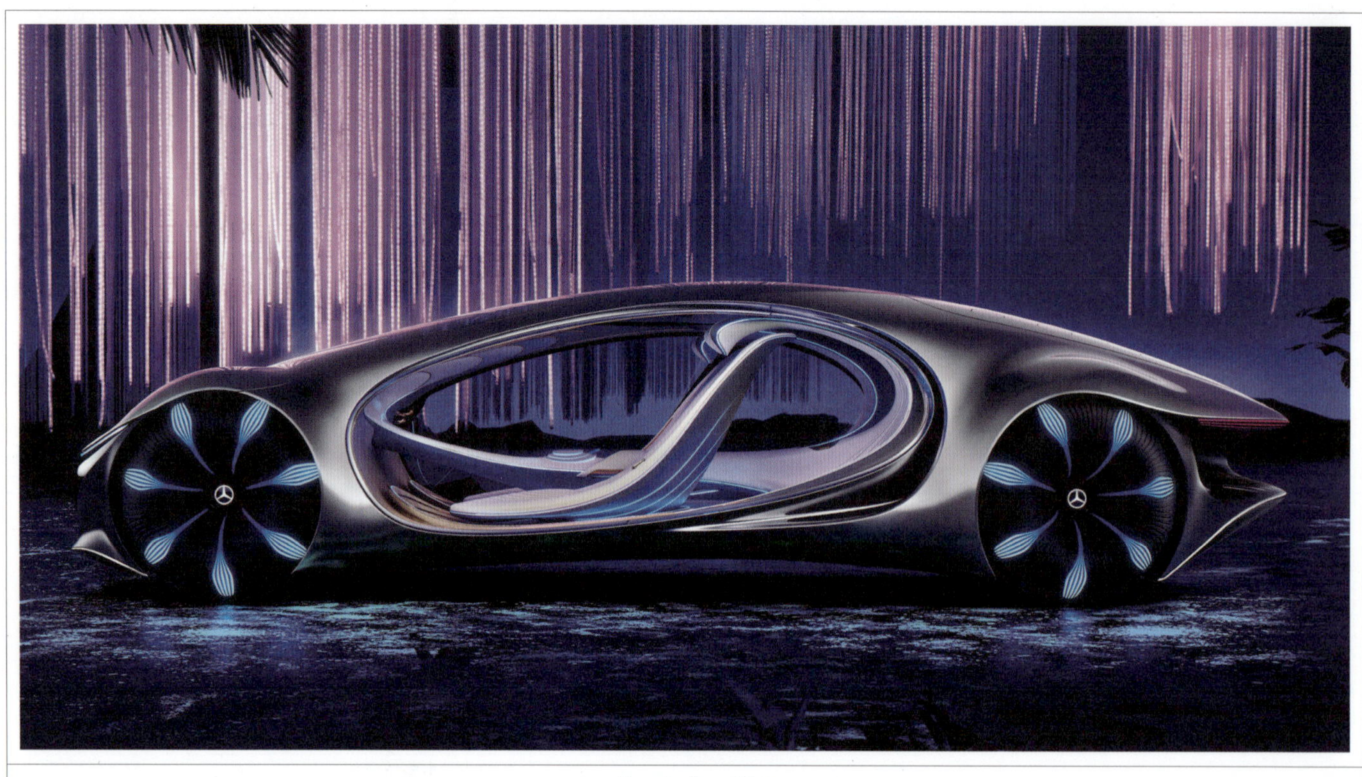

Mercedes-Benz AG

The vision is of a "zero impact car," a car that can merge with both its environment and driver. It has thirty three movable "bionic" flaps on the back of the hood which enable the car to have a more harmonious relationship with its surrounding environment. For the exterior, the car features a stretched, sporty, one bow design. The interior of the car can become a fully immersive space, giving the driver the choice between driving through the real world or the world of Avatar, Pandora. Color-changing fabric further immerses the driver and passengers with their surroundings. There is also a multifunctional control center that can recognise the driver from their breathing or heartbeat, and allows them to drive with their hand, no steering wheel necessary. A menu selection can be projected onto the palm of the driver's hand for easy access. There is an emphasis on sustainability that goes beyond the superfluous with features such as vegan leather and organic battery technology made of recyclable materials. The innovative technology allows the battery to recharge in fifteen minutes. Another ambitious element of the car is the Diagonal drive. This function allows the car to move sideways by 300 degrees. The Mercedes-Benz Vision AVTR combines elements of the fantastical and the real to create what appears to be a totally unique driving experience.

THIS CONCEPT VEHICLE EMBODIES THE VISION OF MERCEDES-BENZ DESIGNERS, ENGINEERS AND TREND RESEARCHERS FOR MOBILITY IN THE DISTANT FUTURE. **Mercedes-Benz**

NOT ONLY IS IT BEAUTIFULLY DESIGNED BUT IT WILL CREATE A CLOSER CONNECTION WITH THE DRIVER AND THE ENVIRONMENT AROUND THEM.

Jon Landau, *Producer of the AVATAR films*

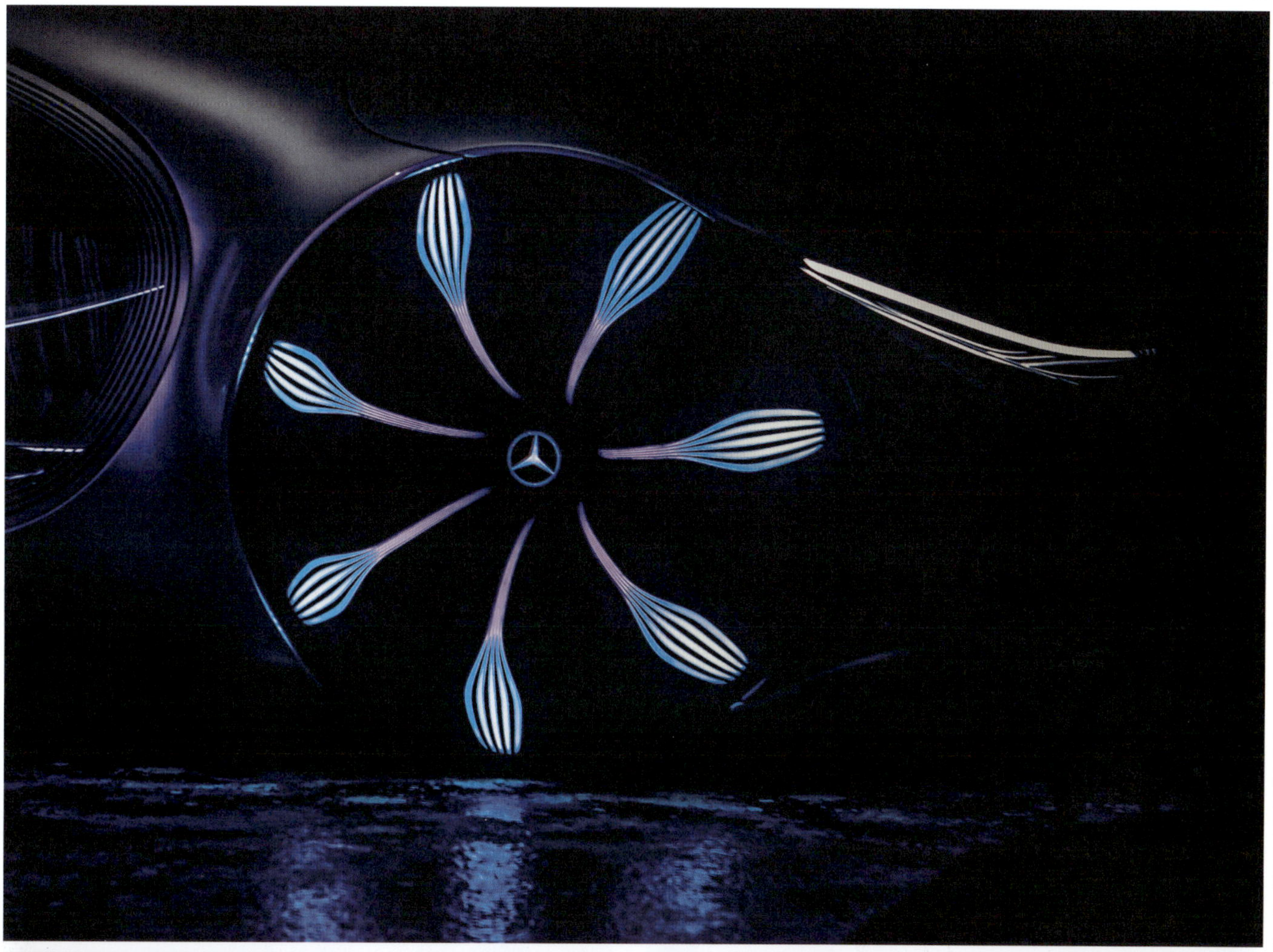

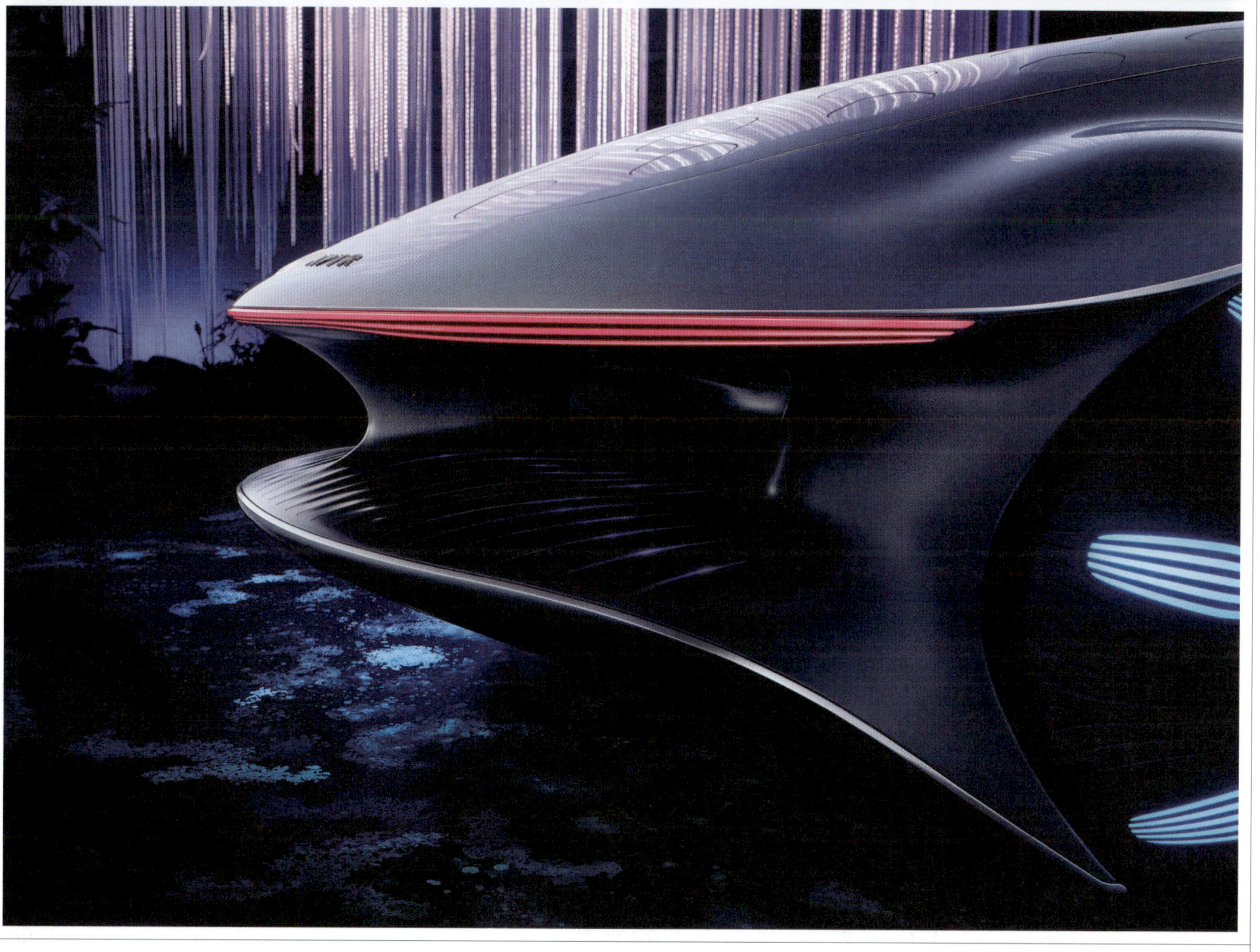

Mercedes-Benz AG

Designed by Russian designer Oleg Soroko of After-Form, the Scate Chair is the first piece of furniture for a Parametric collection that started in 2014. Being the first piece in the collection, the chair was the beginning of a long journey for Soroko; he started experimenting with shape modification. Made from birch plywood, cut by a CNC machine, and combined with metal bars inside with separators between sections, the Scate Chair is very unlike the common armchair. But it is still comfortable to sit in, and can fit one or two people at a time. Its dimensions are 1530mm L, 1370mm W, 1030mm H, and it's made with Rhino 3D and Grasshopper 3D software.

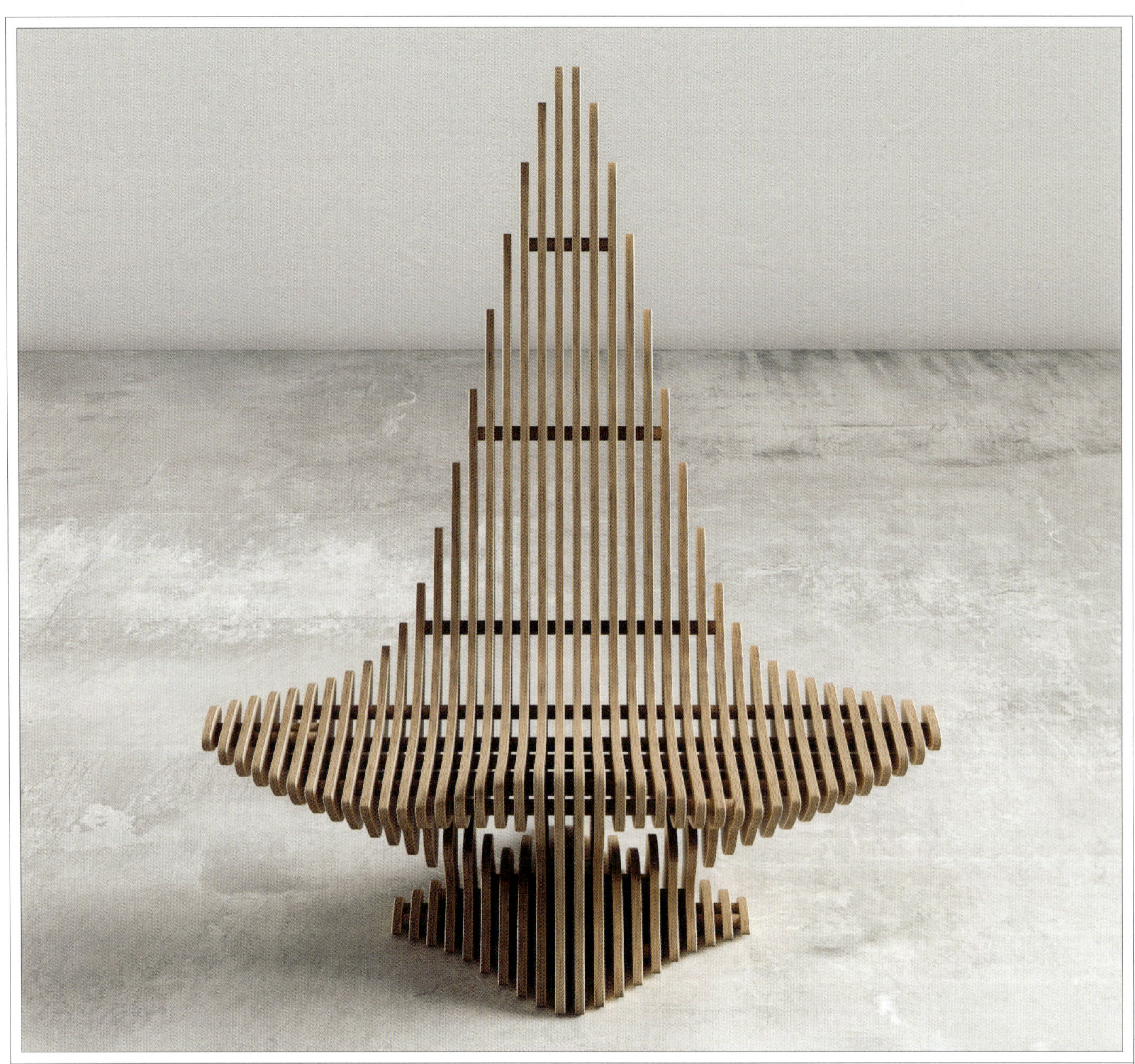

(Above) @after_form / (Opposite page) @maisondada

(Opposite page) Maison Dada, a design firm created in Shanghai, has designed the *Little Eliah Pending Lamp*. French designers Thomas Dariel and Delphine Moreau, founded the company with the goal of creating the unexpected from simple everyday objects. This lamp has versatility that most lamps don't have when it comes to its position. It can be suspended from the ceiling, or rest on a closer surface. The cable cord has a maximum adjustment length of 2.4 meters and comes in 2 color combinations: BlueDeep/YellowChick, and OrangeFlamingo/GreenPeacock. The interior and base combinations allow this object to bring a burst of color into your home.

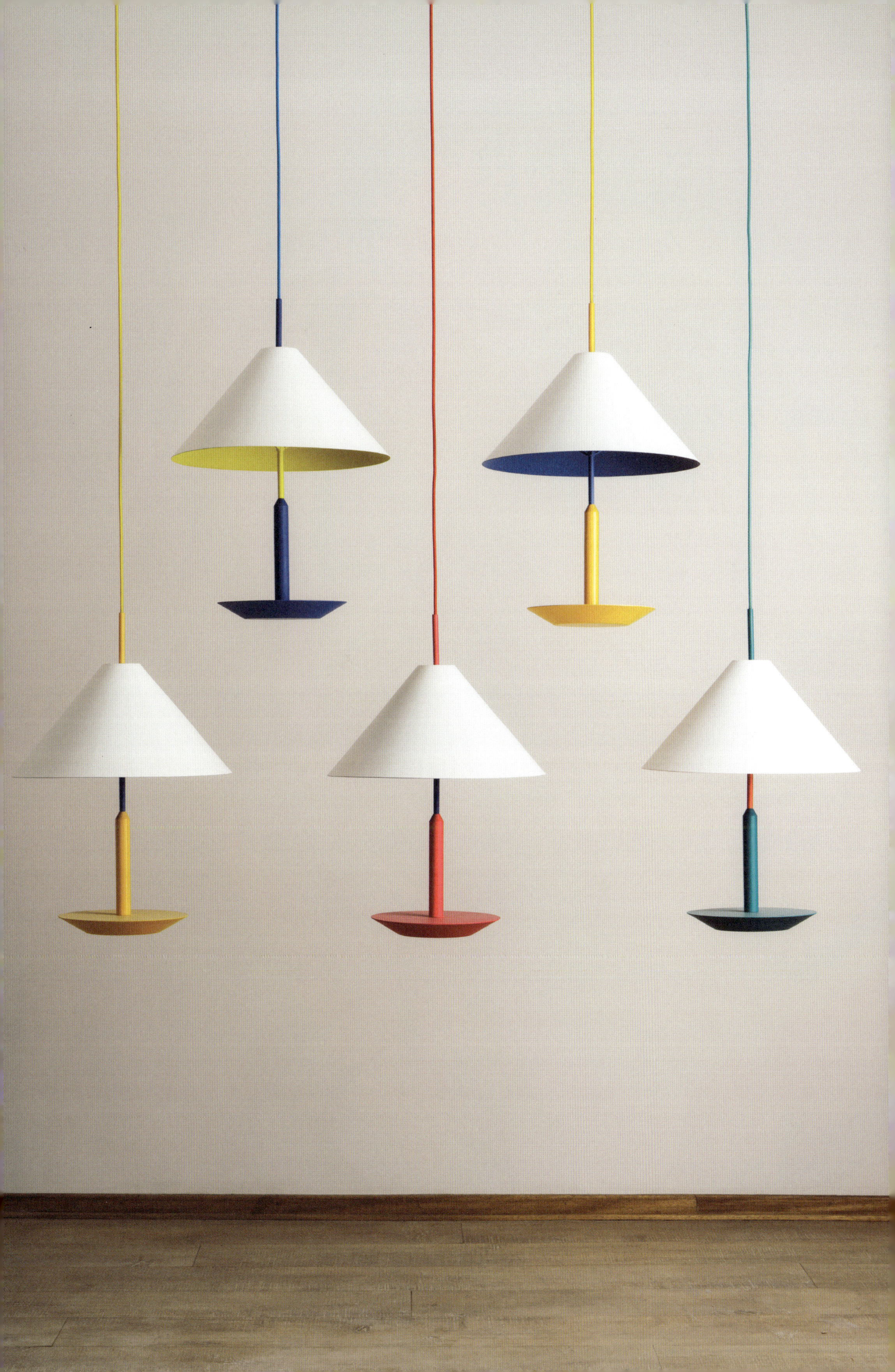

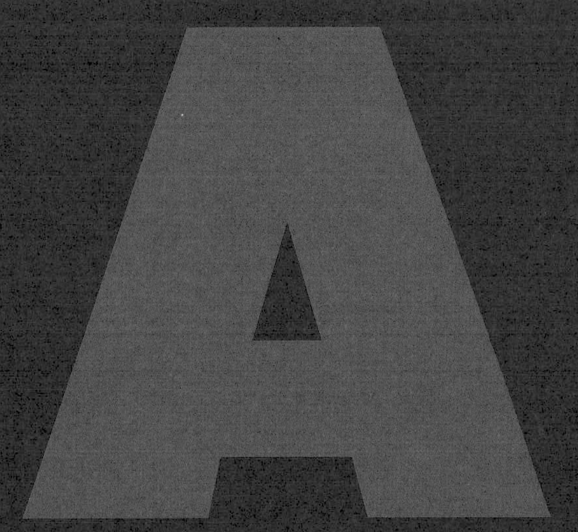

ARCHITECTURE & EXHIBITS

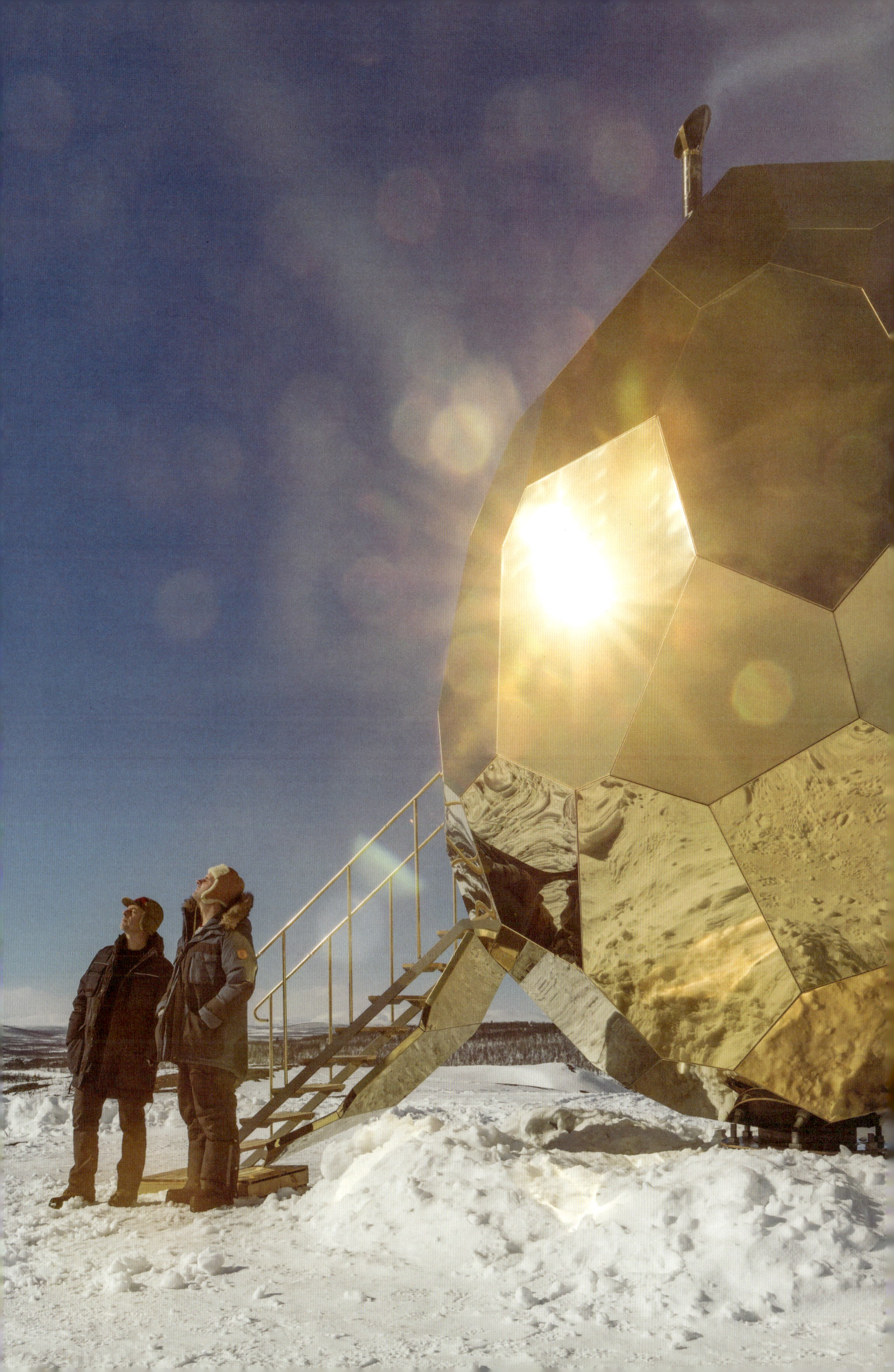

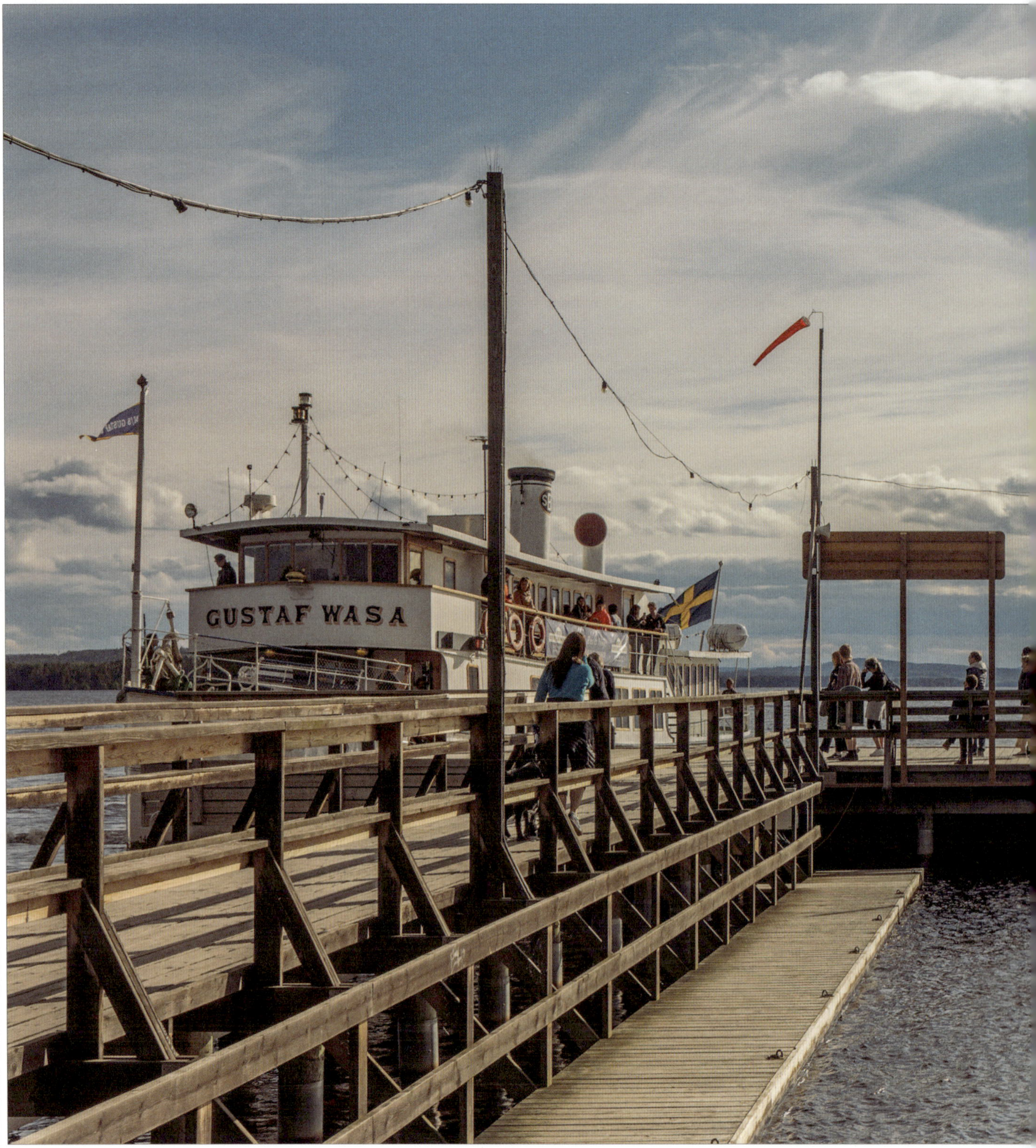

The Solar Egg by Swedish designers Bigert & Bergström for Riksbyggen (Swedish housing company) is a sculptural sauna shaped as an egg which has been installed in various locations around the world. Photographed by Jean Babtiste Béranger, the egg's first location was in Luossabacken in Kiruna, Sweden's northernmost town, in 2017. Made out of 69 pieces of stainless golden mirror sheeting, which form to make the oval shape, the egg reflects a variety of different mirror images. The interior is made from wood; the

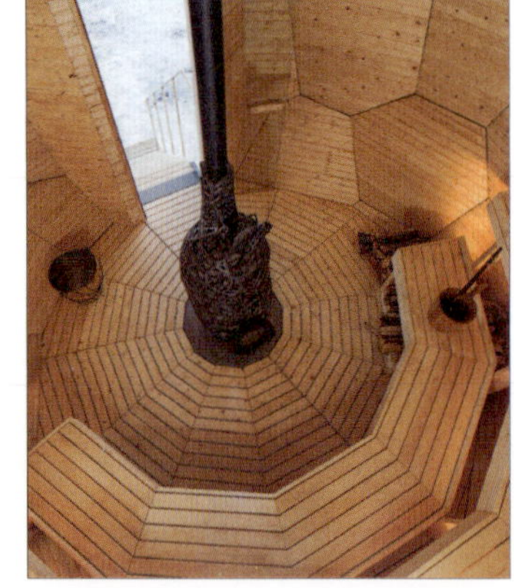

paneling in the walls and floor are made of pine, and the bench, which has room for up to eight people, is made from aspen. At the center of the egg is the wood-fired burner, inside an iron cage in the shape of an anatomical heart. The burner is full of large stones that manage the heat, and the temperature is between 75° and 85° Celsius. Outside the egg, there is a flight of drawbridge stairs that are directly in front of the doorway, which are able to be lowered down into the snow so visitors can enter.

The finished product was deliberately

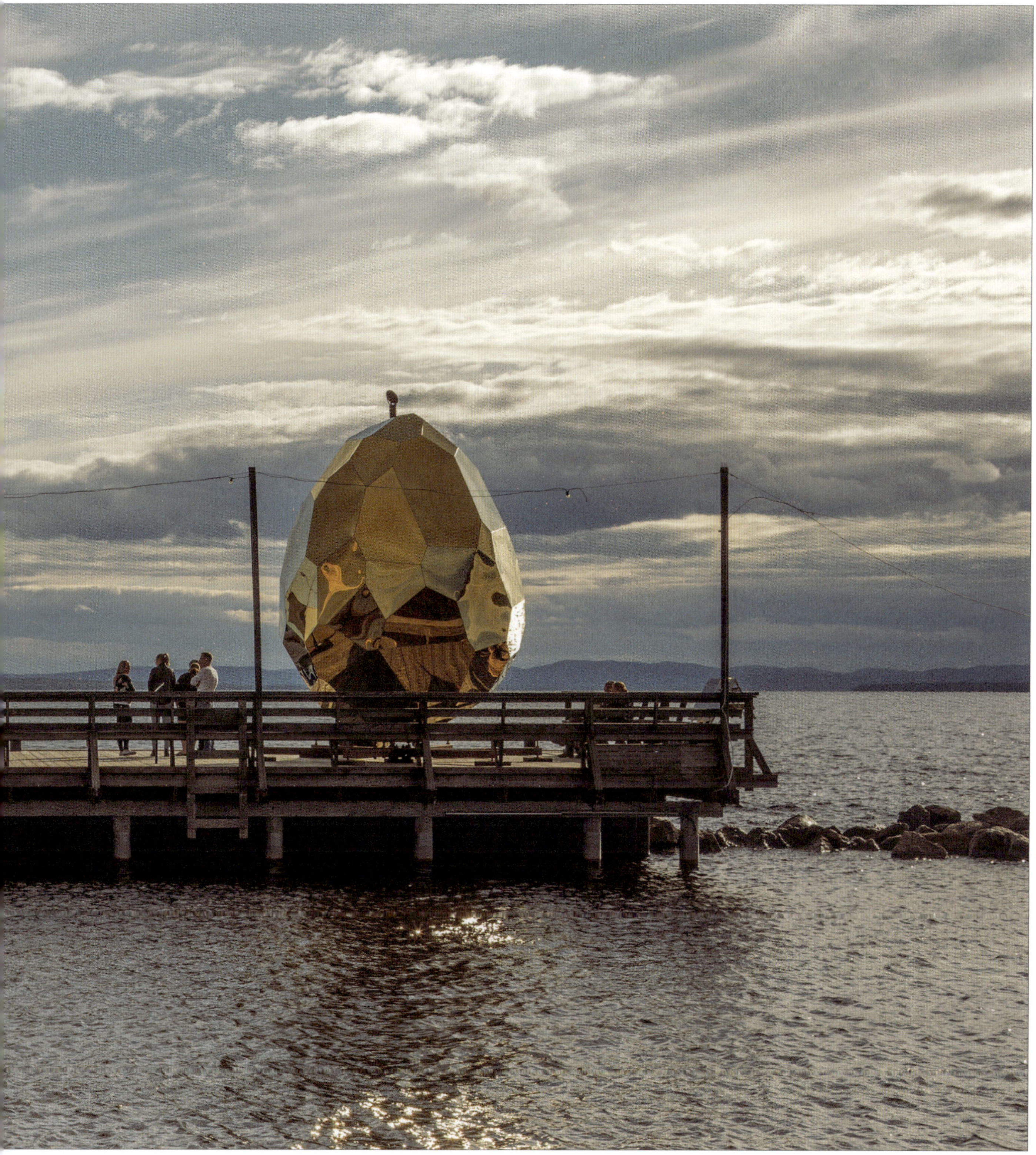

Riksbyggens' Solar Egg by Bigert & Bergström

placed in a cold climate, to have the snowy environment reflected in the mirrored surface on the outside of the egg. When the Solar Egg was first created and placed in Kiruna, the town was in the middle of an ongoing debate; the local people had to move due to the mining company LKAB. The company wanted to take out more of the iron seam cutting downwards underneath the town, and will continue to mine for the next 20 years. Mining has been a vital source of income for Kiruna and Sweden, but that also meant that the land

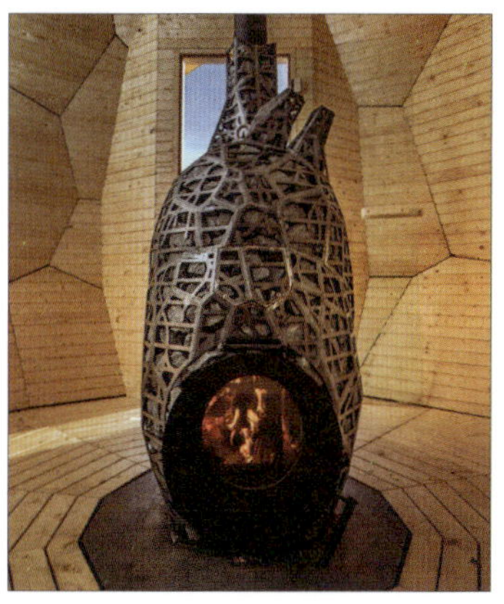

would be heavily altered in order to do so, and a debate about the environment and architecture began. For the townspeople, who expressed worries of losing community spirit after having to move, the Solar Egg is a place for people to come together and share their ideas on these issues. Bigert & Bergström have made this as a way to integrate the environment with the artwork, and is an extension of a project started in 1994 called Climate Chambers, featuring five chambers with extreme climates in each one: freeze, storm, heat, light, and steam.

Li Xiang is a Chinese architect and designer who established her own firm, X+Living, after studying in the UK and Malaysia. She has won awards such as the SBC Green Architectural Design Award of Malaysia, and Interior Design's Best of Year award in 2016. Since then, she has designed many interiors and successful theme parks including, the Shenzhen Neobio Family Park.

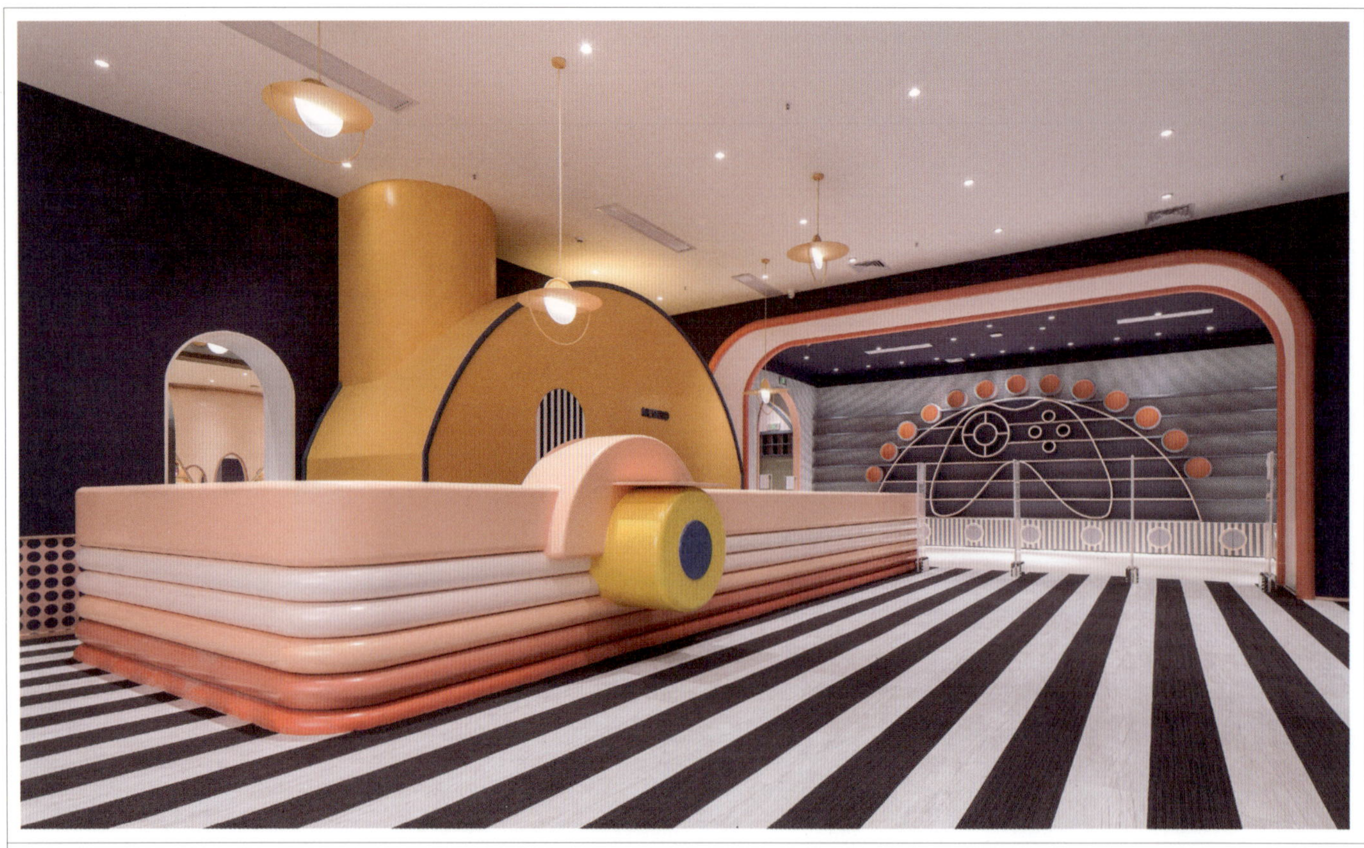

Photographer: Shao Feng

Completed in 2019, Li Xiang has created the perfect environment with dual functionality for the needs of parents and children. Designed with project directors, Ren Lijiao, and Wu Feng, Shenzhen Neobio Family Park is a family entertainment plaza located in Shenzhen China. This structure takes up the first floor of the shopping mall, Hangzhou Star Avenue Phase II, with a project area of 6000m^2. The park layout uses interchanging elements such as space and height along with an open plane, to ensure that the different play stations feel connected as one. The four distinct divisions of the park were each made based on age group; each includes educational experiences, and accommodations and entertainment for the parents. The divisions are marked with oversized, stylistic parasols and carousel-dome seating. Pastel colors were the palette of choice when designing the theme park and features the additional touch of navy blue, black, red, and purple. With this consistent color pattern, the buildings alternate from an abstract of stripes, polka dots, and solid colors. Examples of this include the Sims City room that features a night sky of stars, a reading room of pastel rainbows, and simplistic elements such as a cardboard playhouse jungle gym. The interactive design of the play park connects the rest of the floors of the shopping mall through a spacious, dining and lounge area. Other floors of the shopping mall can be seen while relaxing. This dreamland fantasy world for kids also caters to parents with activities they can enjoy together, including rest stations and restaurants to sit at while their children play.

THE DESIGN OF NEOBIO IN SHENZHEN CONTINUES THE CONSISTENT DESIGN STYLE OF THE NEOBIO BRAND. **X+Living**

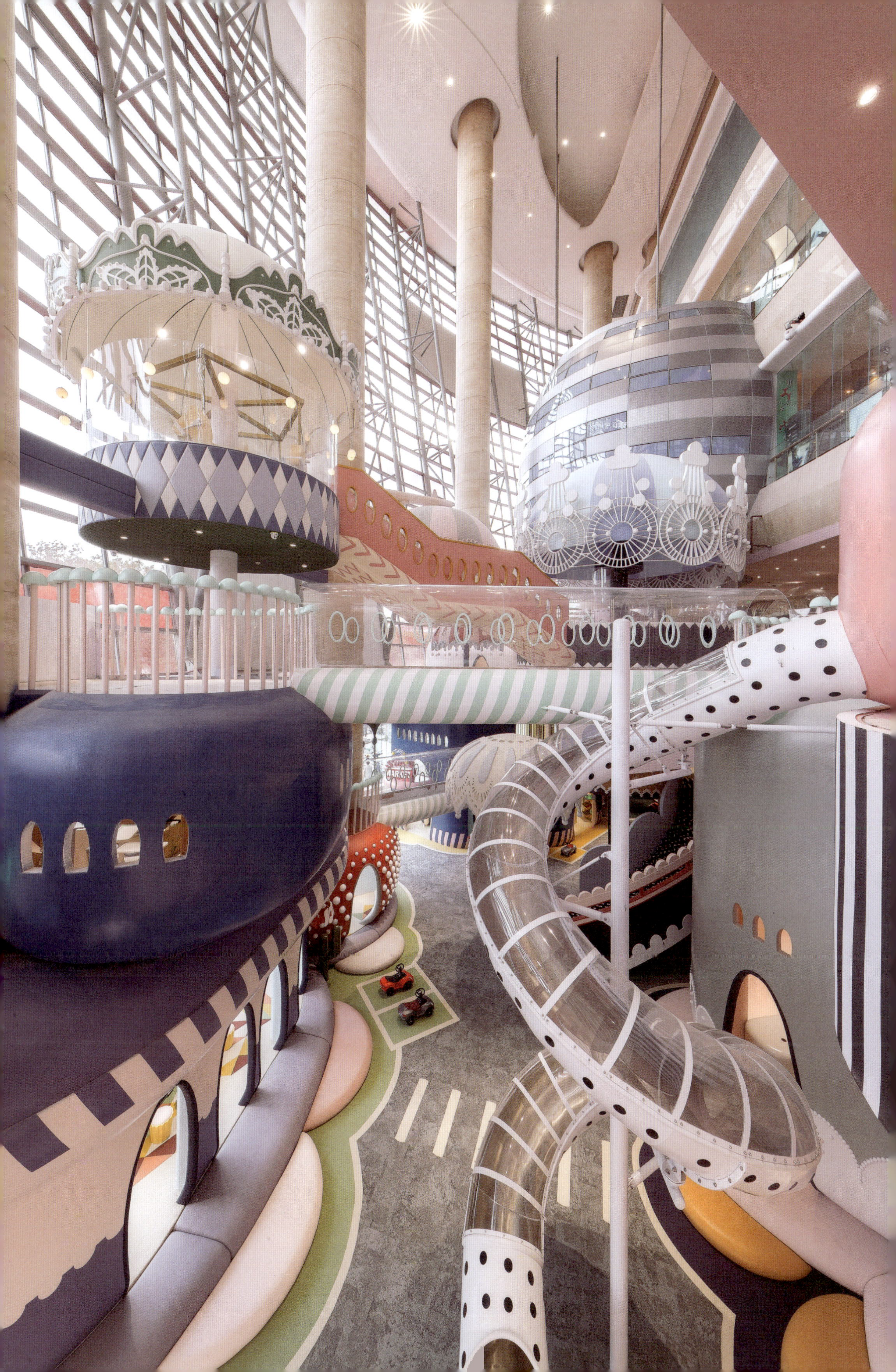

AZURE

DESIGN
ARCHITECTURE
INTERIORS
ART

JAN 2012
205

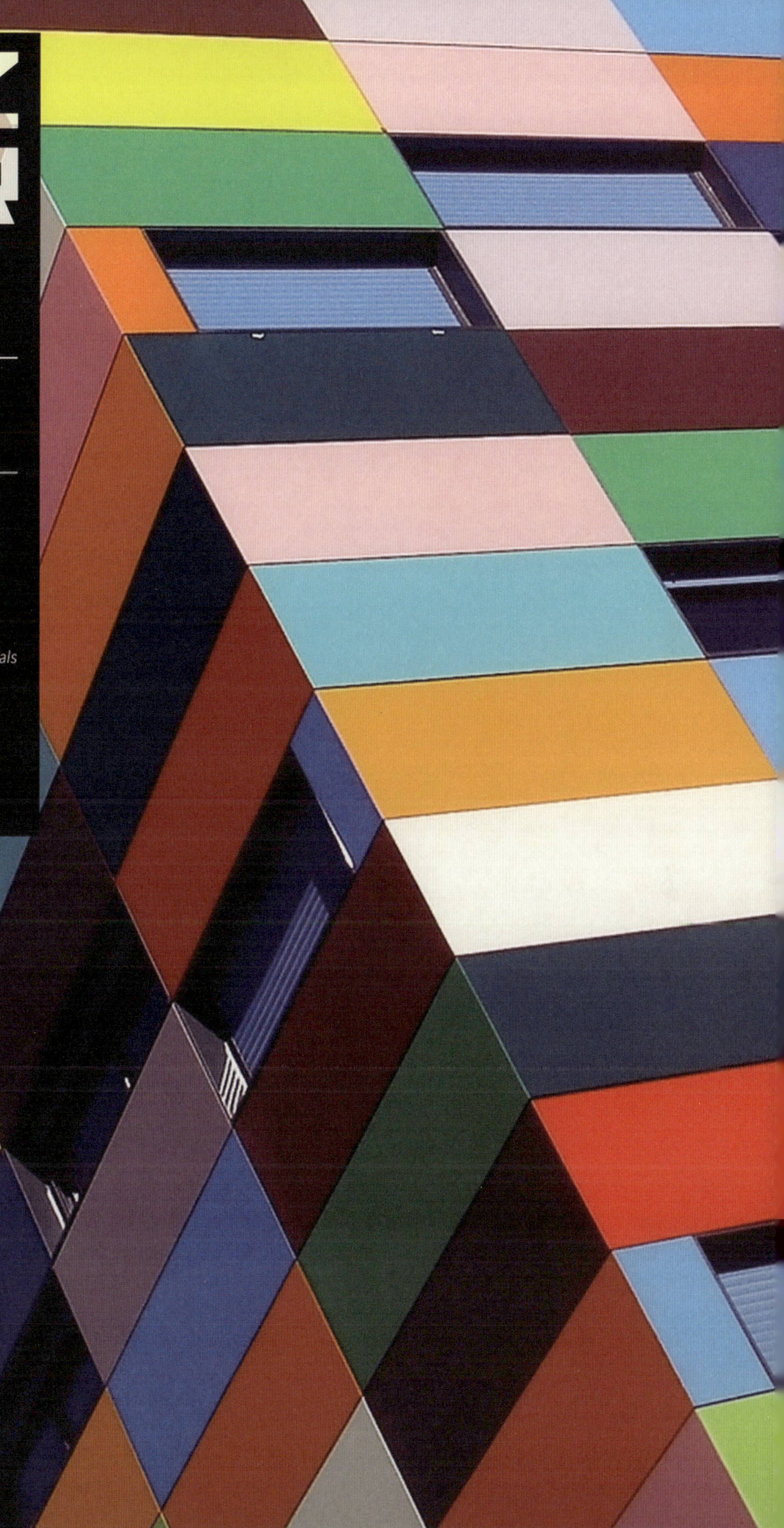

ADRIAN IS A FORMATIVE PRESENCE IN MY CAREER AND MY LIFE. HE TAUGHT ME MOST OF WHAT I KNOW ABOUT DESIGN. HE SOMEHOW MANAGED TO BE INCREDIBLY DEMANDING AND DEEPLY SUPPORTIVE AT THE SAME TIME. HE SET US OFF TO FLY.

Maria Petrova, *Student, Freelance Graphic Designer/Art Director*

THE BFA DESIGN PROGRAM AT BYU IS ELITE AND DEMANDING, BUT WILL PROVIDE A PORTFOLIO THAT CAN GET YOU INTO THE BEST FIRMS. A LOT OF THAT IS DUE TO ADRIAN. HE'S BUILT A PROGRAM WHERE IF YOU WORK HARD AND TRY, YOU WILL SUCCEED.

Erin Scardena, *Student/Graphic Designer*

HE'S INFLUENCED SO MANY DESIGNERS IN SUCH PROFOUND WAYS. HE HAS NEVER STOPPED WORKING TO MAKE THE WORLD A BETTER AND MORE BEAUTIFUL PLACE THROUGH DESIGN AND TEACHING.

Enoch Palmer, *Former Student, Partner at Case Agency*

HE SHOWED ME THAT DESIGN ACTUALLY MAKES YOU FEEL SOMETHING, IT'S NOT JUST SUPERFICIAL. IT'S SOMETHING YOU NURTURE, AND HAVE TO WORK AT. ADRIAN LOVES IT. HE LIVES IT. AND INSPIRED ME TO DO THE SAME.

Tony Yumul, *Former Student, Partner at Case Agency*

ADRIAN WAS AND STILL IS A BRILLIANTLY TASTEFUL DESIGNER WHO WORKED WITH ME AT PEDERSEN DESIGN INC. FOR 8+ YEARS. ANY CLIENT WOULD BE VERY FORTUNATE TO ENGAGE WITH HIM.

B. Martin Pedersen, *Publisher & Creative Director, Graphis Inc.*

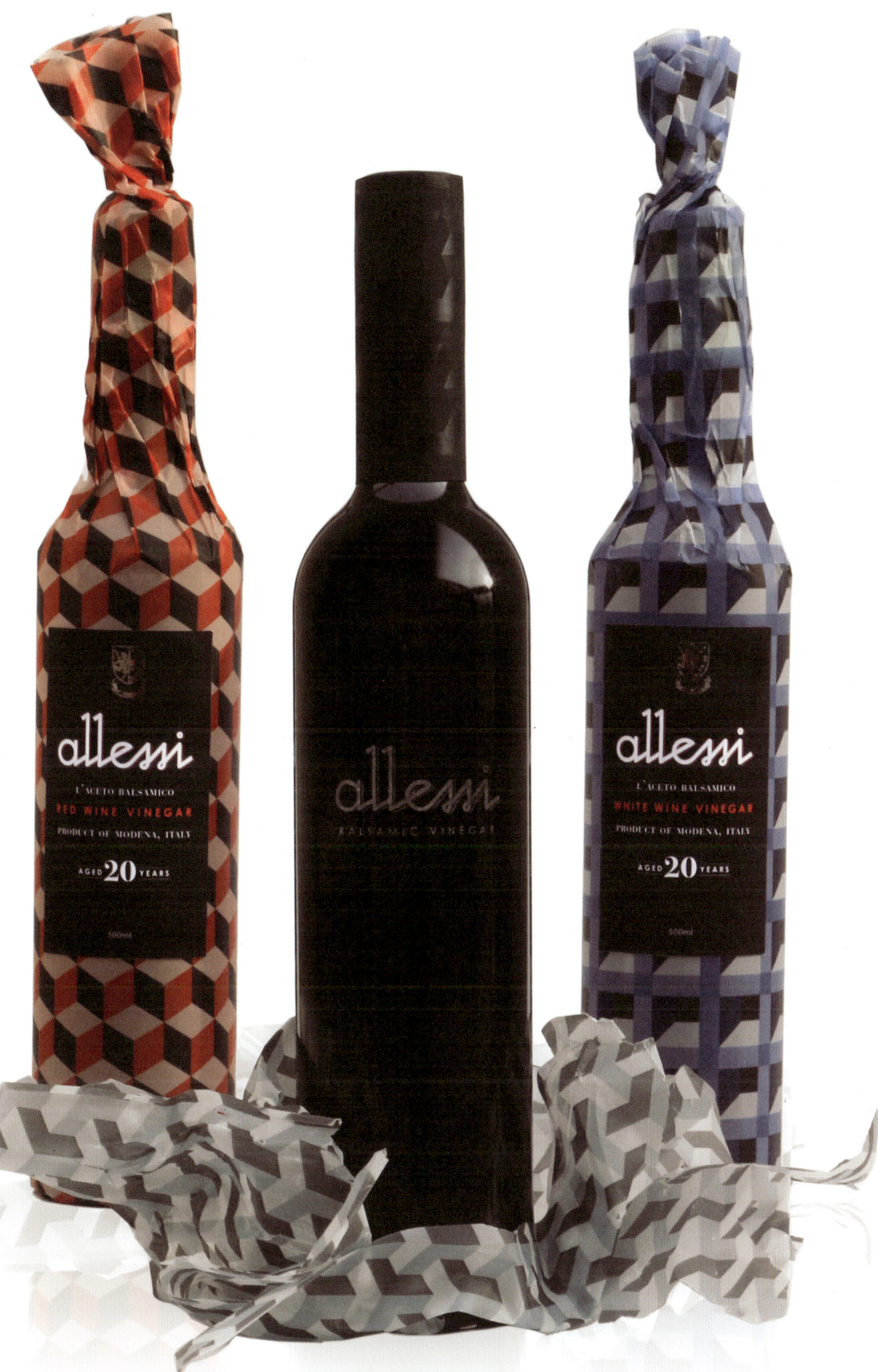

(Page 119) "Azure" New Talent Annual 2012 Platinum-winning Student: Kenji Ishigaki / (Above) "Alessi Balsamic Vinegars" New Talent Annual 2014 Gold-winning Student: Sam Wood

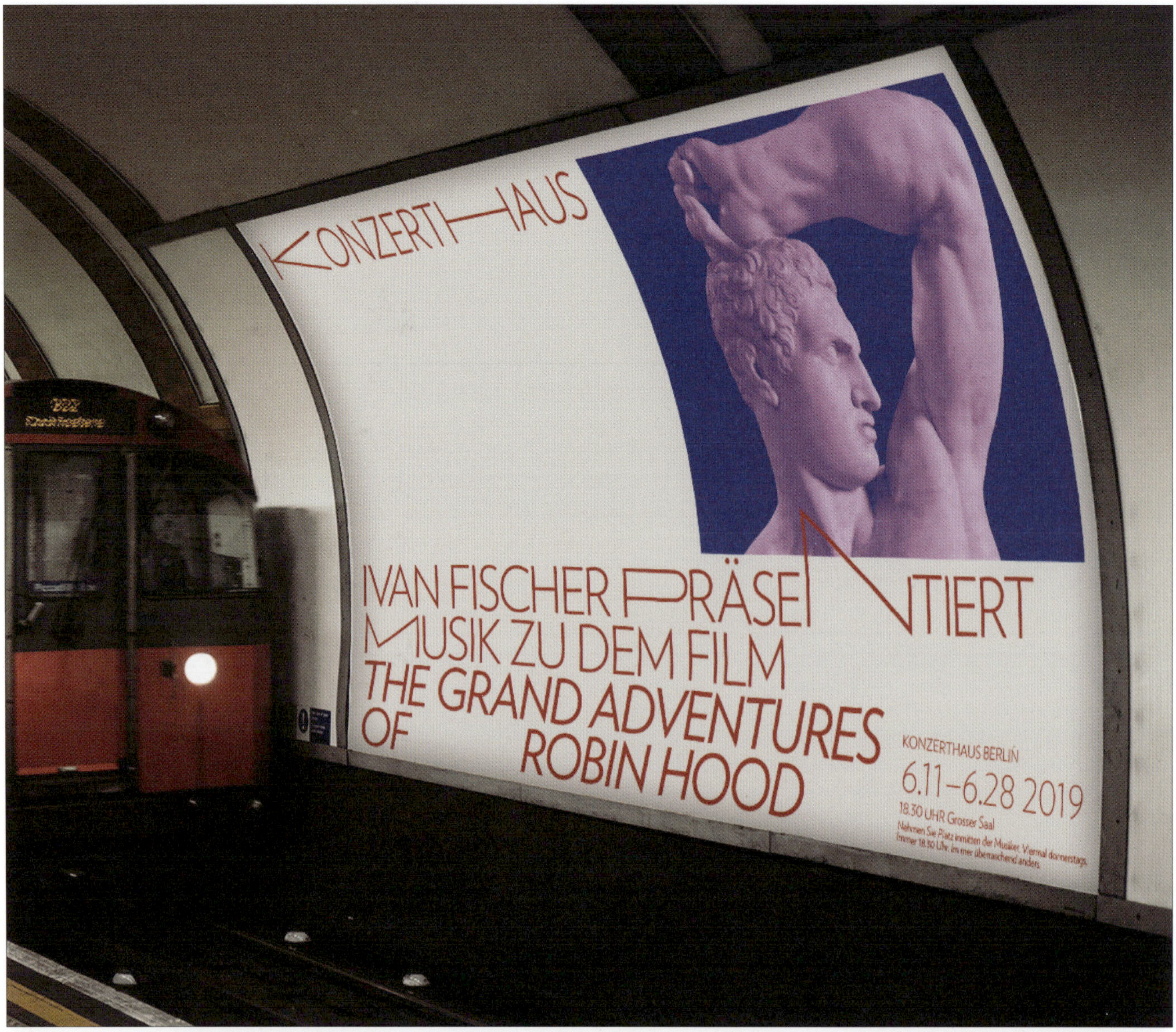

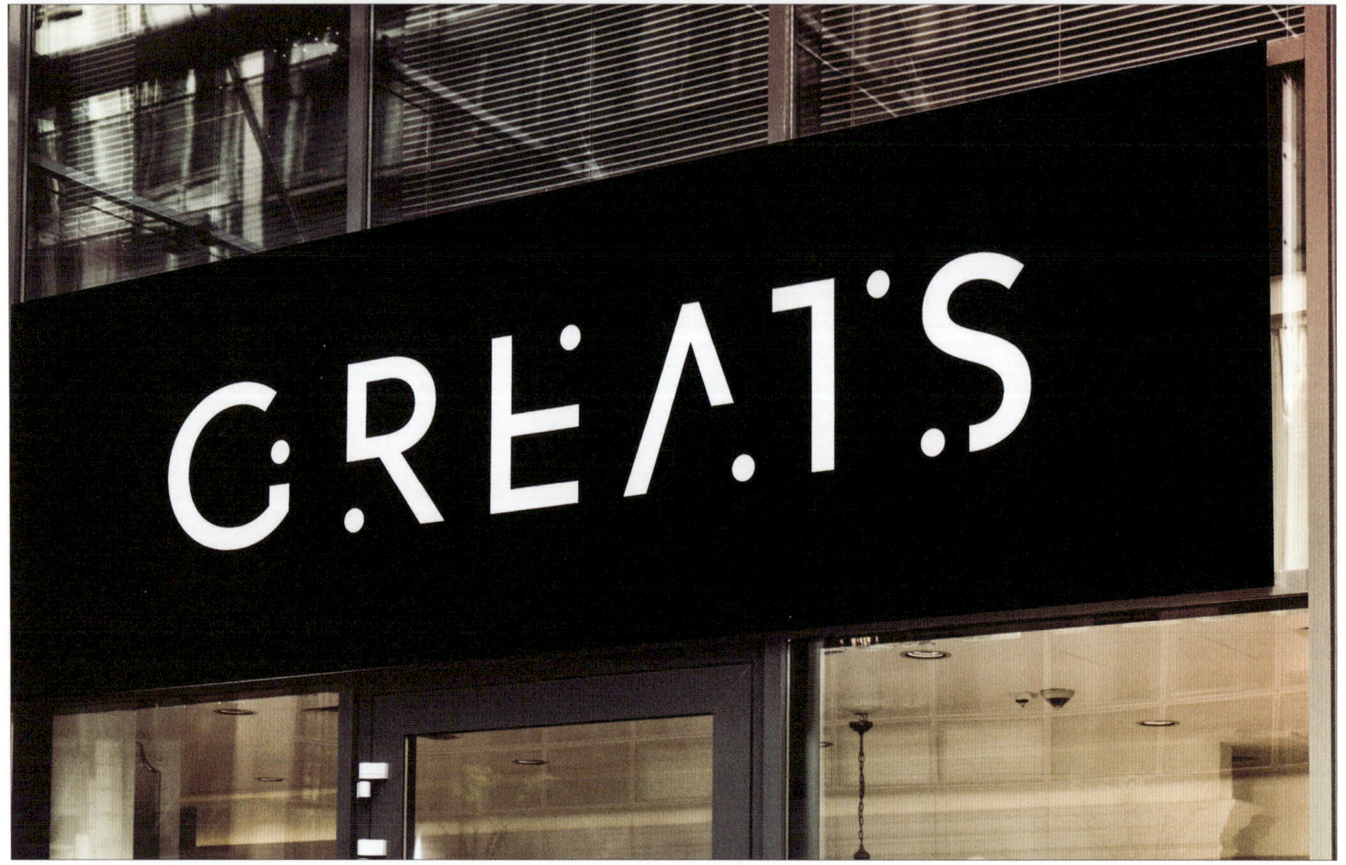

(Top) "Konzerhaus" New Talent Annual 2019 Gold-winning Student: Dallin Diehl / (Bottom) "Greats Branding" New Talent Annual 2020 Gold-winning Student: Dominique Mossman

Introduction by Eric Gillett *Chair of Dept. of Design at BYU*

Long before a student enters his classroom, the mystique of Professor Pulfer has been imprinted in their young minds by upperclassmen. His carefully modulated Australian accent captures their attention on day one and then fades into their consciousness. ▪ Instead, they learn a dialect unique to his critiques. "It's a start" is the polite way to say a rough comp may still be salvageable. "Tricky feathers" refers to an overwrought design that may not. Like an Ittens-like Bauhaus master, he uses the socratic method to instill within each student a deep reverence for good design. Throughout the semester, a show-and-tell of seemingly random objects, like a hand-forged axe or a pair of designer scissors, coalesce into master classes on hierarchy, restraint, or sustainability. ▪ During prolonged critiques he patiently draws out opinions and suggestions and can often be heard extolling the virtues of "typography, typography, typography." Scissors in hand, he cuts away at a student comp, revealing possibilities where none existed before. As the critique draws to a close he pauses to emphasize his point, right-o mate, well, at least it's a start.

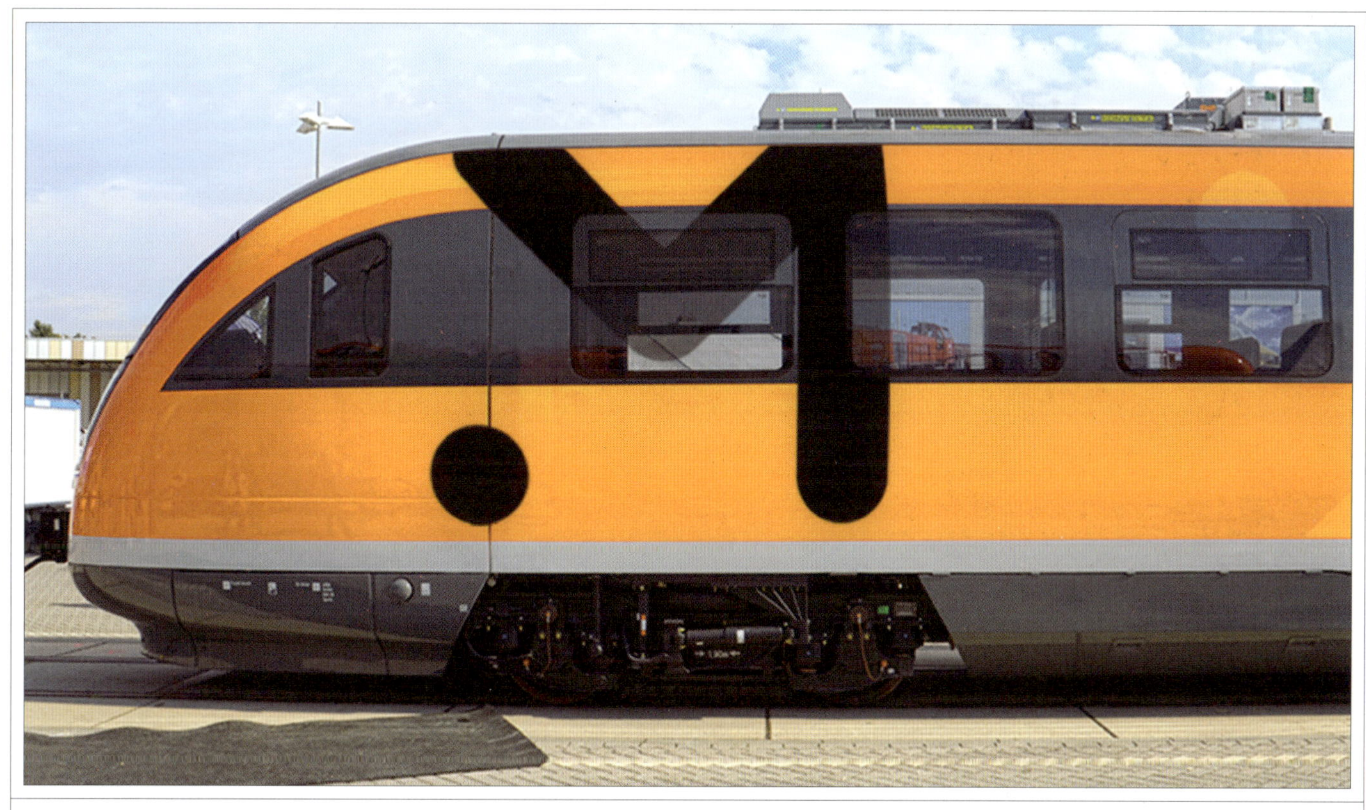

"Seoul Metro" New Talent Annual 2015 Gold-winning Student: Bomi Lee

HE IS AN INSTITUTION IN THE BYU GRAPHIC DESIGN PROGRAM. WE OWE MANY OF THE RELATIONSHIPS AND SUCCESS IN OUR PROGRAM TO HIM.

THE STUDENTS APPRECIATE HIS CONCERN FOR THEIR DEVELOPMENT, AND THEIR SUCCESS AND HAPPINESS IN LIFE.

Brent Barson, *Graphis Design Area Head/Associate Professor at Brigham Young University*

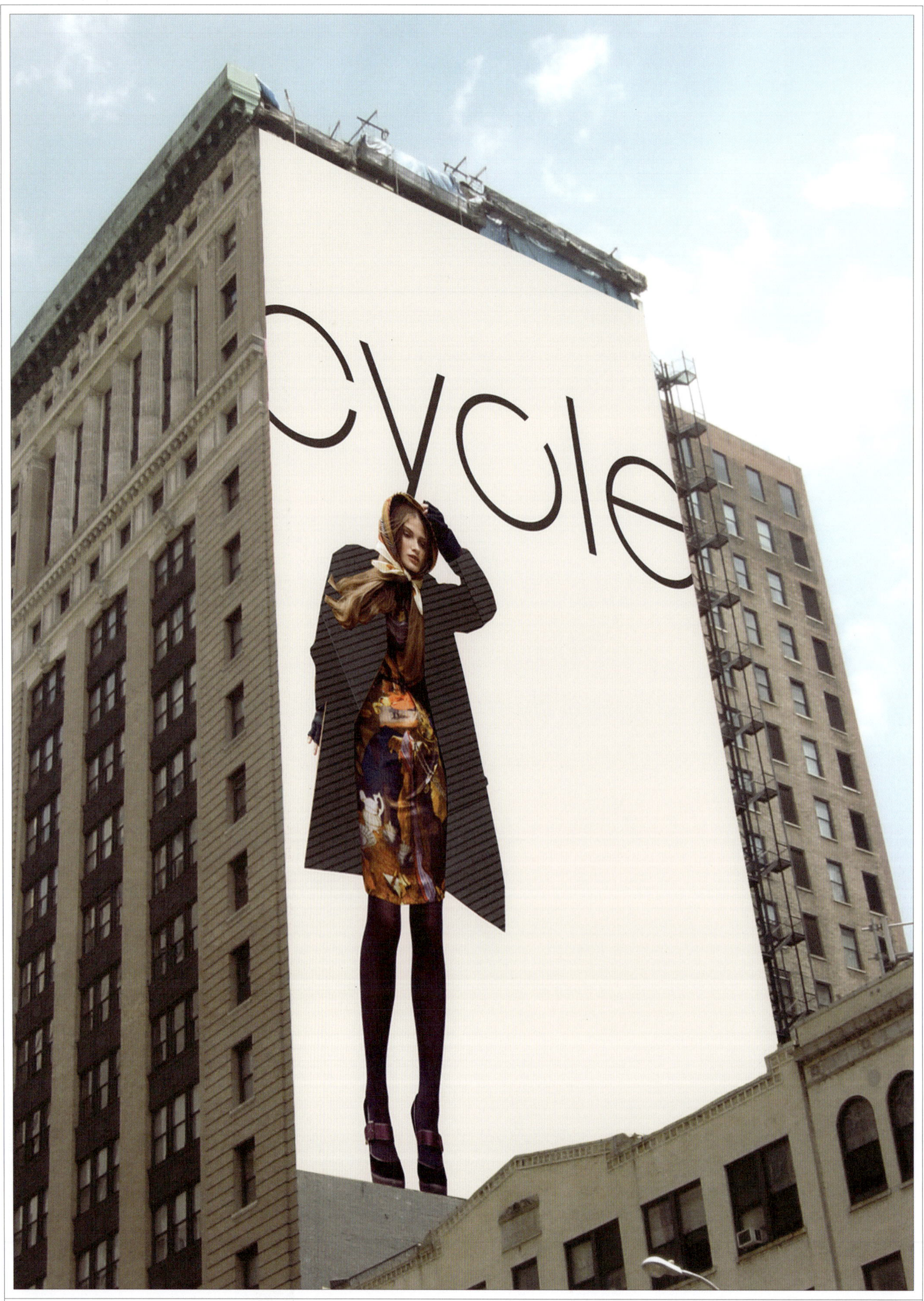

"Cycle Clothing Brand" New Talent Annual 2010 Gold-winning Student: Analisa Estrada

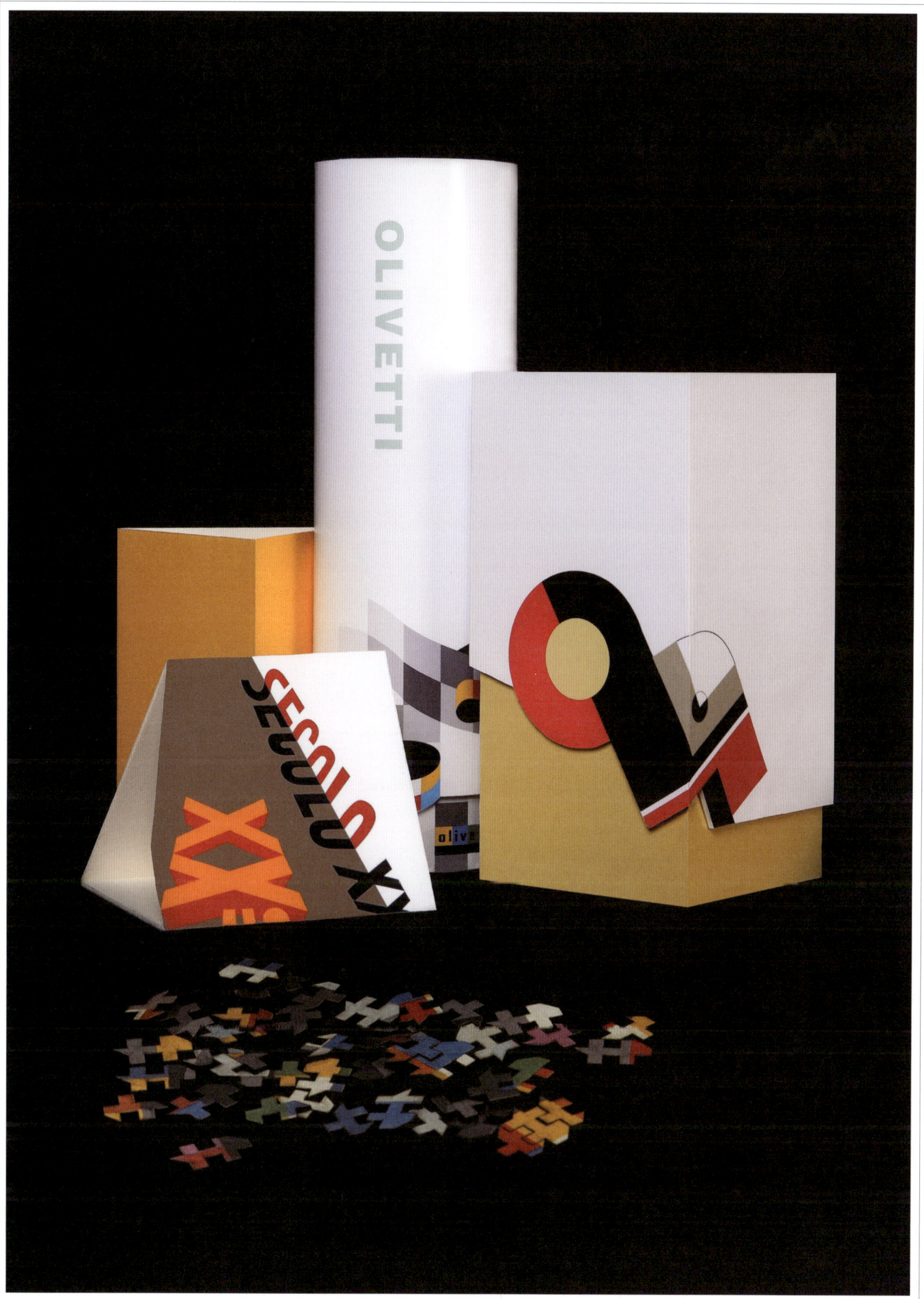

"Design Puzzle" New Talent Annual 2012 Gold-winning Student: Hang Hyun Lee

What is your process for selecting a student for your class?
Our design program is housed in a liberal arts university, which is not unique but it does pose some unusual challenges in that the classroom hours for a student to graduate with a BFA in design are quite limited. Subsequently, the freshman and sophomore years are for foundation classes only, and at the end of those two years, students are required to apply with a portfolio for entry into the BFA track. Typically, we have around 90-100 applicants each year and only accept between 15-20. Once accepted, the junior and senior years are extremely rigorous and the students spend most of their design classes together until graduation.

What are the qualifications you require?
Design is principle based. Therefore, there are fundamentals we look for in the portfolio application process. I call them the three C's: composition, concept (ideation and an ability to think conceptually), and content (what the individual student has to say in their work).

What are the disqualifications?
There are probably several - certainly a lack of the above mentioned principles. Attitude also becomes important; our students have to be teachable. Because of the unique environment, the small number of accepted applications, and the fact that they are required to be in the same classes for two years, the students require good chemistry. They have to be able to get along not just with the faculty, but also with each other.

What might be a typical first assignment?
The first assignment I give is a publication design or traditional print assignment. They have to redesign a current magazine and book series. These are both intensely rigorous projects for students who've only had a handful of foundational classes. The magazine assignment encompasses all the complex principles they'll need in order to succeed on every other project and assignment, both in the classroom, and professionally.

Are real clients suggested?
Yes, all projects are based on real clients and existing products and/or companies.

Might you also ask students to choose a passion of theirs for the assignment?
Yes, in the senior year, one of their major assignments is to do a passion project. It is unique and differs from all their other assignments in that this is a more personal and intimate project based on their personal life and/or family experiences, personal interest, etc. This assignment has produced some very successful portfolio pieces which helps position the student uniquely when interviewing for a job.

Do you work with students individually? Or...
Yes. Because of the smallness of the program, teaching is heavily based on one-on-one mentoring for a lot of the class critique time, and also individual mentoring. My philosophy for a very long time has been that I also believe in the "master's apprentice" approach to teaching and learning.

Do you present their work so that you and the rest of the class can participate in criticism?
Yes, because of the concentrated time that we have with our students (2 years only), constructive critiquing is a major component of every classroom experience. I have found this to be one of the most valuable ways to teach the principles and have the students understand how to implement them in their work. This also prepares them quite well for the professional world.

How do you develop and raise your student's visual and verbal standards?
There are a number of ways I do this. I have a substantial personal library from which I use resources such as, books, movies, documentaries, and objects of beauty, to teach with and expose students to a wide range of principles from all design disciplines. I also take field trips with the students. Because of our geographic location (Provo, Utah), the faculty organizes annual field trips to New York and San Francisco where the students are introduced to many of the major studios and agencies. I also take them to a ranch in northern Utah where we conduct a workshop in regenerative agriculture and design. In addition, industry leaders in design from around the country and the world are invited to the campus to conduct workshops with our students on an annual basis.

What percentage of the whole class reaches award-winning work?
I enter student work into a number of major national and international competitions, including Graphis. Marty called me several years ago and said that we have the highest per capita acceptance rate of work into the Graphis show than any other school in the world, so our acceptance is fairly high in a number of competitions. I would expect that about 50% or more of our students have their work published in these venues annually.

Have you ever dismissed a student or students from your class?
It has happened on rare occasions, but not for some time. As mentioned, our vetting process is quite thorough. In addition, we are fortunate in that we attract a high caliber of students, young men and mostly women these days, who are committed to learning, and value the opportunity they have been given. Seats are limited and they recognize what a privilege it is to be in the program.

With the semester's end, what kind of advice do you give to the class?
I suppose I wax a little more philosophical at the end of the school year as our students are graduating. We do become good friends in that short two-year time span because of the intimacy of our program. I encourage them to stay true to the principles they have learned; to create beauty, disseminate truth and authenticity, and to use their gifts to make the world a better place. Design has that power.

Adrian Pulfer
See his Graphis Master Portfolio on graphis.com.

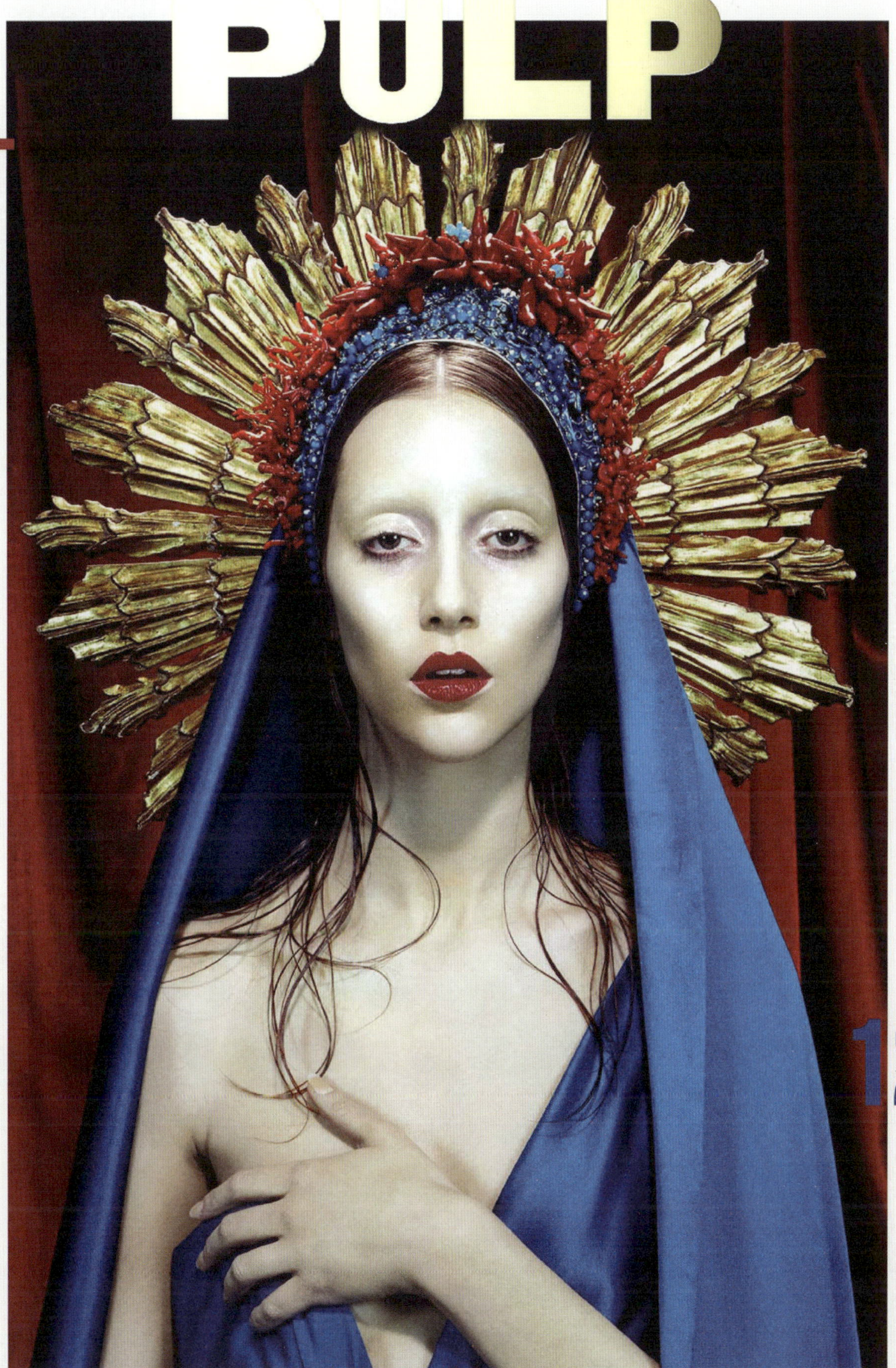

"Pulp Magazine" New Talent Annual 2018 Platinum-winning Student: Haley Stoneking

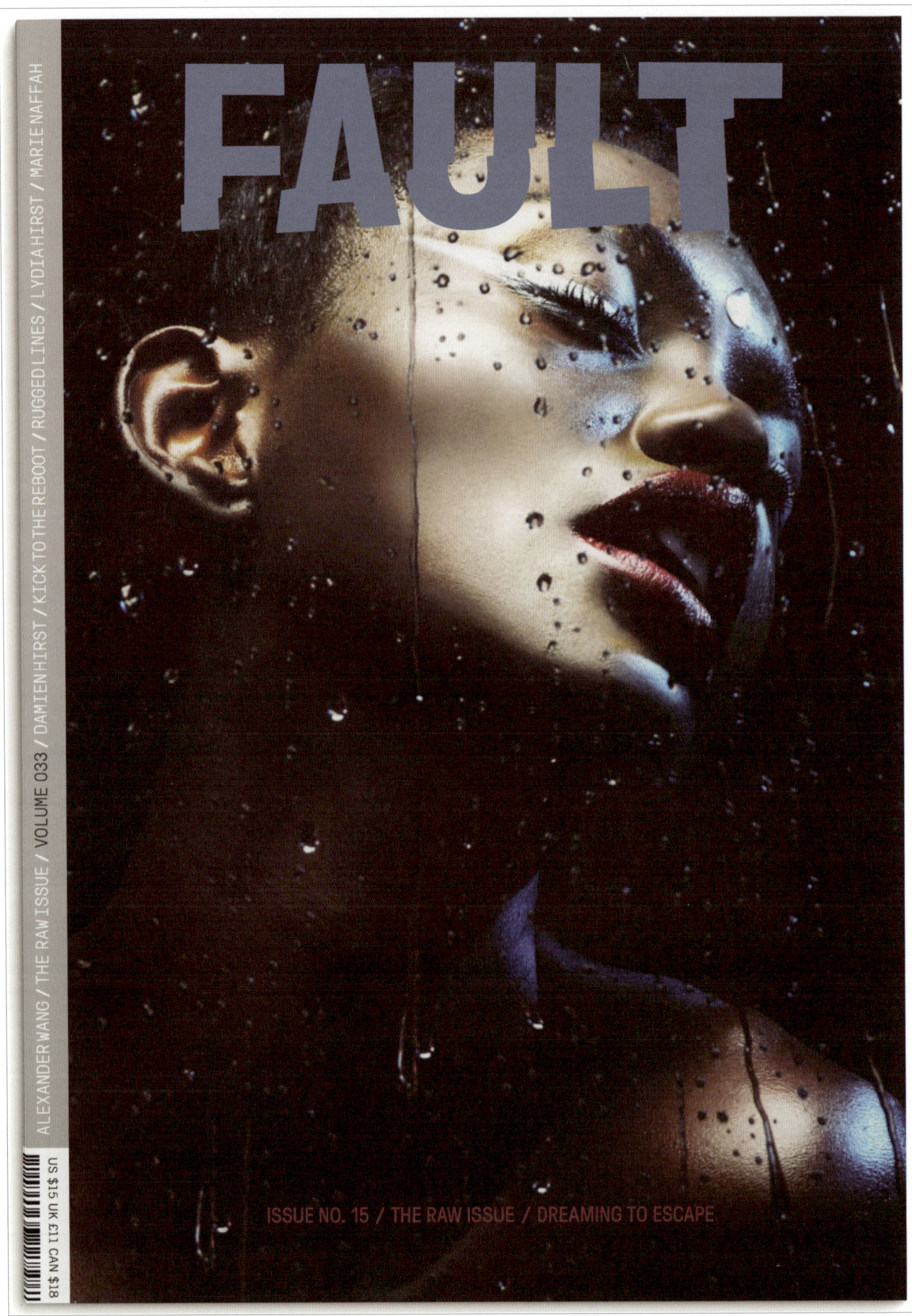

"Fault Magazine Redesign" New Talent Annual 2016 Platinum-winning Student: Evan Chang

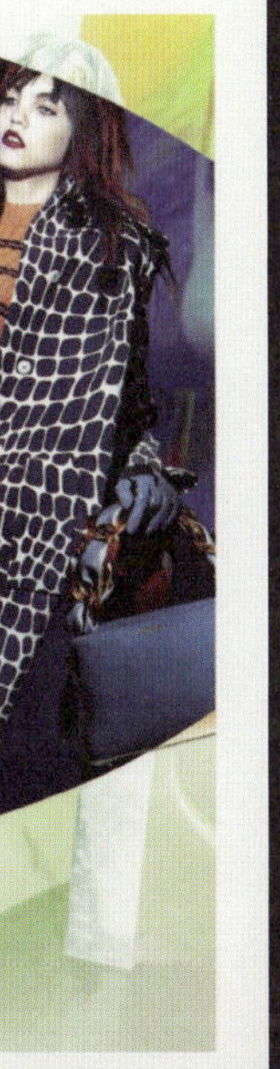

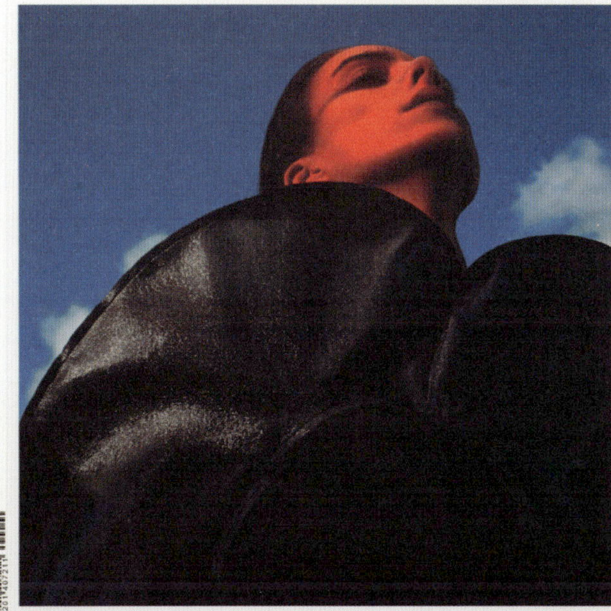

"Muse Magazine" New Talent Annual 2017 Gold-winning Students: Travis Wu

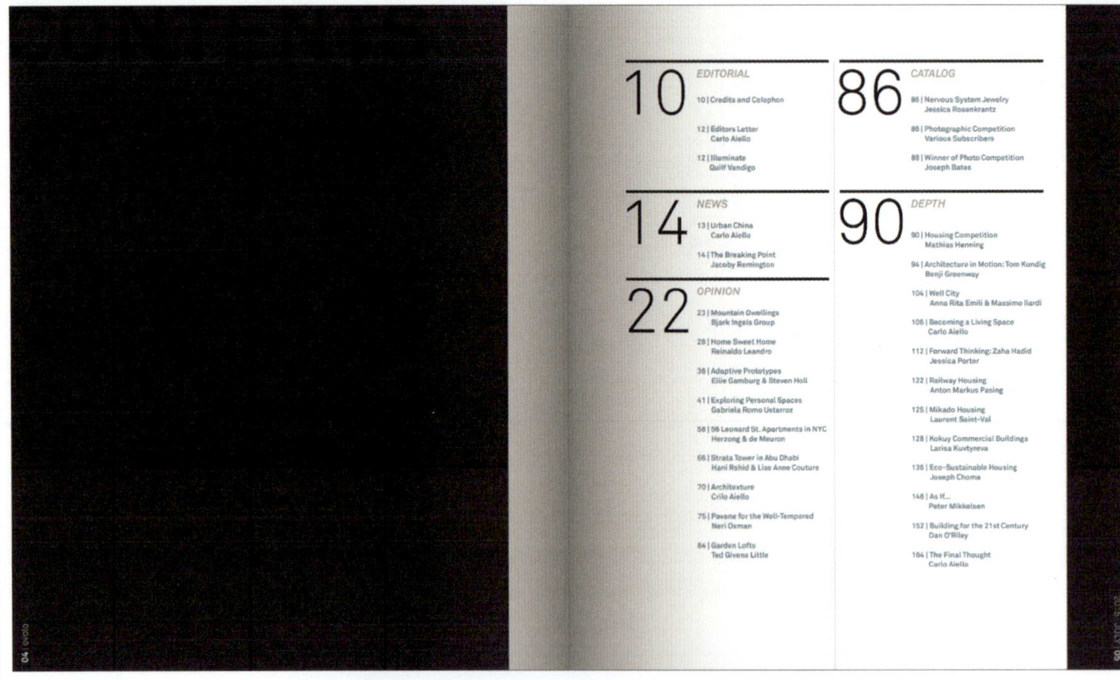

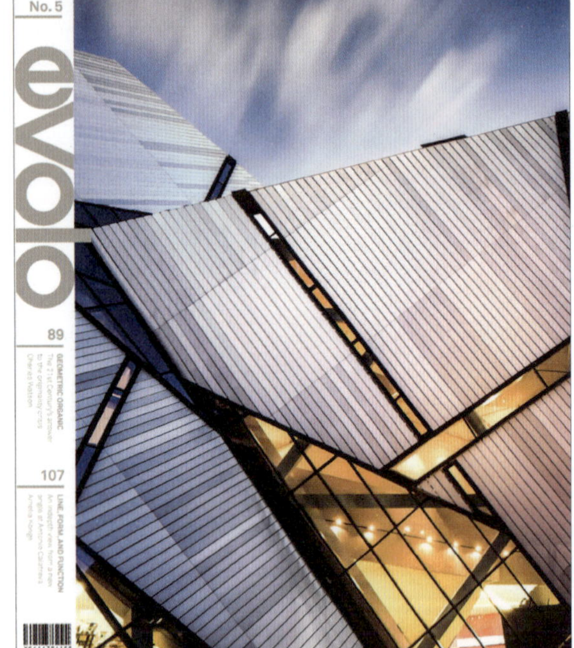

FORWARD TH

The future is on the "tidy" drafting table of Zaha Hadid

TO ADMIRE THE SPLENDOUR of the prodigiously expensive Aquatic Centre, built for the 2012 London Olympics, you have to forgive its shortcomings. Its roof structure required 10 times as much steel as that of the velodrome, which torpedoed the organisers' claims for sustainability.

During the Games, the need for thousands of temporary additional seats which was always a basic part of the brief – was accommodated with extreme awkwardness, which meant that whatever might be good about Zaha Hadid's design could not be fully appreciated until after the Olympic crowds had left. There were complaints about sightlines that, even though in line with the official specifications, cut off views of the top of the diving board from the upper tiers, in a way that seemed gratuitous. In its current state there is some confusion: what the architecture strongly suggests is the front door, beneath a boldly overhanging portico, is not in fact the front door, and visitors have to seek out a more obscure en-

The Galaxy Soho Mall located in Beijing, China

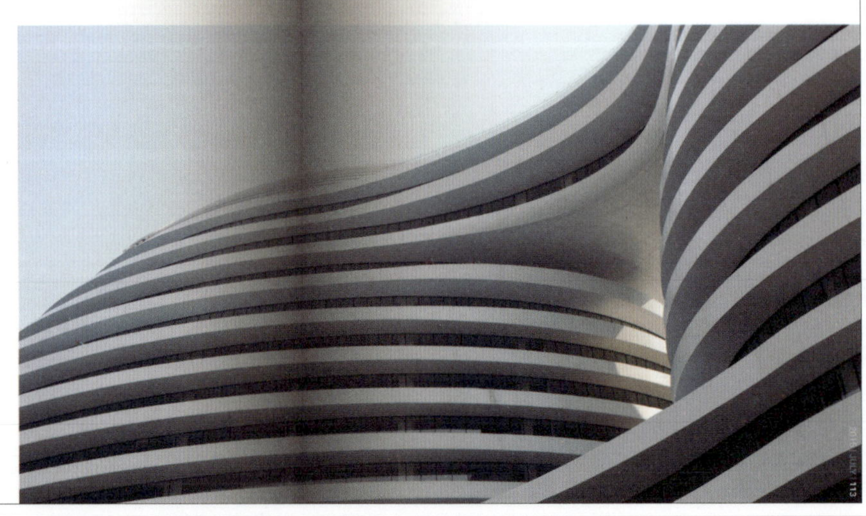

"Evolo Magazine" New Talent Annual 2017 Platinum-winning Student: Connor King

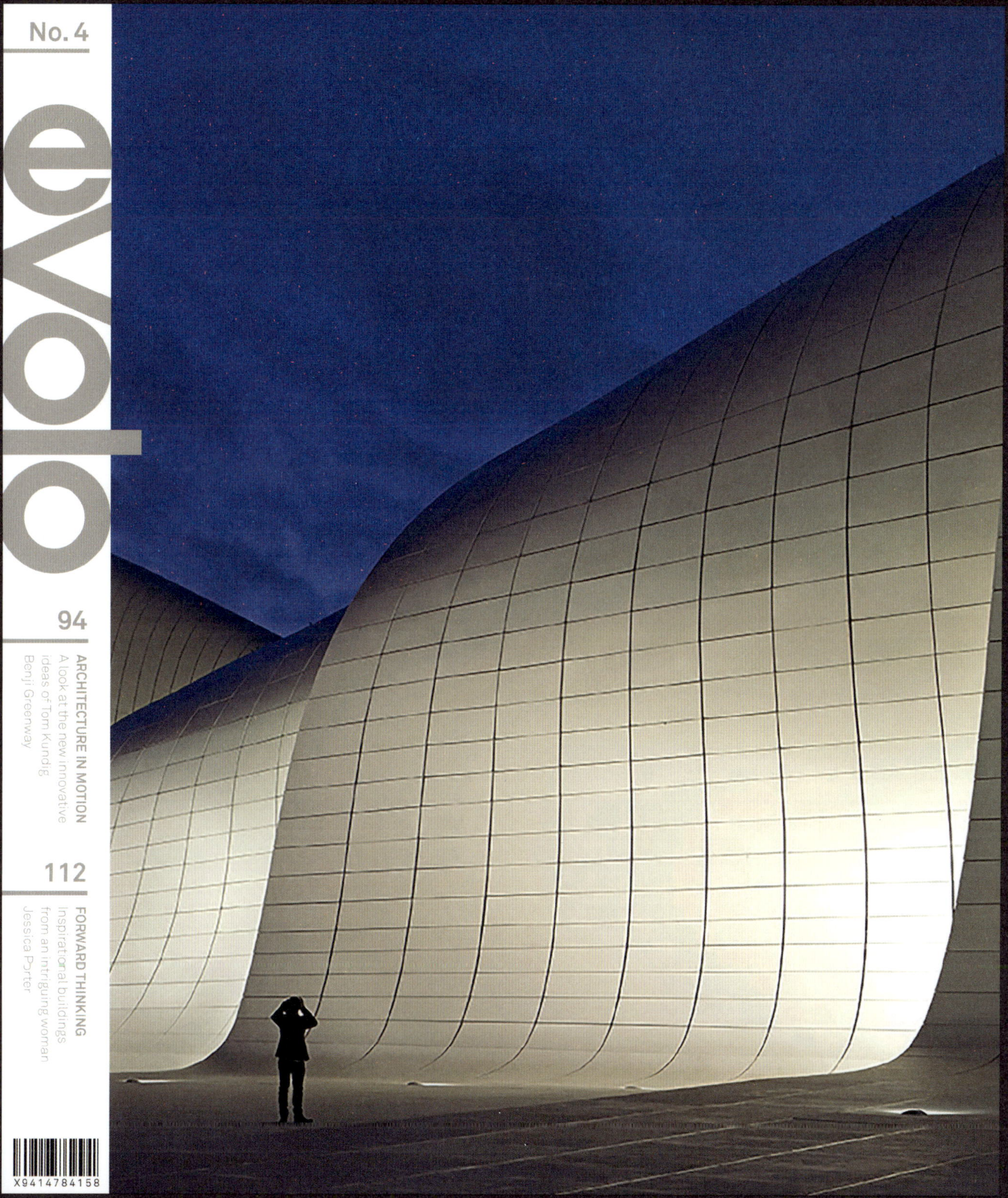

No. 4

evolo

94

ARCHITECTURE IN MOTION

A look at the new innovative ideas of Tom Kundig

Benji Greenway

112

FORWARD THINKING

Inspirational buildings from an intriguing woman

Jessica Porter

"Evolo Magazine" New Talent Annual 2017 Platinum-winning Student: Connor King

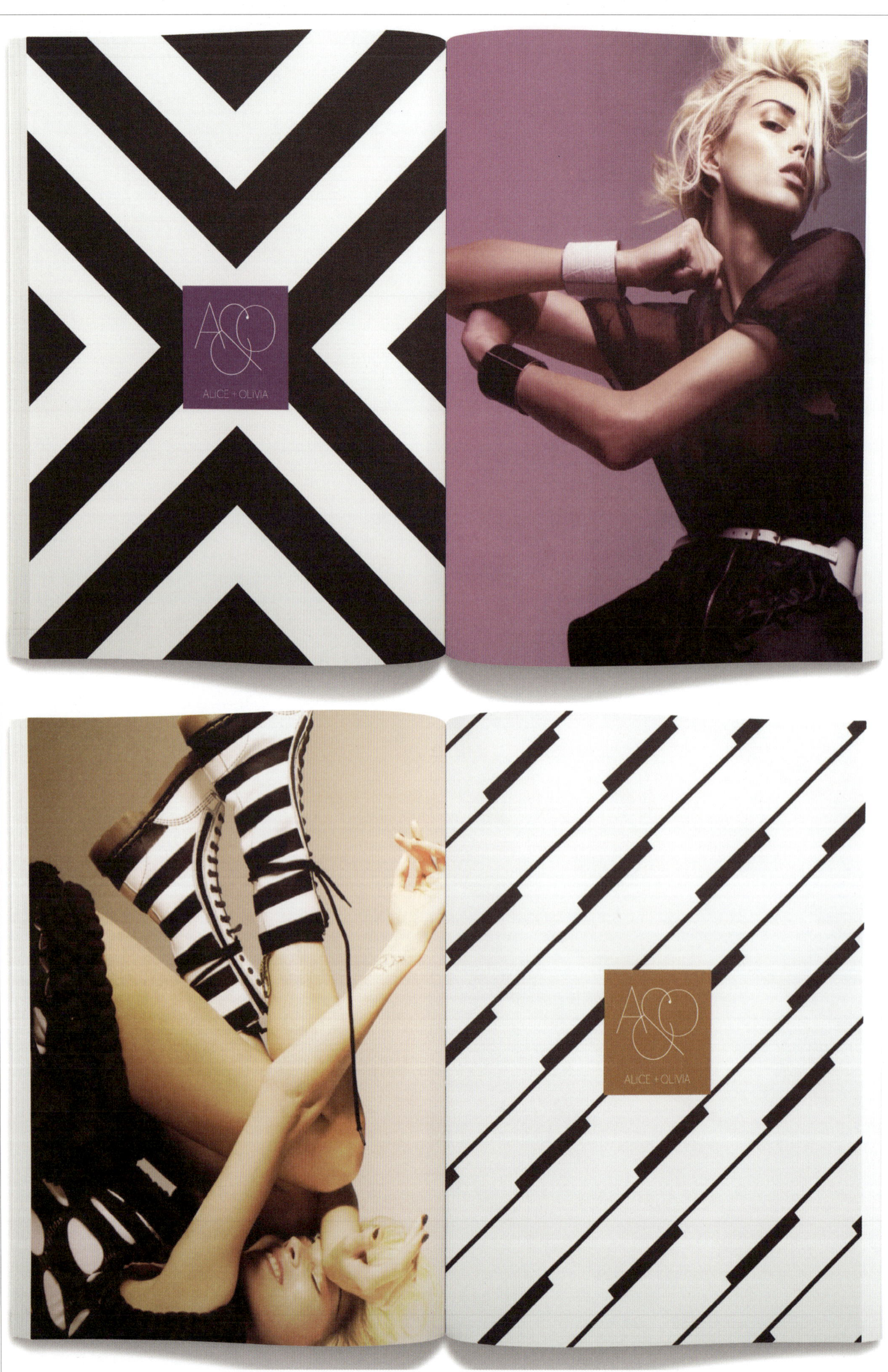

"Alice + Olivia" New Talent Annual 2012 Platinum-winning Student: Paris Wilson

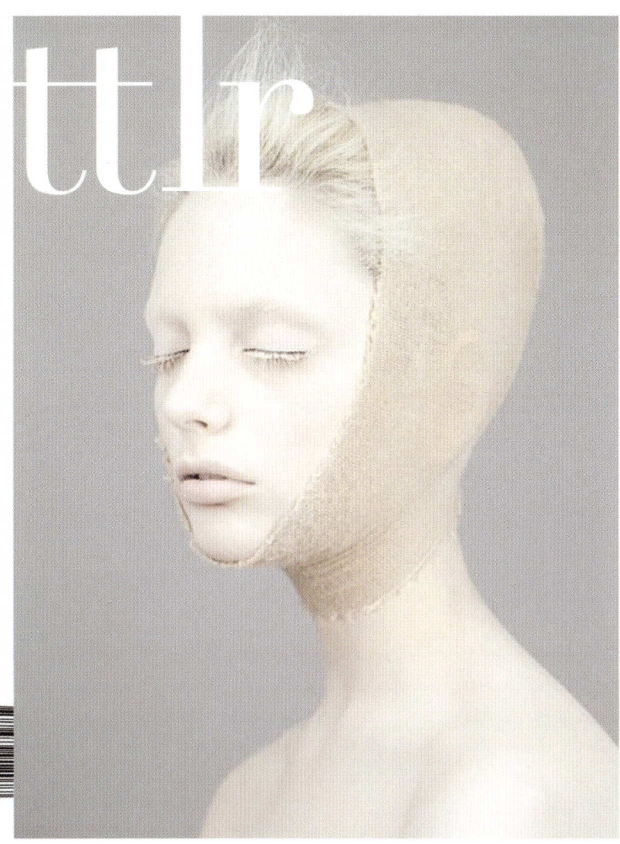

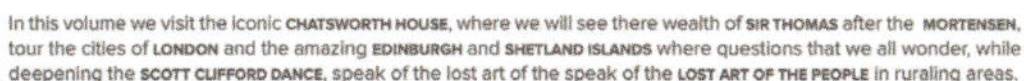

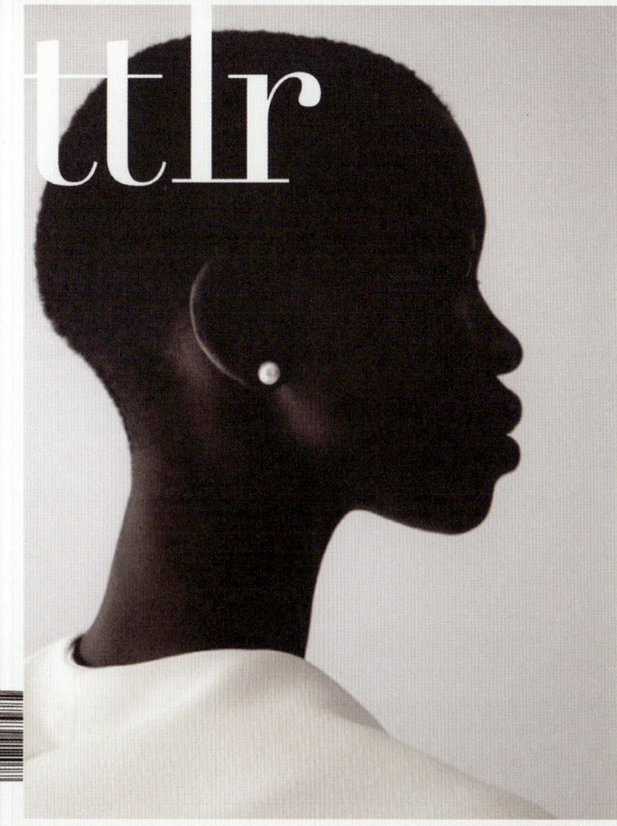

"Tatler Magazine" New Talent Annual 2018 Gold-winning Student: Camrie Smith

Graphis Books

POSTER

DESIGN

ADVERTISING

PHOTOGRAPHY

NUDES

TYPOGRAPHY

PROTEST POSTERS

New Talent Annual 2020

GraphisNewTalentAnnual2020

I believe we have some very fine, new talent on the horizon.

Students who know what they are doing.

2020 *Trim: 8.5 x 11.75"*
Hardcover: 272 pages *ISBN: 978-1-931241-86-1*
200-plus color illustrations *US $90*

This Annual presents work from award-winning Instructors and students. **Platinum:** Advertising: Josh Ege, David Elizalde, Antonio Fragoso, Tu Phan, Vinny Tulley, and Mel White. Design: Peter Ahlberg, Nelson Carnicelli, Tina Fong, Seung-Min Han, Natasha Jen, Ken Koester, and Dong-Joo Park. Photo: Taylor Bareford. This year we awarded 19 Platinum, 179 Gold, and 359 Silver award-winning work from students whose professors have influenced them to create distinct and unique works. We award up to 500 Honorable Mentions, encouraging new talent to submit. All winners are equally presented and archived on our website. This book is a tool for teachers to raise their students' standards and gauge how their school measures up.

Photography Annual 2020

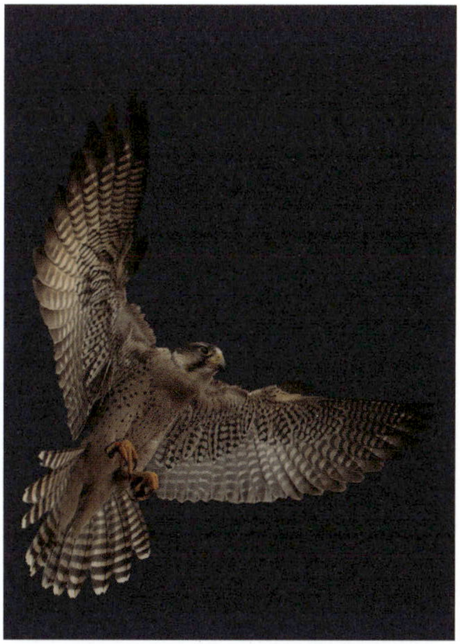

2020 *Trim: 8.5 x 11.75"*
Hardcover: 256 pages *ISBN: 978-1-931241-85-4*
200-plus color illustrations *US $90*

Awards: Graphis presents 12 Platinum, 94 Gold, 117 Silver Awards, and 65 Honorable Mentions in this annual.
Platinum Winners: Craig Cutler, Bruce DeBoer, Nicholas Duers, Nick Hall, Vincent Junier, Jonathan Knowles, McCandliss and Campbell, Lennette Newell, Joseph Saraceno, Howard Schatz, Michael Schoenfeld, Sarah Ward.
Judges: Work was judged by a panel of Photographers who had been past winners such as: Graphis Masters Athena Azevedo, Andreas Franke, and Ricardo de Vicq de Cumptich as well as Colin Faulkner and Frank P. Wartenberg.
Content: Photos from judges, and award-winning photographers. Also included is a retrospective on the past decade of winning photography, and a list of international photography museums.

Advertising Annual 2020

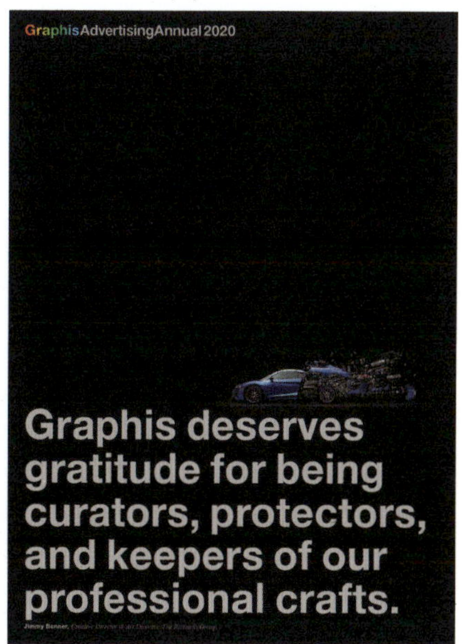

2020 *Trim: 8.5 x 11.75"*
Hardcover: 224 pages *ISBN: 978-1-931241-83-0*
200-plus color illustrations *US $90*

Awards: 10 Platinum, 89 Gold, 59 Silver awards, totaling more than 180 winners, along with 22 Honorable Mentions.
Platinum Winners: ARSONAL, AUDI USA, Brunner, daDá, The Designory, Duncan Channon, Fabian Oefner, FBC Design, INNOCEAN USA, PPK,USA, and Shine United.
Judges: Benjamin Bailey of Doner, Jimmy Bonner of The Richards Group, Matt Herrmann of BVK, Jinsoo Jeon of BRAND DIRECTORS, John Peed of Cold Open, and Xosé Teiga of xosé teiga, studio.
Content: Designs by the judges and award-winning advertising agencies, Q&A's from Platinum-winning instructors, and a special feature on a decade of excellence in Advertising.

Design Annual 2020

GraphisDesignAnnual2020

PLATINUM WINNERS:
ARSONAL
Carmit Design Studio
Carter Hales Design Lab
Dalian RYCX Advertising Co., Ltd.
Dankook University
IF Studio
Michael Pantuso Design
Morla Design
Omdesign
Sherry Matthews Group
Studio | Peteet Design
Ultra Creative
White & Case LLP

2019 *Trim: 8.5 x 11.75"*
Hardcover: 272 pages *ISBN: 978-1-931241-82-3*
200-plus color illustrations *US $90*

Awards: 12 Platinum, 163 Gold, and 268 Silver Awards, totaling more than 700 winners, along with 273 Honorable Mentions.
Platinum Winners: ARSONAL, Carmit Design Studio, Carter Hales Design Lab, Dalian RYCX Advertising Co., Ltd., Dankook University, IF Studio, Michael Pantuso Design, Morla Design, Omdesign, Sherry Matthews Group / Studio | Peteet Design, Ultra Creative, and White & Case LLP.
Judges: Fa-Hsiang Hu, Toshiaki & Hisa Ide, Jennifer Morla, Shadia Ohanessian, Michael Pantuso, and Rene V. Steiner.
Content: The best of design with 716 winners, as well as Platinum and Gold-winning work by each of this year's Judges. Our Design Museum Directory and annual In Memoriam are also presented.

Nudes 5

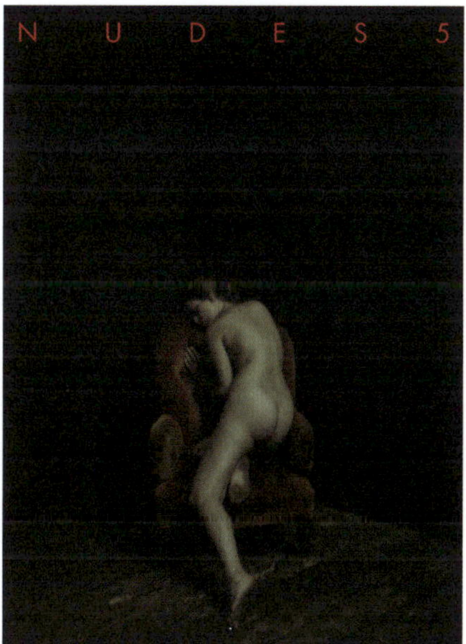

2019 *Trim: 10.06 x 13.41"*
Hardcover: 256 pages *ISBN: 978-1-931241-84-7*
200-plus color illustrations *US $90*

The fifth volume in this series, Nudes 5 continues to present some of the most refined and creative nudes photography. Just as this genre helped elevate photography into a realm of fine art, one will find that many of the images on these pages deserve to be presented in museums. Award-winning Photographers include **Erik Almas, Rosanne Olson, Klaus Kampert, Howard Schatz, Phil Marco, Joel-Peter Witkin, Chris Budgeon**, among others.

Poster Annual 2020

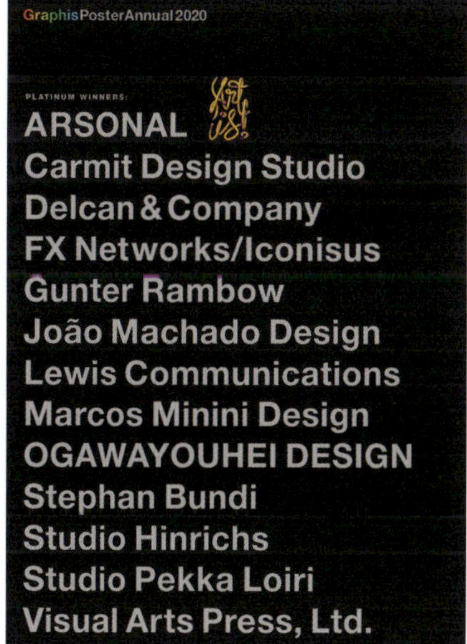

2019 *Trim: 8.5 x 11.75"*
Hardcover: 240 pages *ISBN: 978-1-931241-81-6*
200-plus color illustrations *US $90*

Awards: 12 Platinum, 107 Gold, and 230 Silver Awards, along with 149 Honorable Mentions. **Platinum Winners:** ARSONAL, Carmit Design Studio, Delcan & Company/Visual Arts Press, Ltd, FX Networks/Iconisus, Gunter Rambow, João Machado Design, Lewis Communications, Marcos Minini Design, OGAWAYOUHEI DESIGN, Stephan Bundi, Studio Hinrichs, and Studio Pekka Loiri.
Judges: Entries were judged by highly accomplished Poster Designers: Takashi Akiyama, Rikke Hansen, Dermot Mac Cormack, Patricia McElroy, Gunter Rambow, and Hajime Tsushima. **Editorial:** Designs by Graphis Masters and previous Platinum Winners, who continue to win awards today: Stephan Bundi, Melchior Imboden, Taku Satoh, and Shin Matsunaga. Their Platinum-winning designs from the Poster Annual 2010 competition are shown in full-page images.

Books are available at www.graphis.com/store

At $90 each, these books present award-winning talent. Become a Professional Member and get a copy for only **$45.**

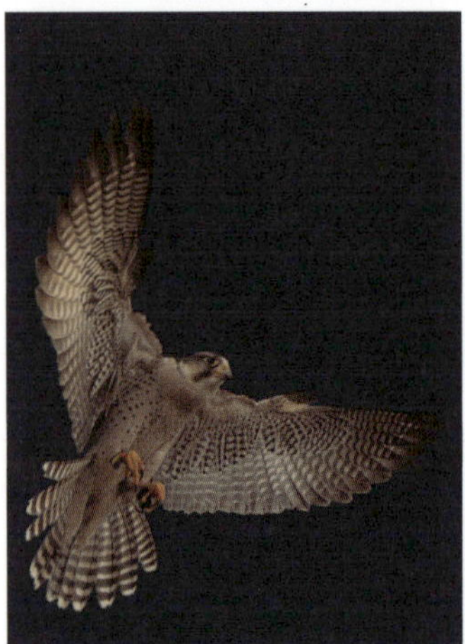

PHOTOGRAPHY ANNUAL 2020 PLATINUM WINNERS:
Craig Cutler
Bruce DeBoer
Nicholas Duers
Nick Hall
Vincent Junier
Jonathan Knowles
McCandliss and Campbell
Lennette Newell
Joseph Saraceno
Howard Schatz
Michael Schoenfeld
Sarah Ward

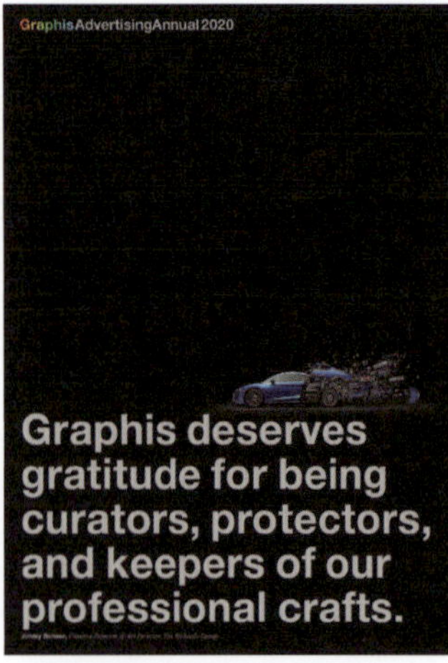

ADVERTISING ANNUAL 2020 PLATINUM WINNERS:
ARSONAL
AUDI USA
Brunner
daDá
The Designory
Duncan Channon
Fabian Oefner
FBC Design
INNOCEAN USA
PPK, USA
Shine United

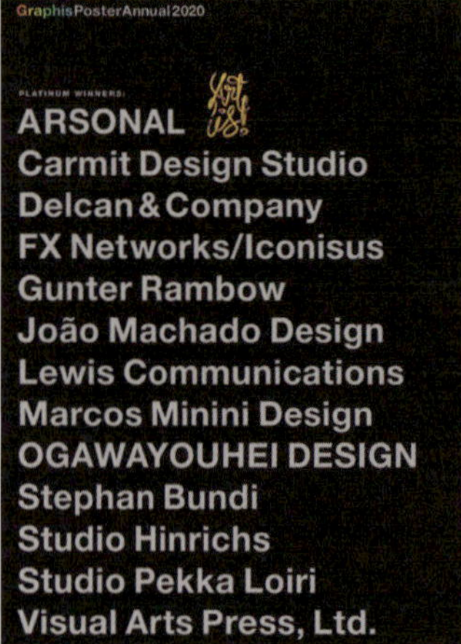

POSTER ANNUAL 2020 PLATINUM WINNERS:
ARSONAL
Carmit Design Studio
Delcan & Company
FX Networks/Iconisus
Gunter Rambow
João Machado Design
Lewis Communications
Marcos Minini Design
OGAWAYOUHEI DESIGN
Stephan Bundi
Studio Hinrichs
Studio Pekka Loiri
Visual Arts Press, Ltd.

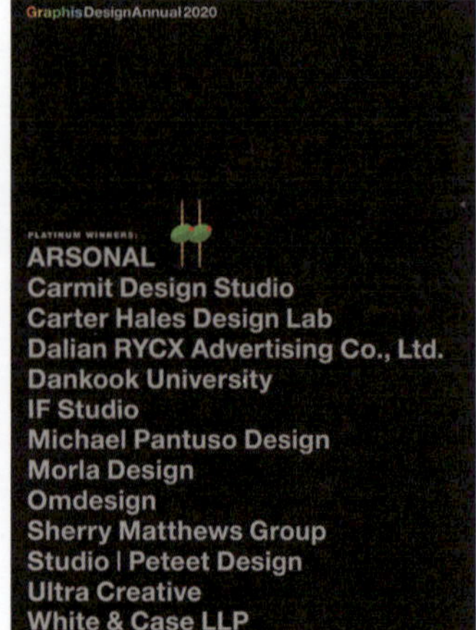

DESIGN ANNUAL 2020 PLATINUM WINNERS:
ARSONAL
Carmit Design Studio
Carter Hales Design Lab
Dalian RYCX Advertising Co., LTD
Dankook University
IF Studio
Michael Pantuso Design
Morla Design
Omdesign
Sherry Matthews Group
Studio | Peteet Design
Ultra Creative
White & Case LLP

Books are available at www.graphis.com/store

YOU SHOULD ALWAYS HAVE A MENTOR NO MATTER HOW EXPERIENCED OR SUCCESSFUL YOU ARE.

Colin Corcoran, *Copywriter & Creative Director, The Independent Copywriter*

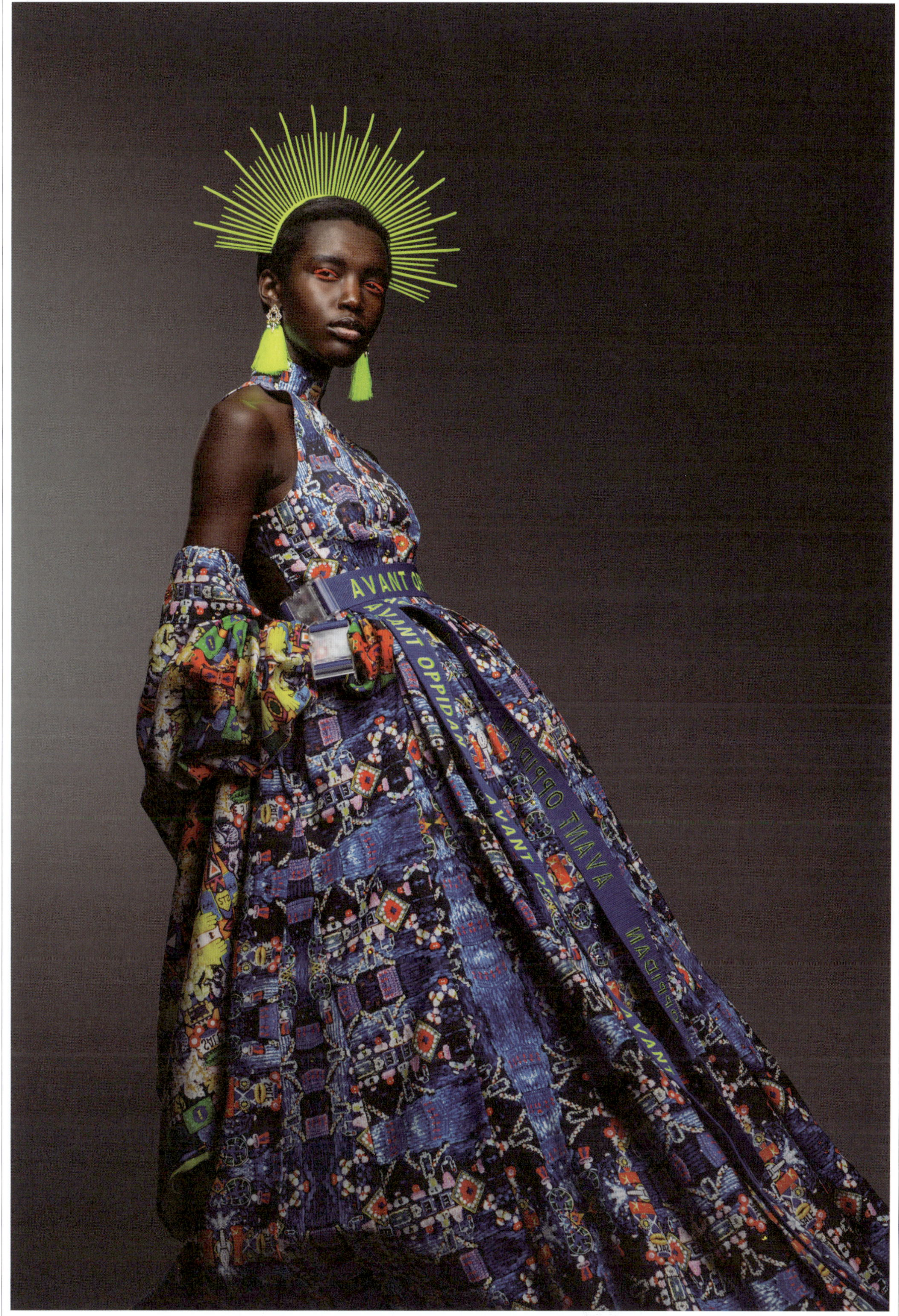

Platinum-winning Photographer: **Hadley Stambaugh** | Client: **Savannah College of Art and Design**

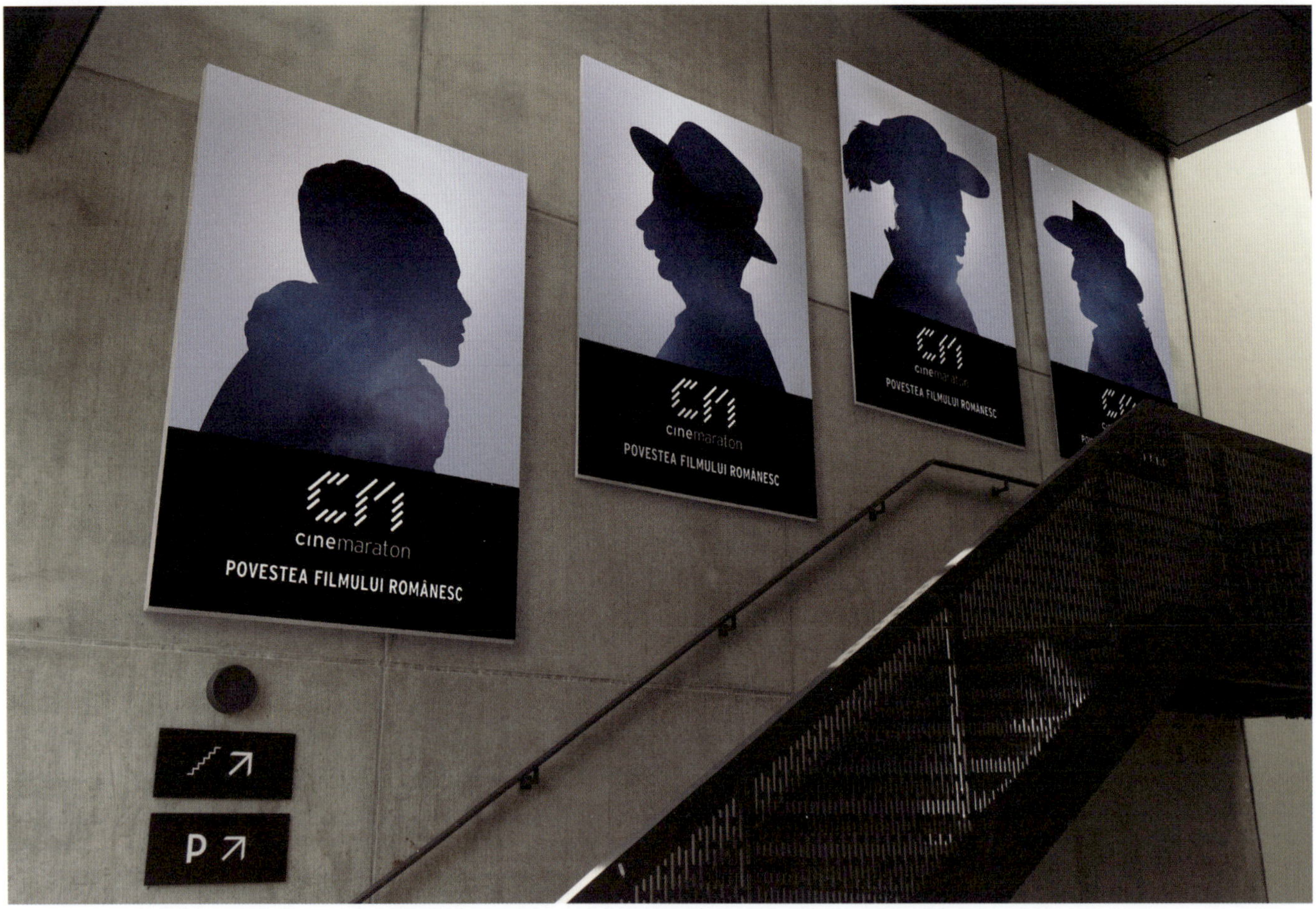

Gold-winning Designers: **Alina Popescu, Andreia Dina** | Client: **AKTA**

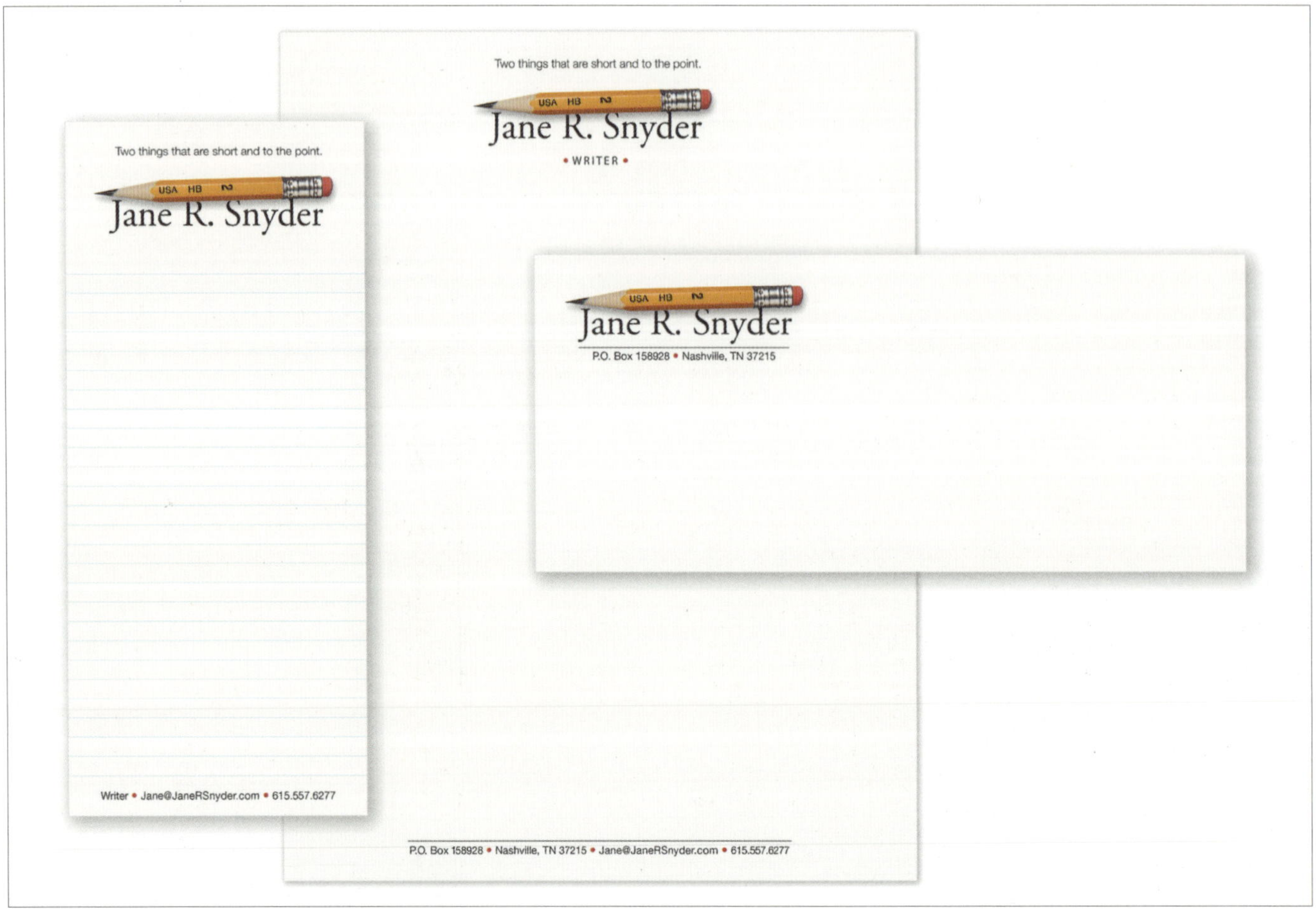

Platinum-winning Design Firm: **Ventress Design Works** | Client: **Jane R. Snyder**

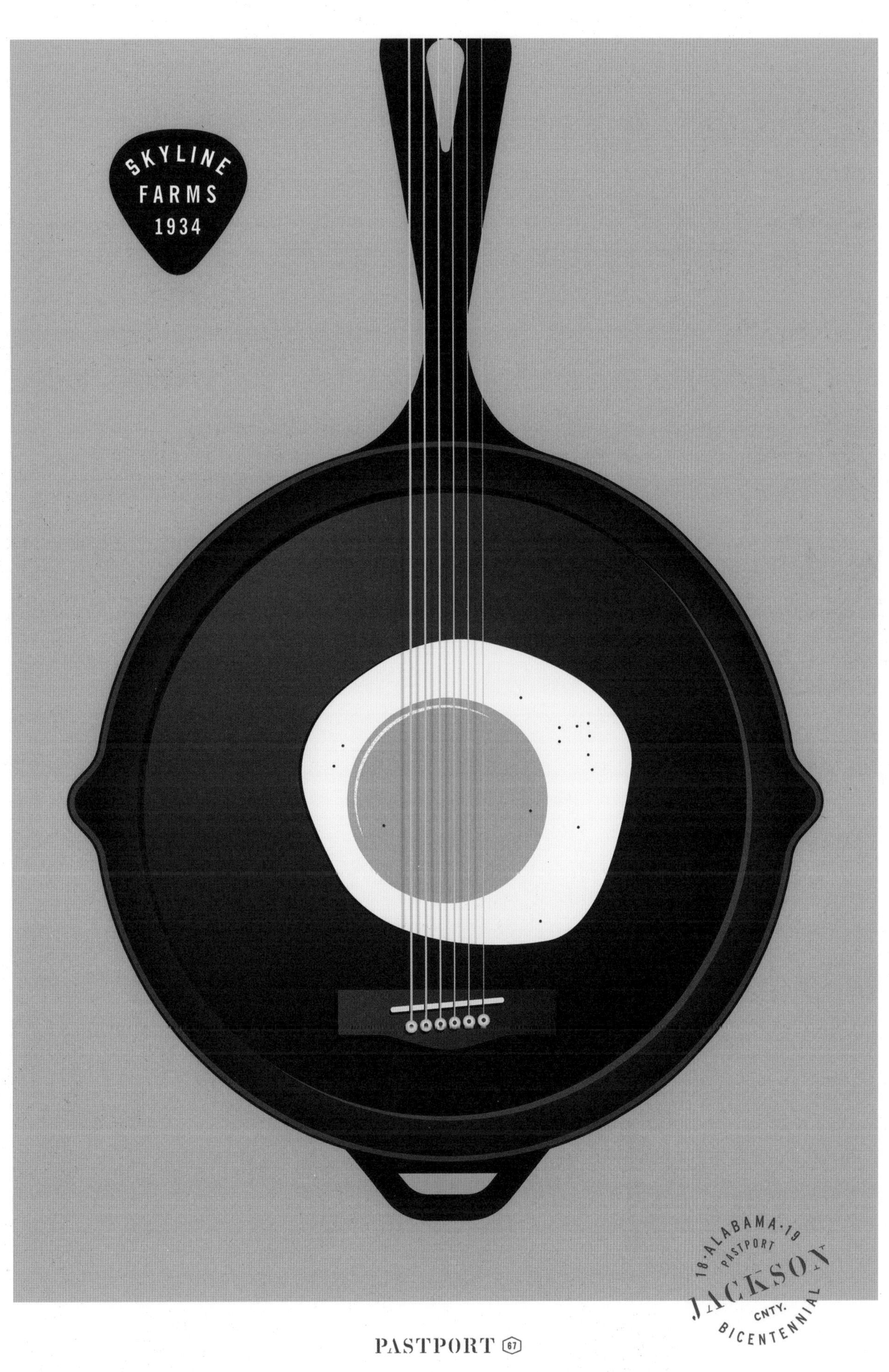

Gold-winning Design Firm: **Tatum Design** | Client: **Alabama Bicentennial Commission**

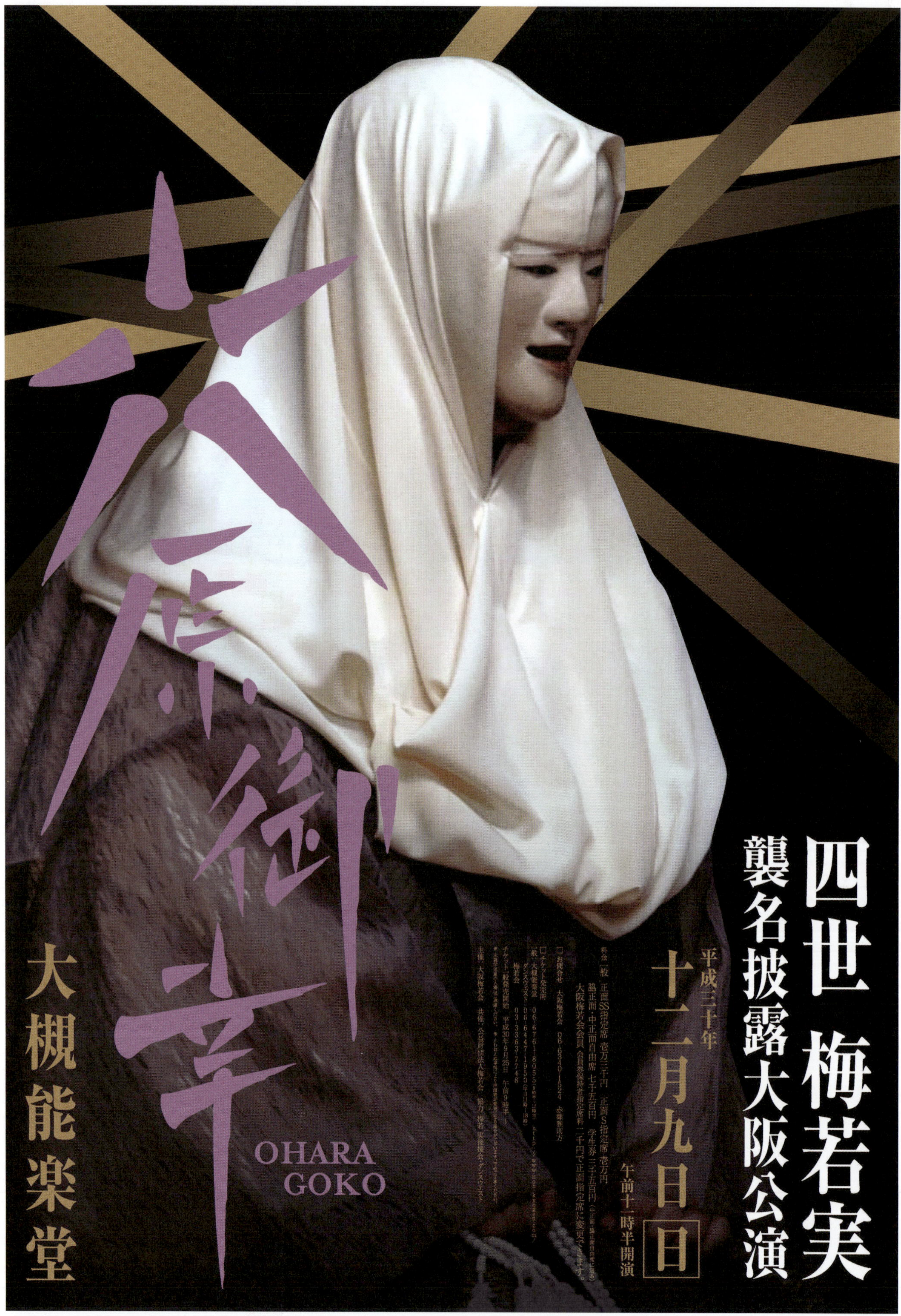

Gold-winning Design Firm: **OGAWAYOUHEI DESIGN** | Client: **DANCE WEST**

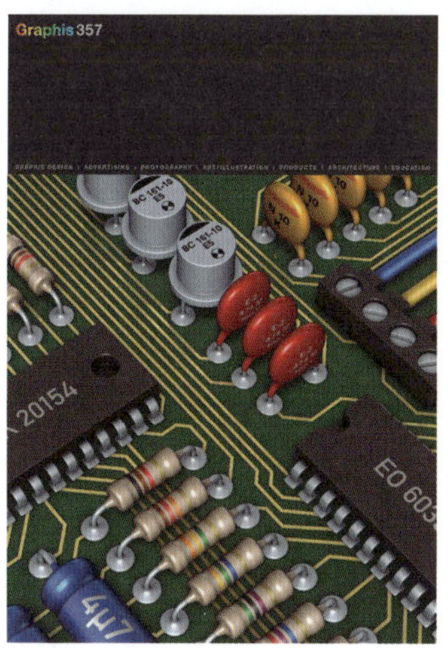
Graphis357

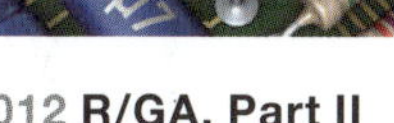

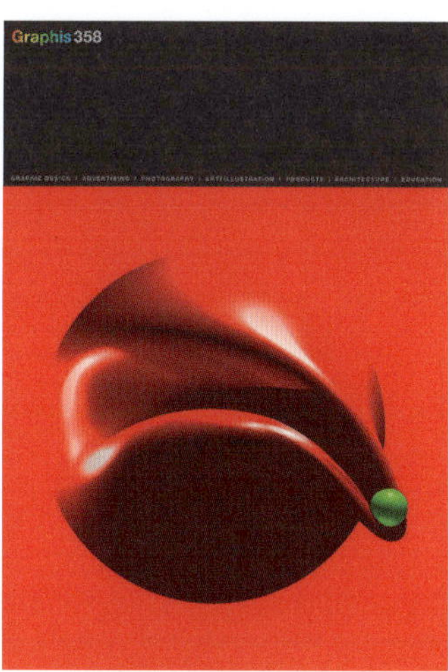
Graphis358

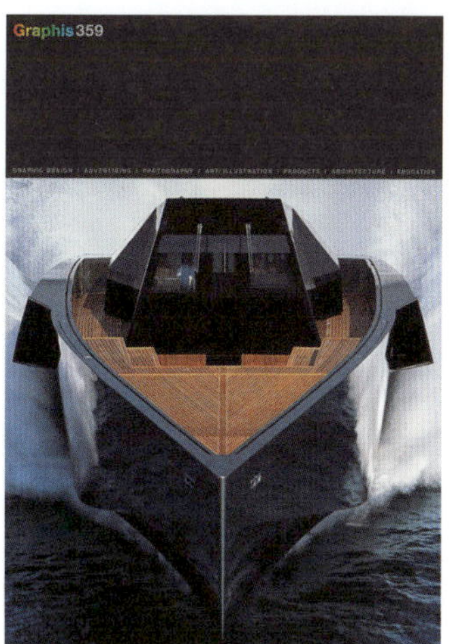
Graphis359

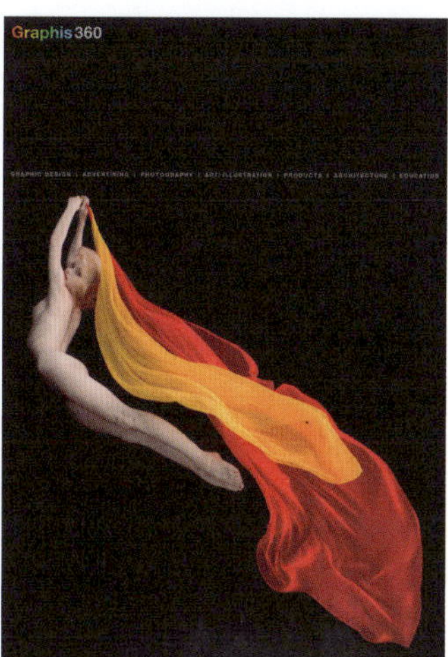
Graphis360

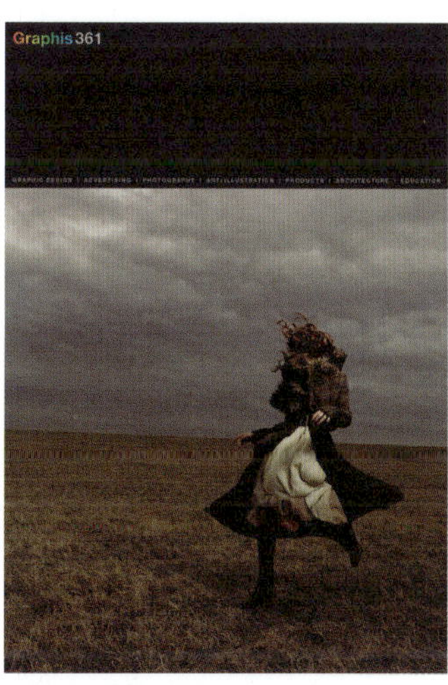
Graphis361

Graphis362

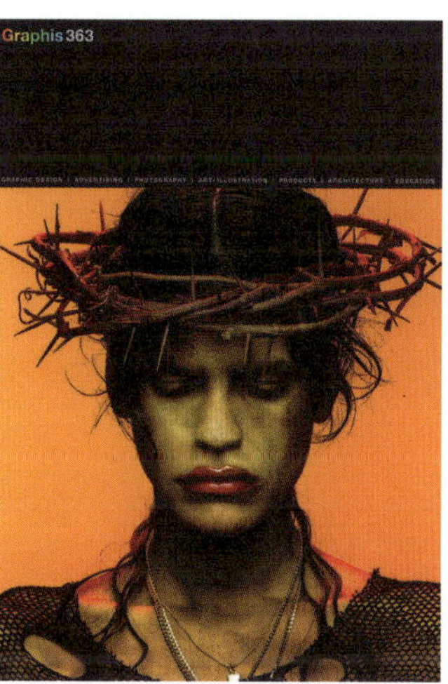
Graphis363

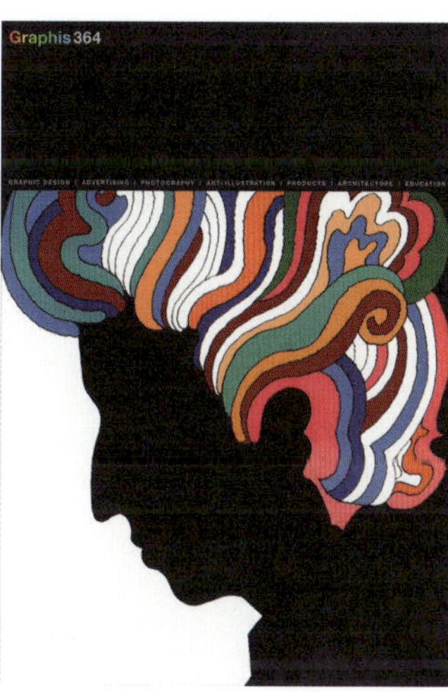
Graphis364

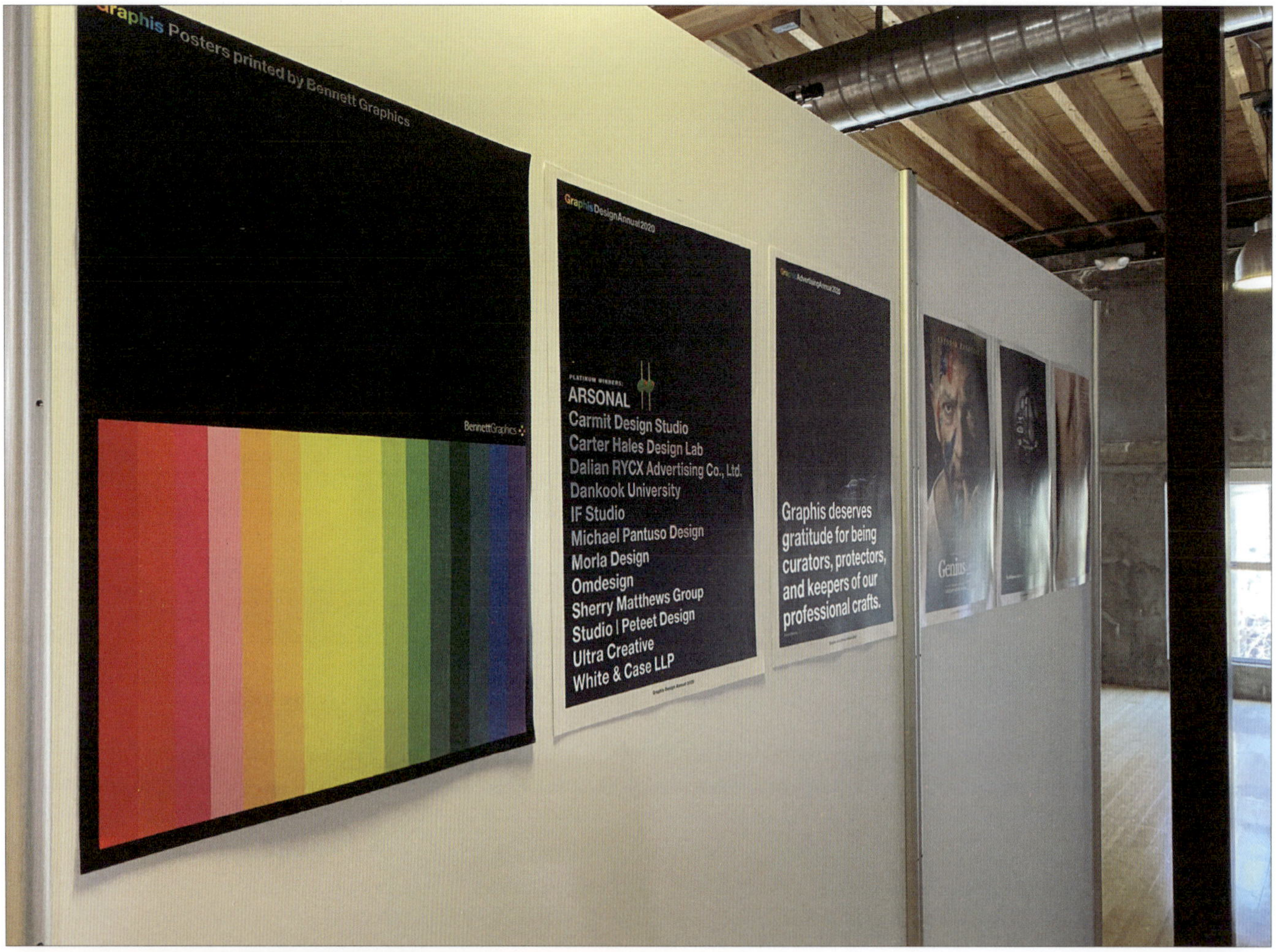

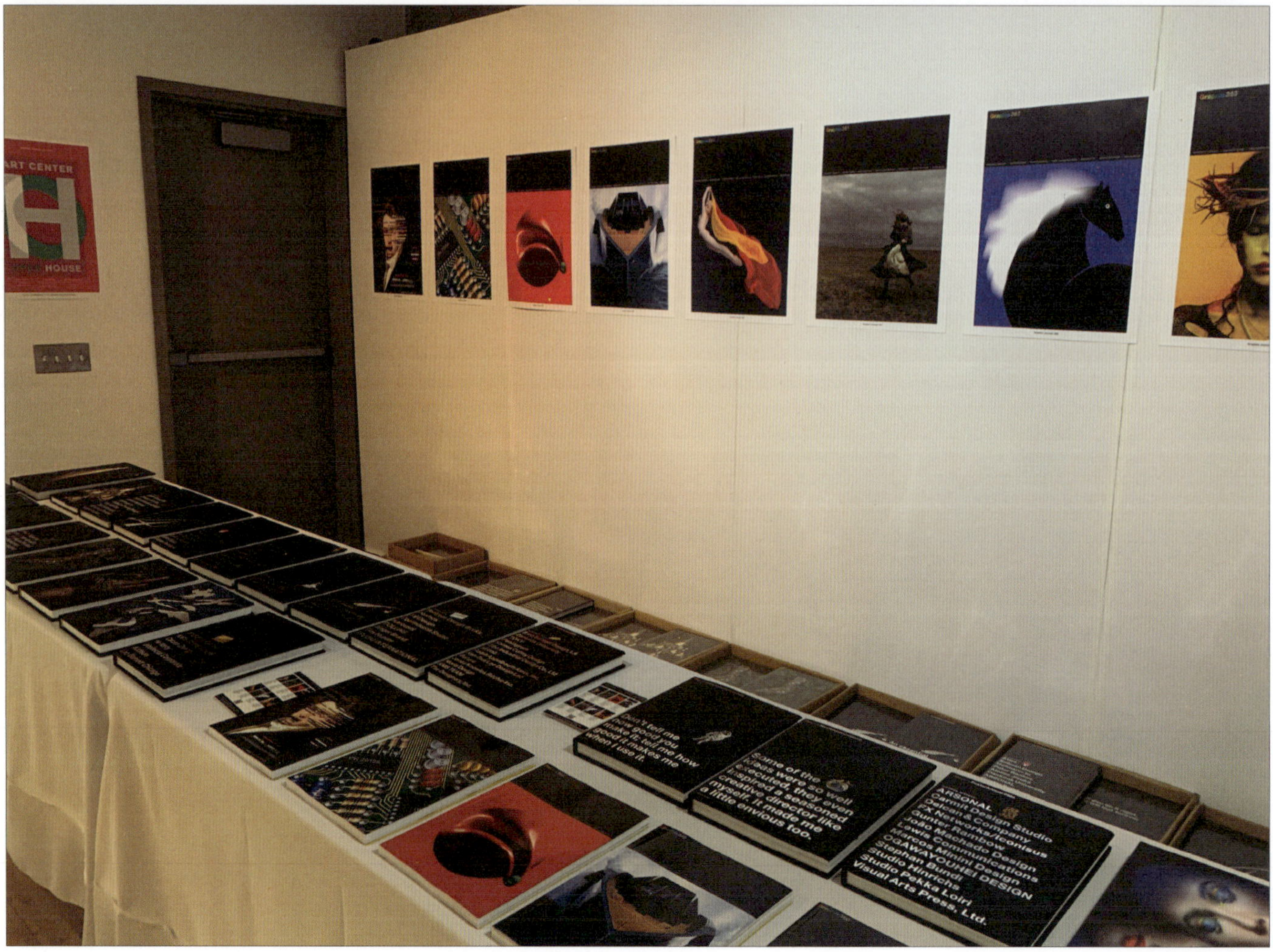

(Top) Bennett Graphics Poster Printer Sponsor / (Bottom) Graphis Journal Cover Posters are hanging on the wall with Graphis Annuals and Journals displayed on the table.

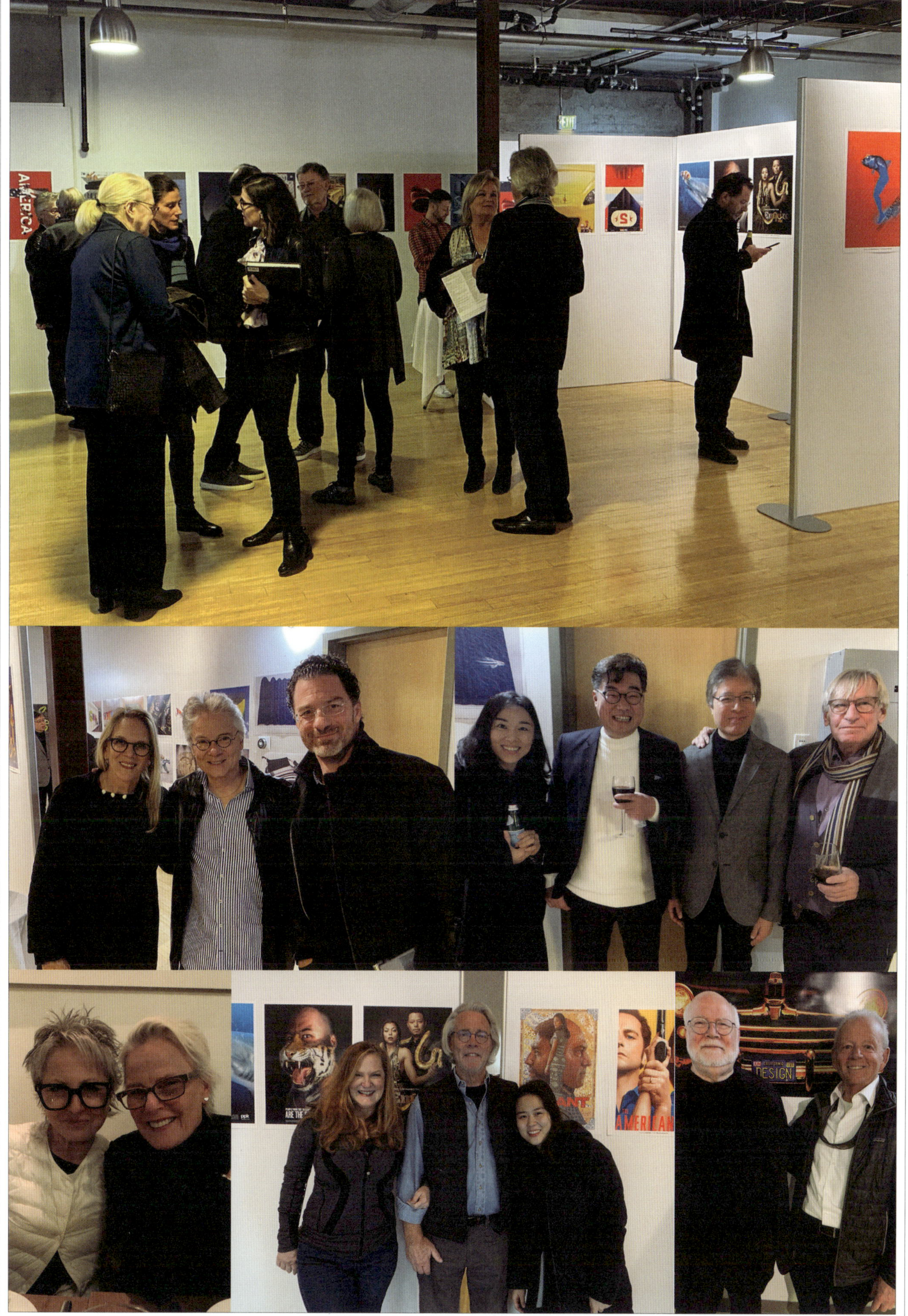

(Top row) Suzanne & Craig Frazier, Michael Pantuso, Dong-Joo Park, Seung Min Han, Earl Gee, Marty Neumeier;
(Bottom row) Jennifer Morla, Kathryn Schwab, Patti Judd, Bob Salt, Heera Kim, Kit Hinrichs, Terry Heffernan

www.Graphis.com